SHANIA TWAIN

Also by Robin Eggar

Tom Jones: the Biography

Shania Twain
The Biography

Robin Eggar

HEADLINE

First Published in 2001
by HEADLINE BOOK PUBLISHING

10 9 8 7 6 5 4 3 2 1

British Library Cataloguing in Publication Data

Eggar, Robin
    Shania Twain
    1.Twain, Shania
    2.Women country musicians – Canada – Biography
    3.Country musicians – Canada – Biography
    I.Title
    782.4'2'1'642'092

    ISBN 0 7472 4786 2 (hbk)
    ISBN 0 7472 5318 8 (tpb)

Typeset by
Letterpart Limited, Reigate, Surrey

Printed and bound in Great Britain by
Clays Ltd, St Ives plc

HEADLINE BOOK PUBLISHING
A division of Hodder Headline
338 Euston Road
LONDON NW1 3BH

www.headline.co.uk
www.hodderheadline.com

As ever, to Jacqui, Jordan and Rowan

✳ CONTENTS ✳

✳ ACKNOWLEDGEMENTS ✳

When I first decided to write a biography of Shania Twain, I was determined that it should be my take on her career and not compromised by being seen as 'authorized'. However, before I wrote a word I met with Jon Landau, Barbara Carr and Jan Stabile from Jon Landau Management and told them of my intentions. My thanks to them for being prepared to listen and then to help – and never hinder – with my researches.

At the very core of the book are some three hours of interviews I conducted with Shania Twain in London in January 1998 and October 1999. These interviews form the heart of my understanding of who she is and where she comes from. It is always easier to withhold co-operation than it is to help; and when Shania learnt I was writing this book, she did not take the easy option. Thus, while Shania and her immediate family chose not to be interviewed for the specific purpose of the book, she never advised me against talking to anybody – and indeed ensured that I had access to the correct facts. Her personal assistant, Kim Godreau, has been unfailingly polite and efficient in answering my frequent queries; for that she has my thanks.

In the past year I have conducted almost ninety interviews, either face to face or over the telephone. My thanks to all the interviewees and also to anyone whom I have inadvertently omitted from the text – the mistake is mine. I have seen northern Ontario in three seasons – autumn, winter and summer – and driven thousands of kilometres in snow, hail, rain and sunshine, which has given me some idea of what the inhabitants of that stunning but tough land live through. The hospitality I received throughout my time in Canada and in Nashville was exemplary, and the reactions of those people who know or have known Shania speak volumes about the person she is.

In Canada, essential and invaluable background work and research was carried out with aplomb, grace and total efficiency by Jeff Silverstein, without whom my job would have been very much harder. Thanks to Declan Hill and Katie and Kees t'Hooft for effecting the introduction.

Extra special thanks to Jeff MacInnis for going far beyond the call of friendship. He provided me with a base in Toronto – plus a taxi service to and from the airport, room, board, skiing, hiking, kayaking, a twenty-four-hour spinning marathon and countless other ideas – all of which helped provide relaxation and an alternative focus away from Shania. Thanks also to John Lucato at Cantel for the loan of a cellular phone.

Searching for Shania's roots would have been impossible without the assistance of her uncle Don Fraser who, with his wife Jan and their children Darlene and Shane, made me welcome in their home. Further memories and information on her mother's family in Manitoba came from the family historian, Roger Pearce, May Thompson and Evelyn Struthers. Despite being rudely awakened one November morning, Jerry Twain's sister Karen (and her daughter Angela) helped me understand the depth of her Native heritage. Jerry's cousin Willis McKay told me of her time spent on the Mattagami reserve as a child while Kenny Derasp told of how he had taught her to play the guitar and gave valuable insight into her early years in Hanmer. In Chapleau, the home of Shania's natural father Clarence Edwards, thanks are especially due to Lori Edwards, to Dan Boucher for his comments, and to Gordon Edwards who was both generous with his time and honest about his own life.

New perception of Shania's life would not have been possible without the personal insights and memories of conductor and producer John Kim Bell, Helene Bolduc, Mike Taylor and Laura Surch, none of whom had previously spoken publicly about the times they spent with her. Nor had Mary Bailey, who believed in a young girl's talent when no one else did and who, despite first nurturing and then losing this once-in-a-lifetime talent, refuses to be bitter and has moved on with her life. Record producer Harry Hinde knows talent when he sees it, but luck and circumstance often conspire against him.

My visits to Timmins were made a great deal easier by Jean-Paul and Charmaine Aube who have set remarkable standards in northern Ontario hospitality. John Emms' knowledge of the local music scene was essential. David Hartt and Mike Chabot, former members of Longshot, shared their memories of those days. Old high school friends Brian Hurst and Rick Thompson gave a different picture. Thanks also to: Lise Dubois, Carole Kiraga, Paul Cousineau, Pam Kardas, Kim Seale, Len Gillis, Gerry Paquette, Claude Gagnon, Roger Richard at the Maple Leaf, Marjan Ilovar, Paul Toffanello, principal of Timmins High and Vocational school, City Clerk Jack Watson, Vic Power (mayor of Timmins 1983–2000), Will Saari, and Georges Quirion, architect of the Shania Twain Center. In Sudbury Colette Del Frate kindly drove me around Hanmer to see the old Twain home and the schools she attended. Thanks also to Lynn Bond for tales of practical jokes and ponies and to Shania's old teachers Ted Evans, John Browning, Laurie Macdonald and Keir Kitchen.

In Huntsville, thanks to Laura Kennedy for sorting out my stay at Deerhurst, and to Gillian Brunette of *The Forester*. The performers and backstage staff (past and present) of the Deerhurst Resort who helped place the era in perspective included Celia Finley, Dean Malton, Mike Degazio, Gilles Lanthier, Marg Reid, Hilda Montgomery and Gary Hubbard. Thanks to the elusive John Kotowski, who finally granted me an interview.

My visit to Nashville, Tennessee, would not have been half as productive as it was without the invaluable advice and help of Country PR supremo Richard Wooton, and of Gillie Crowder, Bob Doyle and Joni Wilson (and, from an earlier but essential background trip, Garth Brooks and Bernie Leadon). At Mercury Nashville, Luke Lewis, Sandy Neese, John Grady and Retta Harvey were generous with their time, while Sandy has continued to answer my nit-picking queries ever since. Thanks to Ron Baird at CAA, Norro Wilson, Harold Shedd, the inimitable Dick Frank, Cecelia Walker at Music Country, and to Joe Chemay and that master of 'American feel and German technology' Paul Leim.

In Toronto, thanks to Larry le Blanc, *Billboard*'s Canadian correspondent, and Brian Robertson, president of the Canadian Recording Industry Association, who clued me up on the Canadian music scene. Thanks also to Samantha Johnson at Universal Music Canada, for help, background information and the Tragically Hip CDs.

Researching Mutt Lange's background would have been much tougher without the assistance of record producer Steve Brown, and Geoff Williams, Ralph Simon, Nigel Grainge, Johan du Plooy, Alison Green, and Adam White at *Billboard* in London. Some of the quotes concerning Mutt's working habits are taken from the Mutt Lange Zone, the only online resource on Mutt worth looking at. Many thanks to George Frazer for putting me in touch with Geoff Williams and Johan du Plooy. Information about Sant Mat came from Lorenz Knauer in Germany and Rachel Storm at Inform in London.

I was first introduced to Shania Twain by Richard Beck at LD Publicity. Special thanks to Richard, and to Bernard Doherty, Claire Singers and all the staff at LD for providing press clippings, support and general background information. Thanks also to Brian Southall at Warner Music International and Jonathan Morrish at Sony Music.

Kate Maiden at Bacall helped arrange my frequent trips to Canada on Air Canada, who flew me there in comfort (and on time!). For helping me track down various numbers and people: Christa Wenzl, Nic Stern, Frances Schoenberger and Elly Houman.

Thanks to my agent, Julian Alexander at Lucas Alexander Whitley, for his advice and encouragement; and, at Headline, to Doug Young for green-lighting the project and to Lindsay Symons and Jo Roberts-Miller for seeing it through.

As usual, I would never have been able to finish the book without the love and support of my family: my wife, Jacqui, who put up with my frequent visits to Canada and the States; and Jordan and Rowan, who know all the words to Shania's songs and still love them.

A Land of Dreams

The first of July is Canada Day. It is an important event for all Canadians. A reminder to the world that they are not just a backward, northern outpost of the United States, that they have their own traditions, their own culture and their own heroes. Canada Day 2001 was the nation's 134th birthday. In Timmins, it was much, much more than that.

Timmins is Shania Twain's hometown, and its people had just spent millions building a museum in her honour. They had also declared Shania Time.

During the build-up to Canada Day, Shania Twain was impossible to escape. It circled overhead like the threatened rainclouds, then settled like a carpet of pigeons over Trafalgar Square. Her face, all flawless cheekbones, dishevelled hair and knowing look, followed you wherever you went. She was omnipresent: on giant billboards, on car stickers, on lapel buttons. The sign outside Casey's restaurant proclaimed 'Shania loves our Veggie Burgers'. In downtown Timmins the streets had been barricaded off so that shoppers could visit the Shania Twain heritage Festival, an opportunistic re-branding of the annual holiday sidewalk sale. The local radio and TV stations seldom stopped chattering about the last opportunities to win tickets to the opening of the Shania Twain Center.

This small town in northern Ontario was preparing to honour its most famous daughter, the Country princess turned international superstar. The centre cost C$4.5 million to build. The town contributed more than a million dollars to that sum, while the rest was raised from a series of federal and state grants and corporate investors. In return, they hope, the attraction will bring in 50,000 tourists a year.

The night before the centre opened to the public there was a gala opening, a black-tie event attended by Timmins' great and good. Of the 200 who attended only half a dozen knew Shania when she was simply Eilleen Twain, a tiny, feisty teenager with a startling voice and a lungful of ambition. While local politicians and the Ontario Minister for Tourism glad-handed each other, scarcely anybody spoke to her uncle and aunt, Don and Jan Fraser, for they did not know who they were. A few acknowledged Helene and Larry Bolduc, but then Helene is known to be one of Shania's closest confidants – her sister Flo works for the mayor and Larry drove the bus on Shania's American tour. Shania's adopted father's sister, Karen Twain, had also been invited to attend, but the Ojibway woman is shy, does not drive and nobody had thought to make sure she came. The event was about Shania the superstar, not about Eilleen's working-class roots.

In many ways Shania Twain remains an enigma in her own home-town. She likes to keep it that way. Many stars would have been in a hurry to forget Timmins. When Shania left town for good, in 1988, she had spent only eleven of her twenty-two years there. Aside from her classmates and those on the local music scene, few knew her and less would have noticed if she never came back. But Shania wanted to belong . . . and Eilleen, the orphan, needed to.

'It's where her family are from. Her mom and dad are still here,' says Helene Bolduc. 'They are buried in the cemetery but she feels that they are still here, so she wants to think Timmins is still very special. Eilleen believes it doesn't matter where you come from, which city you're from, which country you're from, how much population there is, it can happen. And Timmins did it for her. Whatever she went through here, it helped her follow that path. Timmins will always have a special place in her heart; her childhood was here, she graduated here. It was a big part of her life. Timmins is very easy to forget if you want to. She doesn't want to forget and by talking about Timmins she has made sure she hasn't.

Right from the moment she signed her record deal in Nashville, Shania brought Timmins into her life. She shot the pictures for the first album sleeve in the snows outside town and gave a concert in the local French high school a year later. Once her career took off she mentioned her hometown at every possible occasion.

In 1996 the City declared Shania Twain Day and renamed a street after her. She attended a massive gala celebration at the Senator Hotel. It was pouring with rain but Shania delighted the fans waiting outside by joining them in the wet and announcing 'We're not made of sugar, we're northerners.' Once inside, recalls local hairdresser Paul Cousineau, 'She went up to every single person, even the bathroom attendants, and did not leave until she had said hello to everybody. She got up and signed autographs. I don't know how she smiles so much. She doesn't forget people; she is very down to earth and fame has never gone to her head . . . if it hasn't now, I don't think it can.'

On Canada Day 1999 she held the last concert of her North American tour in Timmins' Hollinger Park. Despite the extra costs involved in bringing her spectacular show hundreds of miles north of the regular stadium circuit, Shania refused to consider giving anything other than the full deal. It was the biggest show the town had ever seen, attracting 28,000 people. They still talk about it today. In the summer of 2000 she quietly drove up from Toronto with her younger sister and arrived unannounced, without a bodyguard, at her high-school reunion, where she posed for photos and signed autographs for anyone who wanted them.

A year later, when Shania was only thirty-five, and the town prepared for the opening of the Shania Twain Center, a palpable aura of disappointment hung in the air. Months previously, Shania had told the organizers that she would be absent from the July celebrations, by which time she would be heavily pregnant with her first child, due at the end of August. In town, though, hope – tinged with blind faith – refused to accept logic. After all, she had shown up unannounced before. Like Kevin Costner in *Field of Dreams*, Timmins collectively believed that if they built it she would come.

The 11,000-square-foot building, designed by local architect Georges Quirion and constructed primarily from local materials, fronted in glass, wood and granite, would be an attractive feature anywhere. Inside, there is light and space, beckoning visitors to 'Come on over, come on in'. Interactive exhibits mean people can play musical instruments and watch an excellent video full of unseen footage of Shania, and these are well put together by the Toronto-based Lord Design Studio who have worked with the Jimi Hendrix Museum in Seattle and the Muhammad Ali Center. But there are not enough of them, making one feel that too much money was spent on the building and not enough on highlighting its contents.

Shania backed the project from the start, when she told the then mayor, Vic Power, 'This looks like it will be an exciting project for the City of Timmins and I am happy to be part of it.' Since then she has lived up to her word by donating a million pounds worth of memorabilia. She has sent so much material, in fact, that only between ten and fifteen per cent will be on view at any one time. Her fans making pilgrimages of many thousand miles would probably prefer it if there was more of her stuff simply housed in an aircraft hangar.

The Shania Twain Center is certainly a testament to her remarkable achievements. There are racks of awards, a fraction of a cabinet bulging at the seams. (She has won five Grammies, nine Junos (Canadian Grammies), one CMA and twenty Canadian CMAs, six American Music awards and, perhaps most importantly to her, fifteen BMI Pop awards and eight SOCAN songwriter awards.) There are costumes, too – notably the leopard-skin-print pantsuit from the legendary 'That Don't Impress Me Much' video. Somewhere in the vaults are her wedding dress; a tan suede skirt with fringes handmade by her Native grandmother, Selina, which she wore as a child; handwritten lyric sheets for hit songs like 'Don't be Stupid' and 'Black Eyes, Blue Tears'; and the skimpy T-shirt she wore for her breakthrough video 'Whose Bed Have Your Boots Been Under?'

The clothes all seem impossibly tiny for a star so impossibly big. In six years she has soared across the music world like a flaming comet that has, as yet, shown no signs of burning out. Shania Twain has shown herself to be a mistress of what video can be; she can deliver a live show to rival those with ten times as much experience. But it is the near exponential curve on the graph of her worldwide record sales that is deeply scary. Her debut album, *Shania Twain*, sold 100,000 copies on its original release; that figure rose to 16 million for *The Woman in Me* and in excess of 32 million for *Come On Over*. After overtaking *The Eagles' Greatest Hits 1971-75* (31 million) and the *Saturday Night Fever Original Soundtrack* (30 million) within the last year, *Come on Over* is now the second-highest-selling album of all time – if a long way behind Michael Jackson's *Thriller* (46 million).

Like that of both those rivals, Shania's music works on a multiplicity of different levels. Hers are classic pop songs that hook into the memory so deep they are all but impossible to extract without surgery; their sound is as close to perfect as money can buy, the result of hundreds of hours spent in the studio weaving instruments and voice together into a seamless whole. They are happiness shrapnel, positive messages appealing across the generations to children, to young teens and to adults – if seldom to the young and trendy.

What is on display in the centre is a physical manifestation of the Shania Twain legend. It is about what she is perceived to be – not what made her. *That* lies outside the walls. Perhaps it is only confirmation of the legend that people want to see, to be reminded of her Cinderella story, her rags-to-riches rise, her triumph over tragedy. To fans, a star is a blank slate upon which our own preconceptions, our own beliefs and desires, can be placed. They become what we want them to be.

Shania herself knows that Shania Twain is an illusion. When she met Timmins City Clerk Jack Watson to discuss the plans for the centre, she told him that she is two people whom she tries to keep separate. Eileen, wife and soon to be mother, and Shania, the superstar. 'Eileen has a private life where she likes to do certain things,' Watson says, 'while Shania Twain is that famous person. And if she can use her to help our community she will.'

Timmins and the seemingly infinite bush and forest surrounding it is an essential part of what made her. Much has not changed since she grew up there. Wednesday night has always been talent night at the Maple Leaf Tavern. Twenty years ago Eilleen Twain dropped in every few weeks, sang some of her own songs, maybe a Country weepy accompanying herself on her twelve-string acoustic. The décor has faded a touch (and they have added Shania memorabilia to the wall) but the crowd, lost under a cloud of cigarette smoke and beer, has hardly changed at all. The Mattagami Hotel, where a timid eight-year-old gave her first appearance for twenty-five bucks, was pretty sleazy in 1973. Now it is a strip club. Don's Pizzeria has a Shania vegetarian special but otherwise its pizzas and the *poutine* (fries covered with cheese and gravy) from Chez Nous taste as good as they ever did after a few beers.

The paraphernalia of the twenty-first century – cable TV, the Internet, cellphones – has brought the thoughts and sounds of the world closer to Timmins. It is no longer a northern backwater forgotten by both high and pop culture. Physically, however, it will always hover on the periphery. It's a hard place to visit, 700 kilometres north of Toronto and above the Arctic Watershed (its rivers flow north into the Arctic Ocean) and just far enough off the Trans Canada Highway to be an unnecessary detour. The roads are a bit better nowadays, but the railroad no longer runs through town and a return ticket on the ninety-minute flight to Toronto can cost more than a transatlantic hop.

On satellite pictures of the earth at night, one can see Timmins clearly for where it is: a single pinprick of light encompassed on all sides by darkness. It is a pimple of civilization, bordered by mile upon mile of bush, spruce and pine trees and as many lakes as there are stars in the sky. Timmins' other claim to fame is that it is Canada's largest city. Its limits sprawl over 3,210 square kilometres, including 100 lakes and rivers within its boundaries, while trees outnumber the 46,000 inhabitants a thousand to one.

Timmins would never have existed at all but for gold. It is a town founded on dreams, a place where fortunes lie unseen, undiscovered, beneath the trees. When the town was incorporated in 1912 few believed it had any more future than the dozens of other abandoned mining camps that litter northern Ontario. It is not a pretty place for it is a working-class mining town whose architecture reflects its history. Row upon row of wooden mine houses that have not changed externally in decades sit alongside shops and office buildings carved from chunks of pre-stressed concrete. The climate can be as harsh and unforgiving as the land is beautiful. Winters last six months – and while the locals say they are easier nowadays, the cold still chews at fingers and toes like a ravenous ice demon. In early summers the mosquitoes and blackflies can drive a man mad.

It is a friendly, hospitable place – in part because nobody has been there long enough to put down roots so deep they need to freeze out visitors. Folks can be a little reserved at the outset, but once they have decided to let go they love to talk. That's Shania, too: a bit distant at first meeting but a major motormouth once she's comfortable.

Timmins has survived but not thrived, for it walks a thin line between riches and extinction. Its population is the same today as forty years back. In the late sixties, just as the Hollinger gold mine was closing down, Texas Gulf discovered huge zinc deposits at Kidd Creek. And without that base-metal strike it is unlikely that Shania Twain would be claiming Timmins as her hometown; perhaps nobody would be. Now, though the mine remains a major employer, Timmins' economy is suffering. The town has an unemployment rate of eight per cent, half as much again as the state average. One day the mine will close – for mines always do – and when that happens, Timmins may wither away and die unless something is done now. Hence the centre.

Timmins needs the attention that a global superstar has brought it. It needs tourists. Until Shania, the celebrities it exported were what one might expect from a chilly frontier town. Tough. A series of rugged ice-hockey stars – currently personified by Steve Sullivan of the Chicago Blackhawks – Olympic gold-medal-winning skier Kathy Kreiner, and multimillionaire entrepreneurs Roy Thomson and Jack Kent Cook. Shania Twain is beautiful, but make no mistake: she is as tough, determined and hard working as any of them and any of Timmins' original prospectors. The only difference is that she has taken words and melodies and turned her dreams multi-platinum.

Yet long before Shania ever existed, another girl inhabited this unlikely land of dreams. Eilleen Twain: a little girl with goofy teeth, a voice from God and a mother who believed in her talent almost to the point of madness.

CHAPTER ONE

Titanic Blues
(and Bootlegging Brawlers)

Accidents make history. Sometimes a missed connection is a vital one. Shania Twain might not exist if her great-grandfather Francis George Pearce had arrived at Southampton docks one day earlier. The 24-year-old soldier had promised his wife and baby daughter that the voyage taking them to a new life in Canada would be on a brand new ship. Fortunately he arrived too late and all the third-class passages had sold out. The *Titanic* sailed without the Pearces. On 14 April 1912 the unsinkable ship hit an iceberg and sank with the loss of 1,500 lives, most of whom were travelling in steerage class.

The Pearces were a solid mixture of English and Irish stock (though they tried to deny their Irish blood for years). Frank, born in 1887, had joined the British army in his late teens and was serving in Norfolk where he met Lottie Louise Reeves, one of eleven children. A few months younger, she was born in Weybourne; where the winds blow straight down from the Arctic over the North Sea. They were married in St Michael's Church, Aldershot, on 2 October 1909, after which Frank was posted to keep the peace in Ireland. Their eldest daughter, Eileen, was born in Newbridge, County Kildare on 10 April 1911. The following year they decided, along with most of her family, to try their luck in the Dominion of Canada.

Frank, Lottie Louise and baby Eileen made the crossing safely on the next available boat and took the trains as far as Manitoba. Frank had been lured by the promise of a quarter-section farm, 160 acres of land to call his own. Until his claim was registered, he worked on the railroads out of Winnipeg, thanks to the man his sister-in-law Mary had met on the boat over and subsequently married. Their second son, also named Frank, was born in Winnipeg, but when war broke out, Frank Snr, an army reservist, was immediately called up. He returned to Europe, leaving his wife, pregnant with Jack, sitting in their new homestead in the wild scrubland outside of Badger, ten kilometres from the US border.

Frank did not worry unduly about his wife. He knew the Reeves women had strength of character, spirit in spades. They knew how to look after themselves and their families. 'Lottie and her sister Cyl didn't take a back seat,' says Roger Pearce, Frank Jnr's son. 'If someone pissed them off, look out. There were three Irishmen, the Ryans, in town. They were raised in hell, fighting all the time, but if they were where Lottie was she would give them a tune up and they would sit in the corner like little boys wouldn't say "boo". They had respect for her because she wouldn't take no BS from anyone. When she and Cyl were older they loved to watch wrestling on TV, they'd get all wild over it.'

Gunner FG Pearce (No. 37417) did not return home for five years. He served in the Royal Regiment of Field Artillery; his special affinity with horses proved essential for driving the guns and ammunition trailers through the mud behind the front line. Gunners did not have to live in the trenches, or go over the top into the machine guns of No Man's Land, though Frank regularly volunteered to carry extra ammunition supplies into the trenches. He returned home in 1919 sporting 'Pip, Squeak & Wilfrid', a full set of medals: the 1914–15 Star, the British War Medal, and the Victory Medal.

He was a quiet, well-mannered, dignified man who never spoke about his wartime experiences and just got on with providing for his family. Two more daughters, Grace and May, arrived and, in 1926, when May was two, the Pearces moved to a new farm just outside Piney. It was a family affair, for Lottie's father, Sidney Reeves, had the farm opposite. The land around Piney was all right but nowhere near as fertile as the Red River Valley where the Great Plains began fifty kilometres further west. Mostly flat scrub and bush enlivened by a few hills and East Ridge with its plunging ravines and towering red pines over thirty metres tall.

Frank ran a mixed farm supporting a few cattle, other livestock, grain fields, enough to feed the family. The cash crops were oats and alfalfa, excellent cattle forage. Frank produced such high-quality alfalfa seed that he was contacted by the University of Manitoba wanting to know how he did it.

During the twenties, while life was tough and money short in rural Manitoba, the Pearces and the Reeves survived well enough. Thanks to Mary's husband there was always work on the railroads – every day Frank walked the three kilometres to the rail head in Piney – and the farm provided all the food they needed. They entertained themselves playing cards, Frank Jnr and May loved to sing, Lottie's sister Cyl (Cecilia) had an excellent voice and was a very good piano player, and several times a year there was a let-your-hair-down hoe-down. While the farm could feed a growing family the adults had to find work outside.

Eileen started working in the kitchens and behind the bar of the Piney Hotel when she was eighteen. There she met Walter Fraser, a lad from a local town. They married in 1932 and decided to chance their luck in the mines of northern Ontario. He found work as a shaft sinker in the Hallnor mine in Timmins where their son Don was born on 7 August 1933. The marriage foundered soon after, and Fraser left town, severing all contact with his family.

Eileen struggled to make ends meet. Money was so tight that when Don was ten he was sent to live with his grandparents on the farm in Piney for the winter. Eileen scrimped and saved from her waitressing tips to buy him a pair of ice skates for Christmas. Things looked up after she fell in love with George Morrison (born 1908), a professional saw filer who sharpened and hammered into shape the huge blades in a sawmill. 'George,' May recalls, 'was very nice-looking. He was a big man, tall and very kind.' He, too, was of mixed ancestry, his father Bert was Scottish and his mother Mary (née Brisbois) was, despite her French name, predominantly Irish with a little dash of Spanish. Their only child, Sharon, was born in Vita, Manitoba on 4 June 1945 because Eileen wanted to be back with her parents. She returned to Timmins soon after the birth to the family house on Poplar Street. Later they moved to a small three-bedroomed, wooden bungalow with white walls and a red roof out on Highway 101 between Matheson and Moose Creeks, twenty kilometres east of South Porcupine. The main entertainment when the Fraser kids came out to visit on Sundays, was the short walk to the gas station in Hoyle where two brown bears, Yogi and Booboo, were kept in cages.

George made a good wage and so the family were well provided for, but like most fathers of his generation he left the child rearing to his wife. Eileen was a gentle woman, happiest milking the cow and tending to her large garden. Her daughter, virtually an only child (Don married and left home when he was nineteen), was headstrong and wilful. 'As a child Sharon was a real handful,' says May Thompson, Eileen Morrison's youngest sister, 'she wanted her way with everything. My brother Jack, who lived in Timmins too, couldn't get over how disciplined our kids were in comparison. Sharon had a nervous complaint of some kind and my sister always worried about her. She would raise heck every morning about going to school on the bus, there was an argument every day about something.'

'She was a bright young girl, very enthused with life,' remembers Don. 'She went to school in Hoyle and then to Roland Michener High School in South Porcupine. She was very headstrong but she was also high-strung, very high-strung, so she would go into depression fairly easily. She was always on the go, a very busy girl.'

In the early 1960s, the Morrisons moved to Field, just outside Sudbury. In a few short years everything went horribly wrong. George suffered a severe stroke which left him ninety per cent paralysed and unable to speak. Under the added pressure Eileen, who had a congenital heart condition, suffered the first of several minor heart attacks. That did nothing to help Sharon's mood swings, and without any male influence she started to look for a substitute. Sharon had always been interested in boys – even at thirteen when she went to help out her mother's pregnant cousin Evelyn Struthers, who was staying up at Nellie Lake. 'She was young happy-go-lucky, a cute girl. She was very outgoing and there was a few younger guys in the island

and she was certainly interested in them.'

At seventeen she was a pretty girl, tall, 5' 7" (1.7 metres) and very slender – perhaps too thin for some – with blonde hair turning to auburn. When she was in a good mood she was wonderful company who loved to talk and talk and talk. When the moods were upon her she could be difficult company as she withdrew into herself. She got engaged to Gilles, a young Frenchman from Sturgeon Falls whom both her mother and brother liked. Just before the wedding he was killed in a car crash. Sharon was already pregnant. Her daughter, called Jill after her father, was born on 19 April 1963.

Sharon, a once indulged child, found herself flooded by a fistful of adult responsibilities, a baby, an invalid father, a poorly mother, no money. She was not yet eighteen and she should have been out having fun. She found it hard to cope, she could not earn enough money to support herself. In 1964, that was a man's job. She needed help. Jill was still a toddler when Sharon met a man who seemed to be the answer to all her problems: Clarence Edwards.

'Those times really hit us all hard, Sharon especially, as she had a little girl,' says Don. 'When she met Clarence she was still very upset. At that time I thought he was a real nice person.'

Clarence Edwards was the eighth of Harold and Regina Edwards' nine children. The Edwards are a sprawling, brawling clan who emigrated from Ireland in the nineteenth century and fetched up farming in the Ottawa Valley outside Renfrew on the Quebec border. Fed up with life in 'Cowshit Valley' Harold's father moved to Chapleau to work on the railroads in the early 1900s.

Timmins, 200 kilometres to the east, had a reason to exist: the mines. Without the railroad, Chapleau had none. For over a century it has been the biggest railway terminal between Montreal and Winnipeg and for many years had its own shop and was home to crane drivers, engineers and drivers. If the railway ever leaves, the town, which is slowly wasting away, will disappear back into the forests. There is logging in abundance, for trucks can go anywhere there is wood and bush road, but little else.

In Chapleau, Harold, who was born in 1906, fell madly in love with fourteen-year-old Regina Benson. Her father was Swedish, while her mother was from an old French family, born and raised in Quebec. Along the way the Quebecois had incorporated some Native genes. 'My mother told me one time when I was young that her mother's mother was part Indian,' says Gordon Edwards. 'Clarence, he don't look Indian, but my brother Walter, you put him beside one of these fellas here in the reserve and they are like twins.' The Bensons decided to move 300 kilometres due north, to Kapuskasing, where the Spruce Falls Power and Paper Plant was promising to build a model town where the needs of the forestry industry could coexist happily with the community. There is nothing but 600 kilometres of river, forest and lake between Kapuskasing and James Bay, so its location was ideal for an internment camp. During the Great War thousands of Eastern Europeans, perceived as a threat to national security, were confined there, treated as prisoners of war. After the war the camp was filled with 'dangerous' left-wing radicals, including the leaders of the 1919 Winnipeg general strike.

The smitten Harold followed Regina to Kap and married her in 1927. They set up home in a small farm six kilometres outside of town. He worked the midnight shift at Spruce Falls Paper, commuting in by dog sled in winter and bicycle in summer, and worked the farm as soon as he got back. As the Great Depression bit, Harold helped support different families, including his in-laws, sending them out into the bush to cut stove wood. 'I saw other little kids with nothing to eat but we lived like millionaires, albeit with no hydro [electricity] and we had to fetch in our own water,' recalls Gordon, the second child and the oldest boy, born in 1931.

The secret to Harold's success was simple. He was a bootlegger, distilling moonshine, brewing beer and selling it to locals, bush whackers and natives. The family was engaged in a perpetual battle to outwit the OPP (Ontario Provincial Police). Despite having no phone, Harold somehow always knew when the cops were coming to search for his still.

'One day, when I was about six, he says, "Come out for a ride in the sleigh with me"', says Gordon. 'We went out in the bush half a mile or so where he had his still, he picked up all the copper tubing and threw them up into the thick snow in the spruce trees., Then he lights a fire and we sit down. All of a sudden I hear these dogs coming and he says, "Don't say a word about anything." The OPPs really scared me, big, big men in fur jackets, fur hats and fur mitts. The first time I saw them I thought they were bears, I was so scared I couldn't say a word. They asked my father, "Where's your still? Where's all the paraphernalia for the booze you're making?" They searched all over the place, then they took off again cursing. All they had to do was look above their heads.'

One time, when her husband was at work, Regina got word the OPP were on their way. A tiny woman of 5' 2" (1.6 metres) she somehow found the strength to pick up a 45 gallon barrel of home brew, stagger out to the porch and flip it over. Then she washed out the barrel and was sitting comfortably on it when the cops arrived.

Bootlegging was a labour of love for Harold. Drinking to insensible excess was more than blue-collar culture to him, for alcoholism was bred into his bones, a poisoned flagon passed down through the generations. 'My father and his two brothers they could have drunk the lake. Everybody they knew was the same. My father's brother was the only one who went in the army during the war,' recalls Gordon, 'and when he came home on leave he'd take whatever he could get to drink and go in the bush and lay there for days until the MPs came to find him.'

The start of the Second World War was good news for Regina's carpenter brothers. They headed south to work for the car manufacturers in Detroit and Windsor. Harold intended to join up or follow them south, but after the army rejected him for having too many kids to support, he stopped off in Chapleau to see his father, who told him the railroad was desperate for firemen and engineers. He never went back to Kap, just sent word home to join him. Regina and the kids packed the wagon with furniture, hitched the horse to it and headed for the station. The train journey was close to 500 kilometres.

The family settled two kilometres out of town on Bucciarelli Road. Backwoods kids who had never seen power lines before, they had no idea what the hydro cables that stretched over the peak of the roof did. One day, after Gordon and his mother had walked into town to buy groceries, Ernie went to play on the roof. He was running down the gable, gathering speed as he went, so he thought he'd grab the wires to break his fall, swing on them like Tarzan. The electricity fried his arms so badly he lost them both, wore steel hooks from the time he got out of hospital. The house was cursed, so they moved into town. The hooks never stopped Ernie having fun: when the boys got into fights, he could lay opponents out with one blow.

Music was always there – 'Irish people have to have music' – part of the furniture. Harold scarcely needed an excuse for a party. He had an old wind-up gramophone and every 78 Hank Snow ever cut, from back when the Nova Scotian could yodel like Jimmie Rodgers, long before *I'm Moving On* made him a Nashville star. Regina's brothers were accomplished musicians, always ready to break out fiddles and guitars. The Edwards boys didn't play anything but they could all sing. Clarence had a beautiful voice but he was too shy to use it. Sometimes, when he was a kid and lost in play, he'd start singing, 'Christ,' says Gordon, 'I'm telling you, he had a voice that would drive you up the wall. So good you didn't want him to quit.'

Clarence was a good athlete, quick and tough on the basketball court and the ice hockey rink. His cousin Dan Boucher reckons he was the best broomball player in Chapleau (shooting around on ice using a broom and ball instead of a stick and a puck). He had a temper, though; one night a spectator gave him so much gyp that eventually Clarence dropped his broom, vaulted the rail and repaid the heckler in kind.

There was always a rebellious, sod-authority streak in Clarence. When he was a kid and did not get his own way, he threw himself on to the ground and held his breath until he turned blue. The only person who could talk air back into his lungs was his father. After high school he joined the army. He looked smart in his uniform but he constantly clashed with the stripes and the brass. When he didn't fancy his latest posting he went AWOL until the MPs dragged him back. Eventually the military tired of his antics, banged him up in the glasshouse for six months and sent him packing with a discharge. For a while he roamed Ontario working odd jobs.

In the fall of 1964, Clarence met Sharon Morrison in a bar in Sudbury. They were physical opposites, which might have accounted for some of the attraction. Clarence was dark, with a heavy build, 5' 9" (1.75 metres, tall for an Edwards), arms like hams. He had so much body hair that as a young man he was too embarrassed to strip off when swimming with his brothers. Sharon was skinny, so thin that she seemed taller than she actually was, a twitchy girl forever lighting another cigarette while its predecessor still smouldered, hoping it might calm her jangling nerves, giving her hands something with which to occupy themselves. Even in a culture where everybody smoked all the time people remember Sharon as a chain smoker. Clarence was a handsome guy, a party boy, full of Irish blarney and bravado. Sharon grabbed on to him, a liferaft in her stormy seas. Needy and lonely, once she had him she was not going to let go.

Gordon Edwards was working underground at the Levack mine and was living in Chelmsford, just outside Sudbury, when Clarence and Sharon turned up looking for a place to stay, to be alone for a couple of days. Although he has been sober for the past fifteen years, Gordon still retains one family trait. He is quick to judge and slow to forgive. Sharon's arrival in the house was akin to throwing petrol on a bonfire.

'Three days later I've had it up to here with this girl, but Clarence, he wants to marry her,' says Gordon. So he called his brothers Walter and Desi together, told them there was an important family meeting that night, and ordered Clarence to send his girl out somewhere, anywhere. The boys got together after work and started downing a few, until Gordon stepped into his elder-brother role and told Clarence, 'You can't marry this girl, it's impossible, you marry her and you'll be in the fucking nuthouse in a year.'

Clarence took the point but all he said was: 'I have to marry her because we are having a baby.' Gordon tried to reason with him, told him he wasn't the first guy to have a baby by accident and anyway she'd already been down that route once and why hadn't the last guy married her? Clarence, who knew about Jill's father, refused to budge, he was going to stand by Sharon and that was it. Gordon told him he was going to be sorry, washed his hands of the affair and they all got hammered.

Eileen Morrison was too ill to attend the wedding in Garson, so Don Fraser gave Sharon away. Soon after, Clarence and Sharon moved down to Windsor, just across the border from Detroit, where the pay in the Chrysler plant was better than the mines. They rented a house and their daughter was born on 28 August 1965. They christened her Eilleen after her maternal grandmother and Regina after Clarence's mother. Little Eilleen was a true child of the New World, more Irish (coming from all sides) than anything else, with a healthy dash of English, Swedish, and Scottish blood, leavened with exotic touches of French, Native and Spanish.

The baby girl might have calmed things for a while, but in truth the relationship was doomed before it began. It was a marriage forged in mistake, transferred on to a never-ending battlefield on which there could be no victors, only damaged offspring. Sharon needed someone preternaturally calm who could still the demons in her head. She craved security. Instead, she had a man from a family who considered her to be a nutcase. The Edwards clan still rail about Sharon. To them she has become the monster who destroyed any vestige of a relationship Clarence might have had with his daughters. But they admit 'he is no saint'. He never was.

Sharon's behaviour became erratic. She needed stability but she felt none, which magnified her mood swings. There are signs of an obsessive compulsive disorder in the way she tackled problems all her life, but in the 1960s the only medical diagnosis for a working-class mother was tranquillizers. 'She was on nerve pills steady, she was always taking pills,' says Gordon. 'I've seen her with the pills because one time I went into the blues. She was the one who helped me out, gave me these frigging nerve pills and actually talked me out of it. I took a couple of pills went to sleep and when I woke up I was OK.'

When she was on an up, there was a hyper intensity to Sharon, her energy was phenomenal, her emotions allowed no half measures. The Edwards say she was jealous and possessive, that she had to know where Clarence was at all times. If his friends phoned, he'd sneak out to join them in a beer. He might neck a couple before Sharon found him. If he stopped by for a drink after a broomball game and came back with a book of matches from an unknown bar, she accused him of having an affair.

'They were living in South Porcupine. Me and three other fellas went to go to the winter carnival,' says Gordon. 'I was hanging around until Clarence came in from work and when he did come in, he said, "I have to go to the bank to cash my cheque so we can go to this thing." Sharon told him, "You have got fifteen minutes – don't forget it." He goes and he comes back and it was sixteen minutes and she says to him, "You were fucking the teller!" It was a fight from then until we went to the carnival and all the time we were there.'

Clarence could not cope. In Toronto he'd go to the gym, run for an hour, dripping with sweat, to get everything out of his system for a few minutes. At times, Sharon's physical demands exhausted him. 'He had to fuck her from the time he went to bed to the time he got up in the morning to go to work,' says Gordon, 'I was there when it was happening and she said, "If you can't do it, you're doing it with somebody else." Another night, Clarence wanted to go and have a drink with me. Sharon told him not to go, but he went anyway. As he was walking down the street she tore off all her clothes and started chasing him and screaming at him – stark naked.'

It was a steady fight from the time they got up to the time they went to bed. Once, as they were crossing the horseshoe bridge, driving into Chapleau, arguing furiously, Clarence crashed the car straight into the town dairy, demolishing both it and the car. On occasion his temper got him into bar brawls ('If he gets mad enough get out of his road,' warns Gordon).

Clarence moved from one job to another though he always put food on the table. From Windsor they moved to Toronto, where he worked for CN (Canadian National Railways) in the car department, and then back to Timmins. They stayed with Sharon's mother in Hoyle while Don, who was a superintendent at Texas Gulf's Kidd Creek mine, fixed Clarence a job.

By the time Carrie Ann was born on 16 December 1967 both Clarence and the marriage were finished. His nerves shot, he committed himself to a mental hospital. Discharging himself after several weeks, he returned home and quickly realized he could not take it any more. One day he went out for a packet of cigarettes and a loaf of bread and never came back. Nobody in the family heard from him for six months until he turned up in Toronto back working for CN in the boxcar department. Eventually, he returned to Chapleau and went to work on the railway as an engineer.

'It was a very sad marriage,' says Don. 'Clarence and Sharon were just bad for each other. She was prone to be excitable and high-strung for sure. They were set staying at my mother's place in Hoyle and he [Clarence] just left and never come back. I'd say Clarence was the worst person she could have married and Jerry was the best.'

Eileen Morrison adored her three granddaughters. After Clarence left, Sharon and the girls lived with her in Hoyle. She looked after them as well as supporting Sharon financially. Knowing how sick she was, she worried about them all the time. 'Sharon got depressed and Eileen worried that she wouldn't look after the girls properly. I imagine that Sharon loved her in her way but she wasn't the easiest person to live with,' says May Thompson: 'Eileen gave her life up for those three little girls. When she was on her deathbed she said to me, "I've been lying here thinking what is going to happen to those kids. I've decided that my sister Grace will take one, my sister-in-law Isla will take one." I said to her, "Which one am I going to have?" and she said, "Carrie Ann." '

That never happened. Sharon had already met the man who would be right for her, a man who wanted to be a father to her three little girls.

CHAPTER TWO

The Man from Mattagami

A bandoned, left high, dry and penniless, Sharon wanted nothing more to do with her husband. With the same intense focus with which she had attempted to keep him in her life she cut him out of it. She refused to let him have anything to do with raising his daughters. She told the girls she didn't need him, that none of them did and that they never would. It was a brave, if foolhardy decision. Aged twenty-four with three daughters under five and no professional qualifications, Sharon's prospects were not great. She stayed with her mother and found part-time work in menial jobs, as a cleaner or in hotel kitchens.

In days when the black clouds went away, Sharon was engaging company. Unlike some Timmins locals, who ranted and raved against the Indians, she had no racial prejudices. In town one day she struck up a friendship with an Ojibway girl called Audrey Twain. Audrey decided Sharon was just right for her younger brother Jerry and determined to set them up. One night in late 1969, when Jerry had returned home after working on a logging contract out west in British Columbia, Sharon was invited over to the Twain home at 294 Birch Street North.

She liked what she saw. Although he was two years her junior there was something solid and reassuring about Jerry. A lot of Native people are very quiet and Jerry was too, a watcher who waited his time; he did not strut into a room and demand attention, but he certainly was not an introvert. He spoke when he had something to say and could carry on a very good conversation. But there was something else there . . . a twinkle, a sparkle behind his eyes. He loved to tease, but gently without malice. He laughed a lot, used his humour to alleviate her dark moments. Above all, Jerry was strong, both physically and mentally.

'He was everybody's leaning post,' says Karen Twain, 'When we were going through so much my brother was always the one who told us, "Be tough." '

Étienne Brulé would have recognized Jerry Twain. To look at, he was all Native. Short – only 5' 6" (1.7 metres) tall – powerfully built with a low centre of gravity, jet black hair with matching eyes carved from coal. The name, the clothes and the language might have changed, but the spirit was the same as the French explorer had seen in the Ojibwe warriors 350 years earlier: the unbending duty towards his extended clan, the love for the forests, the physical presence and the pride, the absolute certainty in who he was.

Although their name lacks the historical and romantic resonance of such tribes as the Sioux, the Apache, the Commanche or even small tribes like the Huron and the Mohawk, the Ojibwe have been one of the largest Native groups in North America for most of their known history. The Ojibwe remain unrecognized in cowboy and Indian history primarily because of their geographical remoteness. Secondly, despite being skilled hunters and fierce warriors, they were smart enough to seldom confront white governments in open warfare.

There were always more Woodland Ojibwe than people realized. They lived in the forests on the east banks of Lake Superior and to the north of Lake Huron stretching all the way up to Hudson Bay. There may have been as many as 100,000 living in northern Ontario when they first encountered Brulé in 1623 at Sault Sainte Marie. Prior to that first contact they were a loose confederation of independent clans bound together by a common language. The Ojibwe are one people with three names – Chippewa, Ojibwe and Anishinabe – as well as dozens of sub-groupings and bands. Chippewa is the 'official' name recognized by the United States government and was used on all their treaties. (Stick an 'o' in front of Chippewa and the linguistic link is obvious.) In Canada they are known as Ojibwe (pronounced 'Oh-jib-way'), the name given them by their enemies back in the seventeenth century. It means 'to pucker' and comes from the way their moccasins were sewn with a distinctive puckered seam to keep out the snow. They refer to themselves as Anishinabe and more playfully as 'nish-nobs'.

Their land was never suited to agriculture. The Ojibwe were expert woodcraftsmen, hunter-gatherers who harvested wild rice and used maple syrup and sugar as seasoning and a food preservative. They hunted moose and partridge, trapped beaver or rabbit and fished for sturgeon. Birch bark was used to make utensils, storage containers, canoes and to cover their dome-shaped wigwams. They dressed in buckskin, adding layers of fur when the snow came.

In summer bands gathered by lakes, living off fish, berries and wild rice. During winter, the communities (at most a few hundred strong) split into extended families living in isolated camps which allowed the men to range for miles without encountering any competition. Perhaps owing to those long winters confined inside their tepees the Ojibwe became renowned as great story-tellers. (In one tale explaining the origin of Chicago the Ojibwe refer to it as 'the Place of the Skunk'!) Henry Longfellow's famous narrative poem *The Song of Hiawatha* tells of a young brave growing up on the shores of Lake Superior. After many adventures he marries a Dakota maiden, Minnehaha ('laughing water'), and eventually departs for the Isles of the Blest to rule the kingdom of the Northwest Wind. Longfellow got his tribal alliances and names mixed up. While the geographical locations and stories are all taken from Ojibwe legends the original Hiawatha was a Mohawk who, like Minnehaha's Dakota Sioux, were their sworn enemies.

Originally hereditary chiefs only had limited authority over their own band. However, direct contact with the French fur traders, who admired the high quality of their beaver pelts, changed the social structure of the Ojibwe for ever. Seeking to fill a seemingly insatiable demand back home, the French offered steel weapons and firearms in exchange for fur.

To the east Dutch and French merchants had encouraged an arms race, which, coupled with the virtual eradication of beaver in southern Ontario, had upset the old balance of power. For the seventy years of the Beaver Wars (1630–1700), the Iroquois Alliance and the Huron squabbled and fought for possession of new hunting grounds. Initially the Ojibwe were too far away to become involved, but when the Iroquois, the best-armed force in North America, started to raid their territory, the Ojibwe did not flee. Instead, they regrouped around Sault Sainte Marie and organized into larger battle groups. In 1662, they surprised a large Mohawk war party just west of Sault Sainte Marie and annihilated it. The place is known today as Iroquois Point, the Ojibwe call it 'the place of Iroquois bones'. Soon afterwards they drove their enemies back east for good.

By 1700, the Ojibwe supplied two-thirds of the French fur trade and Ojibwe had become the unofficial trade language. The larger bands continued to extend their hunting grounds south and east of Lake Superior – an area then of little interest to Europeans – eventually, after a hundred-year war, wresting the lakes and wild rice-growing areas in Northern Michigan, Wisconsin and Minnesota from the Sioux. In 1820, the Ojibwe were the largest and most powerful Great Lakes tribe and quite probably the strongest in North America.

As French power in Canada waned after 1763, the British established strong trading links with the Ojibwe. During the British–American war of 1812, they helped defend Ontario from invasion. After 1815, the Ojibwe signed a peace treaty and were seldom in direct conflict with the United States – they always preferred to fight the Sioux – though north of the border some did support Louis Riel's Métis (mixed French-Cree-Ojibwe) forces in the Red River Rebellions of 1869 and 1884.

The last official battle of the Indian Wars did involve the Ojibwe. On 5 October 1898, US army troops were sent to the Leech Lake reservation in northern Minnesota to arrest Bugonaygeshig, a dissident elder. As his braves gathered around, an army rifle was accidentally discharged, and the soldiers found themselves surrounded and under fire. Eventually a truce was agreed and the army withdrew without their quarry. To save face, Private O. Burchard was given the last Medal of Honor awarded in an Indian campaign. As historian Lee Sultzman remarks, 'A soldier got the medal, but as was the case with almost every enemy they had ever faced, the Ojibwe had won the battle.'

While they were never beaten in war, economics, disease and the slow, inexorable, advance of European settlers proved more effective in destroying Ojibwe power. The total collapse of the fur trade in the mid-nineteenth century destroyed their economic clout and a series of treaties – fifty-one with the USA and thirty with the British – slowly whittled away their lands. Western diseases, notably smallpox epidemics, killed thousands, while the insidious effects of alcohol sapped their spirit. However, the Ojibwe remain numerous. There are currently 130,000 in the United States and 60,000 in Canada. Of the 600 plus First Nations recognized by Canada, more than 130 are Ojibwe (at least in part), spread across Ontario, Manitoba, Saskatchewan and Alberta.

When Jerry Twain was born on 24 September 1947, years of social and economic neglect had eroded much of the Ojibwe's self-respect. Primitive living conditions on the reserves resulted in high infant mortality and low life expectancy. In town many Indians – they were still called Indians then – found it hard to get jobs and lived off welfare. Inherently shy, coming from a culture where it is impolite to look people straight in the eyes, their problems were compounded by booze. After a few drinks, retiring personalities would flip, leading to fights.

Indians were often dismissed as dysfunctional, unreliable and lazy, an image founded on ignorance and fanned by prejudice. When the Twain family first moved to Timmins in 1964, there was only one other Native family in the town. 'My brother and I had pretty much a hard time,' says Karen Twain. 'When my mother took us and enrolled us in school, people just surrounded us. They kept asking us where had we lived before and did we live in a tepee. People were ignorant back then. We'd lived all over but I don't remember being teased anyplace else, maybe because there were other Native families in most of the towns we moved to.'

The Twains were a long way from the shiftless Indians of public imagination. Jerry's father – also Gerry (born 9 February 1922) – was brought up on Bear Island on the Lake Temagami reservation an hour out of North Bay. He first met Selina Luke (born 10 July 1923), whose friends called her 'Chi Jo' ('It means squirrel or something like that,' says Karen), when she and her mother came down from Mattagami to visit. He was only eight but told her firmly he was going to marry her. They eventually married on 25 September 1944. Between 1945 and 1958 they had four children (Audrey, Jerry, Karen and Tim) and moved from small town to small town – Shining Tree, New Liskeard, Latchford – in search of work. Gerry worked as a line cutter and claim staker and instilled in his family such pride in his heritage that his eldest son refused government welfare all his life.

'My dad wanted the family to do well,' says Karen. 'He liked the bush but he wouldn't sit in the reservation taking welfare, we were taught to try and make it on our own.' Gerry moved the family to Timmins after he was hired by the legendary prospector Don McKinnon to stake claims in Kidd Township, twenty-nine kilometres north of the town. (The area he staked became part of the valuable Kidd Creek mine, which produces zinc and silver to this day.)

Ojibway culture had been systematically eradicated. Traditional names were replaced by Tims, Ricks and Harriets, while, like the slavemasters did to their African American slaves, surnames were imposed at random. Karen has no idea where the Twain surname came from. 'I went back to my reserve,' she says, 'where they were making a family tree, but it's hard to trace back because there were no birth certificates and records.'

While Gerry and Selina spoke Ojibway and were determined to keep the old tales and traditions alive, their children spoke only a few words. The language, bedevilled with dozens of different dialects, was deliberately targeted by the Canadian educational system. 'Our parents couldn't speak it at school. If they were caught, they were punished,' says Jerry's cousin Willis McKay, 'so they spoke to us in English. After Grade 6 my brother and cousin and I were sent away to a residential school in Sault Sainte Marie – 400 miles away – and our parents didn't have no say in the matter. There we weren't allowed to speak anything but English. And that is how we lost our language. It is now spoken only by the elderly people and I can't speak or understand it.'

The Twain children all attended normal high schools. Jerry was smart, although his schooling was constantly interrupted by the family moving about, and despite attending Timmins High and Vocational School, he never graduated. On his return from BC he buckled down and studied accounting at night school. During the day he worked at the Ministry of Natural Resources marking logs. For all they lived in towns the Twains never lost their love of the bush. Close to their ancestral lands they found relief in the old ways. Woodcraft was woven into their being like birch bark. All his life Jerry hunted and trapped, as much for love as for survival. It defined who he was.

Jerry had had a few girlfriends, but nobody serious until he met Sharon. 'He took an immediate liking to her, I guess,' laughs Karen. 'He asked her out on a date straight away. He took her out to dinner – he invited me as well but I wouldn't go – well, they went out and from that night on they were inseparable, it was really quick.'

Unlike many other men it didn't bother him that Sharon was white, nor that she had three little girls. From the beginning they connected, though it wasn't always love's young dream. 'I used to laugh at them,' says Karen, 'because they used to get into a tiff. I knew there was something wrong, because one would show up at my place and then the other would show up a little later, but they were always so close.'

Like any other ethnic group, Native Americans have been marrying outside their tribes for centuries. In white society a Native wife was a cause for social stigma and so the information was often buried and then denied. That is what Shania believes happened in the Edwards family. 'She [my mother] told me they were ashamed of it and would never admit it,' she told Q magazine. 'Apparently, my great-grandmother was Indian and married a white man. In those times it was not unusual for such women to have to renounce their Indian status and leave the reservation, so it's very, very believable that she had to leave her family and never associate again.'

It was less common for Native men to marry white women. Sharon's choice of second husband certainly incensed Gordon Edwards, who to this day refers to Jerry as 'that Twain fella' and, with little foundation, in fact, dismisses him as an alcoholic, claiming 'show me an Indian who isn't an alky, there is something they can't handle in alcohol.'

In 1971 such prejudice was the norm in a blue-collar town like Timmins and an air of tacit disapproval hung over Jerry and Sharon's relationship for years. Gerry senior did enjoy a few drinks but was so severely beaten up by three youths one night after leaving a bar that he ended up in intensive care.

Sharon's divorce took a while to come through, but they were married on 4 June 1970, after which Jerry formally adopted the three girls. They were members of the Temagami Anishinabe Bear Island First Nation Band, registered as fifty per cent Native Canadian and entitled to the same medical, dental and welfare benefits. Natives did not have to pay eight per cent Provincial Sales Tax. Until the law changed in 1986, a woman marrying a Native man was automatically accepted into the band. Regardless of their genetic bloodlines, Jill, Eileen and Carrie Ann were, still are, legally Native. To Jerry's Ojibwe relatives it was more than that, they were true kin raised in the same nest, if not from the same egg.

Mark (someone had a sense of humour) was born two years later, on 18 August 1972. Darryl was born on 21 February 1974. He was Audrey's son, whom they adopted after she committed suicide in March 1975. Despite this tangled family tree, nobody batted an eyelid; traditionally, Ojibwe childcare has always been spread across extended families and there is no stigma on adoption.

From the start Jerry announced, 'There will be no step-anything in this family.' A pledge he never broke. All the Twains embraced the responsibility of being family, so that the ties of love became closer than those of blood. The girls had few enough relatives. The Edwards family were at the time little more than names to them. Bert Morrison had died in 1968, his last years spent in a nursing home, trapped inside his body, scarcely moving and unable to communicate. Eileen died in 1971, only sixty, a kind woman worn out by misfortune, worrying to the very end. 'My mother on her dying breath said, "Don, please take care of them little girls",' says Don Fraser, who had five children of his own to raise. 'That was her last breath to me and I've told the girls that. If they were ever in need they knew that Uncle Don was always there. If they ever asked me, my home was there . . . but they were always independent.'

Little Eilleen took an immediate shine to Gerry and Selina Twain, who in their turn loved the girls back, as if they were their very own and they were welcomed as family by Jerry's other relatives. Of the three sisters Eilleen was always the closest to Jerry – she adored the outdoor life which Jill never took to. The family visited the Mattagami reserve all the time – it was midway between Sudbury and Timmins – staying many weekends and most of the summer. Jerry's cousin Willis McKay remembers Eilleen: 'She was four or five when she was first out here. She was always chasing after the other kids. Mostly they played hide and seek at the time, as this place was all bush then.

'Everybody knew Sharon and Jerry. They were devoted to their children. They were raised well even though there wasn't much money. They were fun to be with, they joked around and they enjoyed people's company.'

When Eilleen first visited the reserve in 1970 it was a primitive, poor place, cut off from the world, and could only be reached along a back road from Gogama. There were no more than twenty houses and a community hall huddled on a point surrounded by Lake Mattagami on two sides and 13,000 acres of trees and bush on the others. The houses were two-roomed wooden shacks built back in 1951, when the Ojibwe were given the land. There was no electricity; in winter the snow was packed tight around the sides and the shacks were heated by wood-burning stoves and lit by oil lamps. Sanitation was 'a little pee pot on the porch' or an outhouse. Running water lasted from spring thaw until around Christmas, when the water lines froze and everyone had to haul water up from the lake until the lines opened up again in April. Mattagami finally got hydro in 1971; at the same time it ceased to be called an Indian reserve and became a 'First Nation', but it took many years to upgrade the buildings and get in proper plumbing.

Mattagami was a small place and, as most of the inhabitants were related, it enjoyed a communal style of living. 'You could sleep pretty much where you wanted and go eat at anyone's house,' recalls Eilleen, 'like it was one big family.' There were singalong parties in the community hall. At Christmas she'd get up on stage and sign a few country songs. (Natives love country music). In the summers they never missed the pow wows, applauding the competitive dancing displays, joining in the drumming and the barbecues. Instead of chocolate-chip cookies treats were chunks of moose meat and partridge cooked over a fire or deep-fried bannock dumplings topped with jam.

Living off the land was essential in Mattagami, whose inhabitants were not bound by hunting restrictions. 'In those days there was still a good return on the fur from trapping,' says Willis McKay. 'My father and some of the older members would go trapping and be gone a week, maybe more. They had to skin them, stretch them and bring them to the Hudson Bay settlement. Jerry loved the bush, he did a lot of trapping around here, he didn't own a trap line but he did live on wildlife for a part of his time here. Back then we were more reliant on hunting. Moose meat, beaver, rabbit were the three main ones, deer, partridge and fish from the lake.'

In wintertime meat was packed, stripped, labelled on paper and stored in outdoor sheds (freezers after electricity came). In summertime the Ojibwe built wells six metres down to keep the moose meat cold. If there was a danger of it going rotten it would be distributed to all the families who would dry and smoke it.

Hunting was a communal occupation. Hunters went out to catch enough for everybody and children were expected to do their bit. Gerry and Selina taught Eilleen how to track and snare rabbits. 'They would take me out into the bush in winter and show me where the rabbit's tracks would intersect. That's where you'd set your snare. The snare was a stick with a loop of wire a bit bigger than a rabbit's head set across the trail, just above the ground. When the animal ran into the loop, it would strangle itself. Like all the children she was taught to use a gun as soon as she was old enough to carry one.

'I was a good little hunter,' says Eilleen, who also claims to be a good shot with a bow and arrow, although most of the hunters at Mattagami only used rifles or shotguns. 'I was carrying a gun when I was eight years old. Hunting for us was very different, not the whole camouflage GI Joe thing. When we needed food, we'd go hunt. It wasn't a sport, it was about surviving.'

Children were automatically taught how to survive in the bush. 'We'd have camping trips, the kids would play, some people would fish. We were all taught how to live in the bush the Native way,' says Karen Twain. 'You can't get me lost in the bush, it's the same with Eilleen. My father taught us that when you are in the bush it all looks the same, so you have to look for certain markers, a mark on a tree, a different sort of rock, and if you keep those in mind you can never get lost.'

There are certain experiences in childhood that never leave, which make such an impression that they colour the adult for ever. Eilleen's time spent in the bush with her adoptive family left her with a yearning that can only ever be assuaged when she is sitting alone among the trees, staring into a fire, watching wisps of woodsmoke dance her memories across the darkness. 'I like being secluded. I like solitude. I never want to let go of it. It's a craving for me. I have to be in the bush,' she has said. 'I like chopping wood. I like making fires. I love smelling like fire. That's my favourite smell. I love it when my hair smells like fire.'

CHAPTER THREE

Late-night Bars (for a Child Star)

There was other smoke that haunted Eilleen's memories, the fug of stale tobacco smoke that hung over the pools of spilt beer in late-night bars. Times when a terrified little girl, dressed in a buckskin dress, handsewn by Grandma Selina, and cowboy boots, hiding behind a guitar almost as big as she was, was woken in the middle of the night and thrust half-asleep on to a stage to entertain a bunch of half-cut miners and loggers. She gave them Hank Williams' 'Kaw-liga' just the way Charley Pride did, belted out Tanya Tucker's raunchy 'Delta Dawn', wrung the beer tears out with Dolly Parton's 'Coat of Many Colours', and left them with Kris Kristofferson's 'Me and Bobby McGee'.

On those late nights at the Mattagami Hotel in Timmins, or whichever bar gig Sharon had found, singing 'Freedom's just another word for nothing left to lose', Eilleen truly did not have much left to lose. The family needed the twenty bucks she earned and Sharon kept telling her she needed the experience. She hated it, really hated it, didn't feel like singing at that time of night at all. She was eight years old. She loved to sing . . . but she hated performing.

Eilleen could always sing. She has no memory of a time before music. She did not sing nursery rhymes like 'Twinkle Twinkle Little Star' with a toddler's lisp and a wandering tune; instead she held the melody and experimented with phrasing and tone. At six she was singing the harmony parts because they were more interesting. 'I remember being put on top of a countertop by my mother when I was three,' she recalls. 'I would always sing out loud to the jukebox.'

For Show and Tell at her primary school, six-year-old Eilleen decided to sing John Denver's 'Take Me Home, Country Roads'. At home everybody loved it; unfortunately, the horde of first-graders were less impressed and they teased her mercilessly, christening her 'Twang' and instilling in her an innate fear of performing in public that was to last a decade. 'All my classmates thought I was being a show-off and it created serious inhibitions for me,' she recalled in a letter to her fans written in 1994. 'From that point on I was afraid to perform.'

Sharon, however, would have none of that. She recognized that her daughter had a special talent – because of the way she would harmonize with songs on the radio – she adored the Mamas and the Papas, the Carpenters and the Supremes – or extemporize new parts to the country songs on the creaky eight-track player – Jerry's favourites: Charley Pride, Waylon Jennings, Dolly, Tanya.

Don Fraser has never been quite sure where Eilleen's musical talent came from, though Roger Pearce insists it's there in the younger generations. 'I don't think there is a musician in our family and as far as I know none on the Morrison side,' says Don. 'My mother couldn't sing but she loved music. She was a wonderful lady, everybody loved her, and I think it was her who Eilleen got her talent from. Eilleen does look like her. Her drive she got from Sharon, for sure. Sharon really believed in Eilleen, it was the one thing she really believed in. I know how much she pushed her, she was the driving force. One year, we had our relatives up from Piney. Myrna Lorrie was performing at the Mattagami Hotel and Sharon said, "Would you like to hear Eilleen sing?" – she was still little. We went down there, she performed and it was just tremendous. At the end Myrna came up to us and said, "That young girl has a lot of talent and she is going to go places." '

The musical branch of Jerry's family was Selina's side. Her younger sister had married Romeo Derasp, a French Métis, the whole family played music – their son Kenny played guitar and sang while Romeo and his brother had a pick-up country band at weekends. Kenny was thirteen at Christmas 1972 when there was a family party at his mother's house in Timmins. It was the first time he had met his cousin Jerry's new wife and family.

'We were having a Christmas get-together at my mother's,' says

Kenny. 'I was singing, my dad was singing, when Eilleen stepped up and said, "I want to sing a song." She was very young but we were all shocked by how good she was. Her timing was good, her pitch was good, it surprised everyone, came out of the blue. She sang her little heart out. My dad said, "This kid can sing, you should bring her down to Sudbury and we'll get her out in public." '

'I have often thought they moved down to Sudbury because of that. Sharon was a real stage mom, she was so enthusiastic about the whole music thing.'

After Sharon and Jerry married, they rented a small house on Bannerman Avenue in Timmins. Jerry had a job on the line in the mines, which he hated; it was physically demanding and kept him inside. The following year the Twains moved down south. They rented a small apartment on King Street in Sudbury; Jerry went to work for a local building supply store and Sharon took part-time work waiting tables at Gus's Restaurant and chambermaiding at the Sorento Hotel. Kenny Derasp lived with his dad on Queen Street, two blocks away across Little Creek, but spent a lot of time over at his cousin's.

When she was ten, Jill was given an acoustic guitar, but somehow it was her little sister who always ended up hugging it. One day, Jerry was fooling around on it and started showing Eilleen how to hold it – no easy task as the little girl was dwarfed by the instrument – so that her left hand could travel up and down the fretboard, while her right hand strummed across the strings. Jerry was not an accomplished picker but he knew his way around a couple of instrumentals – the old Carter family classic 'Wildwood Flower' and 'Under the Double Eagle', a standard based on an old German march – and taught her the basic chords. Soon she could play Stompin' Tom Connors songs as well as he could.

Stompin' Tom Connors is a Canadian icon, yet nobody outside the country has a clue who he is. Born into utter poverty in Saint John, New Brunswick, to a single mother, he was taken into care before being adopted. At fifteen he took off with his guitar and for the next thirteen years hitchhiked across the country subsisting on menial jobs and handouts. His big break came in 1966 at the Maple Leaf Hotel in Timmins (a coincidence which was not lost on Sharon). When he discovered that he was a nickel short of a beer, the bartender, Gaet Lepine, suggested Tom play a few songs instead. He was such a hit that he ended up playing at the hotel for the next thirteen months. CKGB, the local radio station, gave him a weekly spot and issued eight 45-RPM singles of his songs. In 1969, he signed with a national label and soon became a star.

There was nothing complicated about Stompin' Tom. His songs were no-frills, three-chord country, Tom in his roll-brimmed cowboy hat strumming a guitar, stomping out the rhythm with his pointed Western boot. Maybe another guitar and an acoustic bass but nothing else to detract from the lyrics. His songs, like 'Sudbury Saturday Night', 'Bud the Spud', 'I am the Wind', 'The Bridge Came Tumbling Down' and 'The Canadian Lumberjack', were not full of poetic images, they were tales that resonated with the drinking men in the Maple Leaf because they were all about ordinary working-class Joes like them – truckers, miners, boatmen who liked to season all their food with ketchup, get hammered at the weekend and watch other big blokes beat the crap out of each other on the hockey rink. (Stompin' Tom is also a dyed-in-the-maple-leaf patriot with a fierce personal integrity. In 1979, railing against the Americanization of the domestic music industry, he handed back all six of his Juno Awards. What relevance, he reasoned, had Dionne Warwick got to Canada. This was not just a symbolic gesture, as he did not tour or release any new records for the next nine years. His legend, however, has continued to grow.) Tom Connors stood for all the little guys, because he was one. Small wonder Jerry Twain loved him. Sharon reasoned that if Stompin' Tom could get his break out of Timmins – and they'd seen him many times – so could her daughter.

Kenny, who had been playing guitar since he was six and was pretty proficient, took over teaching Eilleen. 'I saw she had a knack for it and so I started showing her chords and stuff., She quickly grasped the rudiments and began practising with the Derasps. One of her first shows was at the Christmas for the Kids' Telethon held in the auditorium at Sudbury High. Her first recordings were just Kenny playing and her singing. 'We didn't know what we were doing,' he says, 'but we were playing the songs at a million miles an hour. We did Tammy Wynette's 'Good Girls Going to Go Bad' so fast we turned it into a rock song. It was hilarious.'

Soon Eilleen and her guitar were inseparable. 'I started playing guitar at eight but I was singing long before then,' she says. 'I was serious about experimenting with my voice harmonies. That was all I wanted to do. I didn't want to play with dolls or anything else but my guitar. I would play until my fingers were bruised. If I'd had it my way, I'd have taken the easy option and remained a songwriter, not a performer. I loved music but I was never passionate about being a performer.'

Sharon was not prepared to let that happen. A determined stage mother who 'lived for my career. She knew I was talented and she lived with the hope that my abilities were my chance to do something special.' When the family moved out to Hanmer they bought Eilleen her first guitar, an Elvegas copy of a Gibson Hummingbird. She was given music lessons by a local guitar teacher. Then they bought a piano and sent her off for lessons. Sharon pumped every visiting band for information. One night, a singer gave her some advice on microphone technique, how you had to learn to back off then come up real close, sing in a whisper one moment and a scream the next. A few days later, Sharon returned home with a small PA system complete with tiny amp, a mixer, two column speakers and a Shure SM58 microphone, determined that Eilleen learn how to work with a microphone. Jerry was furious, so Sharon had to get a part-time job pumping gas until she paid for it.

Sharon and Jerry sacrificed a great deal so that Eilleen could have access to everything she needed. They drove her the twelve-hour round trip to Toronto for voice lessons. Sharon needed her daughter to succeed, for that meant not only escape from the drudgery of her life but a more fundamental affirmation of her worth. Over the next few years she lapsed into long depressions often triggered when Eilleen's career was not going well.

In the mid-1970s the Woodland Hotel in Val Caron was one of Sudbury's premier country gigs – a bit faded around the edges but it could attract out-of-town artists of the calibre of Myrna Lorrie. Sharon convinced the owners to let Eilleen come and perform. To do that she had to wait until after they had finished serving liquor at 1 a.m. By that stage half the audience were too soaked in beer and whiskey to care. 'When there was a good band in town, my parents would get permission and ask the club if they minded if I came in to sing,' Shania remembers. 'Lots of times the band would play past after they started closing the bar and they'd stop serving. But the band would usually play while everybody finished their last-call drinks. There's about an hour there and the band would be tired then anyway and everybody was drunk. So they were happy to have me come up and sing. I would do that quite often.'

'I was scared shitless. I had terrible stage fright. My parents forced me to perform, which in the long run was the best thing, because I was quite a recluse,' she admits. 'If not for them I'd still be singing in my bedroom. From the age of eight, I was doing weekends, the odd gig here and there. I did everything my parents could get me on. Every TV station, every radio station, every community centre, every senior citizen centre. My great-grandfather Twain was in one, so I'd go and entertain him. I'd have some people going – "I can't hear anything – is she playing anything?" and others complaining that it was too loud.'

'I wasn't just a kid trying to sing, I was actually a musician. I basically taught myself. I used to write out all of my chord charts to my original music. I was very serious. I was actually a professional by the time I was eleven. Sure, I was doing the telethons, little fairs and country shows locally, but I was getting paid and I was working.'

Sudbury was certainly a better place than Timmins to launch the career Sharon knew Eilleen deserved. The local bar culture was thriving, as Stompin' Tom had recognized in 'Sudbury Saturday Night'. Those after-hours shows were the gigs Eilleen always dreaded the most. Sometimes she was so tired, plucked from the depths of dreamtime, standing up there defenceless and all alone that when she sang 'I'm So

Lonesome I Could Cry' there was hardly a dry eye amidst the beer and cigarette fumes (small wonder that she had never smoked and seldom drank). The bar owners paid cash under the table or passed the hat around to those not too drunk to forget where they had put their wallet. When she turned eleven she went legit. 'The police were either going to have to arrest me or ban me from being in there,' she says, 'or give me a proper permit.' The permit meant she could sing in the bars but had to be given a separate room . . . and it meant an end to the 1 a.m. shows.

'Our mom had a lot of faith in her,' says Twain's younger sister, Carrie Ann Brown. 'She was always on the phone trying to book things, taking her to talent contests, travelling out of town to shows, getting her lessons.'

At times, Eilleen must have wondered why it was her doing this, not Jill, nor Carrie Ann, nor any of her friends, wondered what her childhood was being mortgaged for. Or perhaps not. 'I wasn't really aware of what was going on,' she says, 'I was just singing and it was my parents who were more aware of everything. I don't remember what I thought at the time, because a singer is what I've always been, it's what I've always done.'

Eilleen was only nine when she learnt an important lesson. Singing like a honky-tonk angel is not enough. To win you do not have to be the best, you have to know the right people. She learnt it the hard way. 'Eilleen was far better than a lot of the singers that they were pushing that were older than her,' says Kenny, who used to go with Sharon and Eilleen to many of the local talent contests. Sometimes he'd play guitar behind her. 'That was where the politics came in, there were so many jealousies going on. It was awful what they did to her, she was only a little kid. I saw bands rehearse with her and do it fine, but when it came to the contest they'd deliberately screw up the song, so it messed her up and she'd be coming off the stage crying. I couldn't believe grown-ups would do that to kids. Sharon and I used to get really mad.'

Angered, Sharon was determined that Eilleen would win talent competitions, believing that was a way forward. 'Mom was so discouraged,' said Shania. 'She couldn't understand why her little girl was unable to win a contest.' When she was nine, she performed in a contest at the Native Friendship Center in Sudbury, where she met the half-Cree, half-Irish singer Lawrence Martin. Smarting at another failure a few weeks later, Eilleen and her parents, along with Lawrence and his fiancée Connie, drove a thousand miles to Brandon, Manitoba for an Aboriginal contest. The drive took almost twenty-four hours and they arrived with barely an hour to spare. Eilleen and Lawrence appeared as a duo and as soloists. They won everything.

For some years afterwards the two would occasionally perform together. Lawrence, though ten years older, came over to her home at Proulx Court to watch music shows on TV and then sit around analysing the moves, the material and how to improve their own. However vindicated Sharon felt, winning Native talent contests meant nothing to a record label (though Lawrence did eventually win a Juno award under the Cree name Wapistan and served as mayor of Moose Factory, up in James Bay). While Sudbury was closer to the centre of things than Timmins, the local entertainment market remained oblivious to her talents. In 1977, Eilleen told the *Sudbury Star*, alluding to her experiences in the sub-text, 'People just don't notice you in Sudbury. They see a lot of performers and you are just an ordinary person. But the first time I played with a band in Toronto, people stood up and took notice. Down there they are always looking for new talent. It is more fun playing with people like Carroll Baker, because you can do what you want. In Sudbury there was no communication with the band.'

While she had struck up a good rapport with Myrna Lorrie at the Woodland Hotel, her best reception was in Toronto, where she gathered some heavyweight admirers. In 1977, she sang with Freddie Fender (which impressed her teachers no end), learning the Spanish verse to his hit 'Before the Next Teardrop Falls' phonetically. She had no idea what she was singing, but the crowd in Rockhill Park called her back for three encores which blew the night's schedule to shreds. She performed with Country Edition in Orchard Park and recorded a demo of ten of her songs with a band called Eastwind. 'They were the cream of the crop of country players down there and they knew she came from a family that didn't have any money,' says Kenny Derasp. 'So they did a demo for her free of charge; none of the musicians charged anything, a lot of people knew she had something.'

It looked like she had cracked it when she was signed to do several appearances with the *Big Country Show*, a travelling concert party sponsored by *Opry North*, the largest syndicated Canadian country radio show. She sang in Ottawa and Sudbury on the same bill as Carroll Baker, Ronnie Prophet (who both had deals in Nashville) and opened shows for Canadian country artists like Debbie Post, Gary Buck and Anita Perras. There was even an offer to go and do a TV show in New York, but Sharon and Jerry decided she was too young for the Big Apple. In 1978 in Sudbury, she opened for Mary Bailey, a young singer from Kirkland Lake – their paths were to cross again and again.

Eilleen's set at the time was pure country. The running order for a show in the Soo (Sault Sainte Marie) on 13 May 1977 featured fifteen songs, including such classic country weepies as 'Crying Time Again', 'Honky Tonk Angels', 'Delta Dawn', 'Jamabalaya', 'What's Your Mama's Name Child', 'Tennessee Mountain Home', 'Me and Bobby McGee', 'Harper Valley PTA', 'Queen of the Silver Dollar', 'Say You'll Stay Until Tomorrow' and finishing up with 'I Wish I was a Teddy Bear' and 'Pure Love'.

In 1978, her biggest break to date was being invited on to *The Tommy Hunter Show*, the country music TV show in Canada from 1965–1992. Everybody who was or indeed wanted to be anybody was desperate to be invited on. For that appearance she was billed as Ellie Twain. Glen Campbell and Ronnie Milsap topped the bill. In contrast to her usual attire she dressed in a dark velvet jacket and a long skirt; around her neck she wore a simple silver chain with an Austrian crystal given to her by her friend Colette. She also made TV appearances on *Easy Country* and *The Mercey Brothers Show*.

Travelling to one show she got on the train from Sudbury and after a while realized she was going in the opposite direction. The conductor told her she could transfer at another station in six hours. She says, 'I said, "You've got to stop the train right now because I'm going to be on TV." So they let me off in the middle of the bush with my guitar, like a little hobo. I caught a train going the other way in half an hour, but I did think, "What if the train never comes?" '

CHAPTER FOUR

The Hungry Years

S udbury lies some 300 kilometres south of Timmins, and at four times the size it is in many ways its bigger brother. It was a major terminus for the Canadian Pacific Railway until some of the richest copper and nickel deposits in the world were discovered in 1883–4. Smelting operations were underway by 1888. Sudbury rapidly became the most important mining centre in Canada, with the majority of its population employed in that industry. Huge nickel concentrators and smelters were erected at Copper Cliff, Falconbridge and Levack. Sudbury and its sprawl of surrounding communities still produce around one-fifth of all the nickel mined in the world and almost all of Ontario's copper.

Like many a mining town it has lain in thrall for almost a century to a single company, Inco (formed in 1902 as the International Nickel Company). Although by the time the Twains moved to Sudbury in 1973 Inco's importance to the local economy had begun to decline, it still employed over 20,000 people (the population of Greater Sudbury is currently 164,000). If Inco sneezed, the whole town caught a cold. Almost everybody had some link to Inco: if they weren't directly employed, their businesses serviced the mines or the workers.

After Jerry landed a job with Indian Affairs, the Twains moved out to Proulx Court, a horseshoe road right on the northern edge of Hanmer. The house was bought with the aid of an Aboriginal housing grant, but there was still a hefty mortgage with high monthly payments to make. (At the time, if a Native chose to go and live on a reserve, the government was obliged to build him a house, so if he wished to buy one off the reserve, the government kicked in some money to help.) It was a three-bedroomed bungalow of 1,400 square feet with a dirt floor in the basement, which, after living with four kids in a small apartment, seemed like a mansion. All the houses around were constructed of wood, dotted on lots with scrub and trees filling in the gaps, which did little to dispel the icy winds which swept across the smooth valley floor. There were lakes in abundance for swimming or skating.

In 1975, the population of the Valley, as the four small townships of Val Caron, Blezard Valley, Val Therese and Hanmer are collectively described, was ninety per cent blue collar. People moved there because land was cheap and the rents were low. Hanmer had one Dominion supermarket and a couple of 'mom-and-pop' corner stores. Behind it the roads were gravel, not tarmac. It was an insular working-class community made more so by language – seventy per cent of the Valley was French, not all of whom spoke English. John Browning, who taught at Pinecrest School in the 1970s, recalls how three twelve-year-olds in his class had never been to Sudbury and how a girl burst into tears when she first saw Ottawa, because 'she never ever thought she'd go somewhere like that in her life'. Miners disciplined their children the old-fashioned way; if a teacher called that meant they were in trouble, even if they weren't. One boy turned up the next morning with his head shaved bald – his father's solution to a minor disciplinary misdemeanour.

Provided they weren't on strike, regular Inco employees earned a good wage; they could afford fishing boats and new trucks. It was the others like Jerry Twain, the casual lumber or forestry workers and the subsistence farmers – there were still a few working farms in the Valley – who were at the bottom of the economic pile. Less than half a mile from the Twain house on Concession 4 (later renamed Gravelle Drive) were houses which still had dirt floors and whose nearest water-pipe was four blocks away.

For Eilleen it was not all work and no play. She was still a little girl, with a little girl's enthusiasms. She had to go to school. She attended Redwood Acres for three years, Pinecrest Junior High for Grades 7 and 8, Capreol High for just one year, and very seldom missed a day. Eilleen and Lynn Bond became firm friends at Redwood Acres when they discovered they both loved horses, and their friendship continued through their move to Pinecrest. Lynn lived five kilometres away in Val Caron and they would hang out anywhere they could see a horse. On Michelle Drive up the road from Lynn's was a house with a little paint pony in the field behind. The ten-year-old girls thought nothing of knocking on the door and asking, 'Can we spend time with your pony?' A warning that the animal had not been ridden much did not deter Eilleen, who leapt on it bareback and rode it back to Lynn's. They tied him up in the backyard and forgot to tell her dad, who woke up and thought he was seeing elephants.

No neighbourhood house with horses was safe. The Dions, who lived on the curve of Proulx Court, also allowed the girls to look after their pony. Lynn's greatest triumph was being allowed to look after Prince Buddy, who unfortunately lived in a farm way down on Highway 69. The girls decided they were going to enter him in a local horse show. Lynn's mother only agreed to take them on condition that on the Sunday morning they both went to church. The potential cowgirls reluctantly agreed and then went off to the show. Eilleen wore Lynn's chequered shirt while she wore one of Eilleen's.

'We didn't know anything, like what we were getting ourselves into,' recalls Lynn, 'but we packed that horse up and we were hot girls, we were going to show what we had. Eilleen took Prince Buddy into one class where they would command, "OK walk, trot," and you had to stop and do this straight away. This pony was a real hothead and went just ballistic. The judges were like "You're going to be thrown off, control this horse," but she was so determined to get him under control and finish her class. That took a lot of guts, because she looked like a real idiot out there. Everybody else was doing their class the way they're supposed to and she's in there, you know . . . but she was staying on her horse whatever. Needless to say we didn't win but we had a good time.'

Lynn was a natural runner, skinny as a whip. Her relationship with Eilleen was always competitive, in Grade 6 they practised doing back flips for hours. They had the same focus on getting things right. Lynn won most of the sports events but she got angry when Eilleen won the standing long jump, telling her friends, 'Well I had to let her win one,' then going back home and complaining to her mother because she was so frustrated at her friend.

While the teachers seldom saw it, there was another, wilder side to Eileen. Like Jerry she enjoyed playing practical jokes on her friends, pretending to throw up green slime at parties. She caught Lynn in one class by offering her a home-made chocolate brownie. After it had been wolfed down she killed herself laughing and admitted to having laced it with Exlax. A few months later, Lynn went for payback with an extra strong laxative. 'I doubled over and laughed, and, no, she didn't think it was very funny either, she was a little upset, but hey, what comes around goes around, right?

'There were a few episodes in school when she would do some kinda mean thing, but it never stopped us being friends. I remember going to my locker and there was this letter in there. I wasn't the prettiest thing in those days, but there was this letter and it was about this boy and how he watched me when we had recess and how cute he thought I was. I'm like "Eileen, look at this, check this out, this guy likes me but I don't know who he is." We'd be out at recess and I'd be looking like, "OK, who's watching me, and . . ." Well it turned out she wrote this letter, so of course the joke was on me again. She did things like that, she had a sense of humour.'

Singing took priority in Eileen's home, for it was the dream rock upon which her mother's fragile psyche rested. At school she preferred to sink into the anonymity of the pack. The only reason that Laurie Macdonald, the music teacher at Pinecrest, knew was that one of her teachers at Redwood Acres told him, 'You are getting one hell of a singer.' Eileen had been asked to sing at a parents evening there and had stunned the teacher by telling her to first check with her mother that she wasn't already booked to perform elsewhere and then asked if there would be a sound system and on-stage monitors for her performance.

During Laurie's first singing lesson, in which the whole class would sing popular songs together, he listened out for her. When he could not distinguish her from the crowd he asked her if she wanted to sing something. 'Oh no, not really,' she replied, perhaps remembering that long-ago First Grade humiliation. Laurie listened some more and realized that most times, if the class was singing a song, he could not pick her out from anybody else. But if she ever wanted to, she could drown them all out – 'Her control was that good.'

Eilleen was convinced to sing in front of her classmates on the Eighth Grade camping trip to Halfway Lake. Teachers Ted Evans and John Browning were in charge of fifty-six young teens, aided only by two eighteen-year-old qualified lifeguards, Wendy Wickstrom and Jenny Saxe-Albert. Eilleen had brought her guitar along and on the first night – in between hands of euchre – she sat down by the campfire and played a small set including Randy Vanwarmer's hit 'Just When I Needed You Most', Kenny Rogers' 'The Gambler' and the traditional scouts' favourite 'Barges'.

It was not enough for Eilleen to play the song, it had to be just right. Says John, 'She would play along for a while and sing, sound just great, and then all of a sudden she'd quit and start over again.' It turned out that Wendy and Jenny were good harmony singers and they started to join in, so the following evening the three of them disappeared off from the fire. They sat around experimenting with different harmonies until long after everybody else had gone to bed. Although Eilleen was the best singer, she did not attempt to exert her will, she just let it slide along. 'Eilleen was not that kind of personality that she would take charge, she would watch and listen, and then suggest,' says Ted.

Well-organized and comfortable in the bush, Eilleen had arranged to share a tent with Leah Mersham, who had turned in early because she was not feeling well. Unfortunately, she had left the zipper undone and the tent was invaded by mosquitoes. John and Ted were enjoying a quiet moment alone by the fire when Eilleen stomped up in a filthy mood. 'Leah's in there snoring like a fool,' she complained, 'the tent is full of mosquitoes, and there's no damn way I'm sleeping in there with a bunch of bugs!' Ted had a truck with a camper in the back, so Eilleen grabbed her blanket and went to sleep in the driver's cabin. Every time she turned over the truck would rock and disturb the teachers in the back.

The next morning, after they had organized the kids to load their gear in the buses, Eilleen made up for giving them a sleepless night. 'John and I were starved, I would have eaten his shoes at the time,' says Evans. 'Eilleen says, "I've a piece of steak in my cooler," so she got out this chunk of pounded minute steak. I cut some sticks and we propped it over the coals, and the three of us shared the steak with some salt, and it tasted like heaven. Eilleen was pretty thrilled. She told us, "This is great, we have real food, we can cook and eat. When my dad takes us camping, all he ever brings is flour and salt!" '

For the two years she was at Pinecrest, Eilleen seldom did anything to show off in front of her peers. 'She was pale, mousy,' recalls Macdonald, 'very small, slight, a cute, nondescript kid who never wore make-up – no eye shadow, no fancy hairdos – she was a very pleasant, nice little thirteen-year-old, with terrible teeth. She never was a fashion plate, just blue jeans and a nice little top, dressed very plainly in clothes that were cheap and easy to look after. She buried herself into the crowd and did her best not to stand out.'

'She wasn't a loner,' agrees Ted Evans who taught her English and Physical Education, 'she wasn't a target, nobody picked on her, but she wasn't a joiner. She did want to join the basketball team, and so she orchestrated this meeting between her stepfather and myself.'

Eilleen was close to a cert for the team – she had balance, poise and strength that belied her size. The problem was that team practice was on Sunday mornings, which conflicted with her doing any out-of-town gigs on Saturday nights. One afternoon when Ted Evans was on bus duty, she asked him to talk to Jerry, who had come to pick her up. Ted offered to pick her up and take her home (in those days teachers were allowed to do such things without need of a chaperon). Jerry was too polite to give an outright 'no' but Ted knew he was not keen on the idea. A week later, Eilleen told him she would not be able to try out. Her schedule, she explained, was such that she had to go home after school, get her homework done, have something to eat and rest, and then she'd be out singing some place that evening, and then, when she came home and everything was done, she could go to bed and start again for the next time. Even in Grade 8 she didn't have very much spare time.

Occasionally, she rebelled against such strictures. On long, cramped car trips she and her sisters might start arguments that brought the car to a halt, followed by a brisk walk allowing everybody a chance to cool down. One day, she and her aunt Karen went into town to watch a fashion show and decided they wanted to go to a movie afterwards (Hanmer only had a drive-in theatre). Karen phoned home to be told firmly by Jerry, 'No, you girls have to come right back. Eilleen, you have a show this evening.' They stayed and watched the movie anyway but there was hell to pay back at Proulx.

That distance between school, where she tried so hard to be just another little girl, and career became increasingly important to Eilleen. Her close friends knew both sides of her and loved to listen to her sing, though she was always uncomfortable playing to those she knew intimately. They joked that if a house had a guitar Eilleen would find it. Lynn Bond begged her to play her own songs but, being a competitive little girl, could never resist teasing her about it. One time at school she crossed the line seriously, called her 'twa twa twa Twain' and made fun of her. Eilleen was very upset and it took a while to be friends again.

Singing was simultaneously her release and her curse. 'Shania would always be singing – even just walking down the street. I'd be embarrassed,' recalls Carrie Ann. At home the radio was always playing and at every song – Elton John, the Carpenters, Fleetwood Mac, whatever came on – she danced around the room crying, 'Oh I love this song.' Laura Surch might say tartly, 'But you love every song,' but that never stopped Eilleen. Singing along to the radio or to Jerry's eight-track was how she learnt to refine, then to perfect her harmonies.

'Eilleen was a very serious kid,' says Kenny Derasp. 'She spent a lot of time in her room. Her and I used to go and sit in her room to get away from everybody and just play.' The art of creating, of actually writing songs, was very different to performing them and became progressively important. That was private, where the loner came out. She was ten when she wrote her first songs. Her first two titles – 'Is Love a Rose?'

and 'Just Like the Storybooks' – were wish-fulfilment fantasies, fairytales in rhyme. In her dreams she waited for Frank Sinatra, the superstar the most removed from northern Ontario imaginable, to kidnap her and take her away from it all. A more down-to-earth fantasy was becoming Stevie Wonder's backing singer. 'I wanted to escape this life I had,' she has said, 'and I knew the only honest way of doing it would be to be kidnapped. Because I'd have felt so guilty if I'd ever left my family willingly.'

Writing songs was her escape from reality. They came out of silence, out of solitude. After one performance in the Soo she sat silent in the back of the car for the whole ride. Then, without a word, she rushed into her bedroom and emerged twenty minutes later with a new song. Sharon admitted to the *Sudbury Star*, 'I always wondered what was going through her head then.' When she was in one of her hyper modes she found it hard to wait, constantly asking her daughter, 'What have you been writing lately? Can I hear something? What have you been doing in there all these hours?' Says Shania, 'I would never play her my music. Very rarely would I let here hear something. Unless I felt it was completely finished.'

In winter she wrote in the bedroom she shared with Carrie Ann. She wrote songs on scraps of paper which, like some absent-minded hamster, she left all over the house. Eventually she learnt to store them in boxes under her bed. When it was warm, she retired to her secret place, hidden out in the woods that straggled around the back of the house. Nobody was invited there, until one day she beckoned her aunt Karen out into the bush then shushed her to secrecy. She led her by the hand into a little grove surrounded by scrub and spruce trees, proudly pointed out her little barbecue set-up, and the rocks that passed for seats grouped around the fire she loved to watch. 'This,' she said, 'is where I come when I want to be alone and to write songs.'

Pinecrest was a small school with no cafeteria, so at lunchtimes the kids ate in their homerooms, supervised by their teachers. They bolted down their food and then rushed off to enjoy whatever activities were on offer. Whenever possible Eilleen made some excuse about her lunch and headed for the classroom which doubled as a music room. There she grabbed a guitar and started singing. The staffroom was right next door, which was how Laurie Macdonald learnt how good she was. Sometimes he played the piano while she let rip and next door those who did not know complained that Laurie had cranked the stereo up too high. What he did not know was that on many of those days she had eaten no lunch at all.

Throughout their years in Hanmer the Twain family were struggling to meet their bills and put food on the kitchen table. In those pre-PC days, Jerry was an oddity, the only Native on the payroll of the Sudbury Bureau of Indian Affairs, and when he proudly showed the pictures of his five children the white staff got more confused. 'He was what they called an Indian agent,' recalls Willis McKay, who is now the Housing Officer at Mattagami First Nation. 'He took care of band affairs, dealing mostly with housing problems and water and membership too. Jerry was really an outspoken person, very steadfast in what he believed in, always pushing to get a better life for himself and his family. He cared for people around here. If we had problems he worked for us, he tried to help everybody. He didn't take no for an answer. If he felt something he didn't agree with, he spoke up, he didn't let it drag by, he stood up for us. At the time it was a difficult and brave thing to be a go-between between Indian Affairs and the Indian people.'

As well as a frustrating job for a man with drive and intelligence it was also poorly paid, involving short-term contracts with no civil-service benefits. In winter, Jerry found himself without steady work, struggling to make the rent, a situation not helped, as Karen remembers, by the casual, endemic racism of the day: 'In Sudbury they would always lay off the Natives first.' Jerry did not help himself either, for he was a proud, stubborn man who refused to accept government hand-outs. He would not go on the dole, nor go back to Mattagami or Bear Island. 'We would have been better off on the reserve a lot of the time,' Shania said, 'but my father had much too much pride for that. He had to be independent of the clan and we starved for it a lot of the time. He must have earned a pittance, because we didn't eat half the time, and he got turned off in the winter, which was not good.'

Winters in Hanmer were long and hard, made doubly so when the electricity got shut off. When cash was too tight to visit the Laundromat, the washing was done in the tub in cold water. 'We didn't have a lot of food, often I didn't have a lunch to go to school,' Shania has said. 'How many days in a row can you not have a lunch? Sometimes I would make up a mustard sandwich because I was so embarrassed, I would make up something, any kind of sandwich I could just to throw the teachers off, or I would get permission to go to the music room for lunch to sit at the piano and write.

'I was very much aware of being poor, because everybody around me had things. My sister Jill and I used to walk home from school and smell everybody's dinner cooking. We were so envious we'd call them "roast beef families". We thought roast beef families were the norm and that everyone with a brick house was rich, because only rich people could afford to have such a sturdy house. Anyone with meat cooking was also rich, because that was not normal to us. If you decided to take an extra potato, someone didn't get a potato at all. They only kind of meat we ever had was ground beef, and in the autumn the reserve sometimes sent a little box with moose or fish – but certainly not enough for seven people. We would snare rabbits and stuff but beef was a luxury.'

Although officially his family were band members at Bear Island Jerry was so respected at Mattagami for what he did for the community there that they were happy to help out in return. 'We considered them more members here than at Bear Island, we recognized them as family,' confirms Willis McKay. 'If we knew they were hurting, we would pass on whatever we had. Moose meat, beaver, rabbit, deer and partridge.' However, living off the land was not a long-term option in the Valley.

'There were definitely hard times, many days when we had to huddle round the stove because we couldn't pay the heating bill,' said Shania. 'We went to bed wearing our coats, literally freezing. It's not the way you want to live, you can die in those conditions. I don't think our parents would have allowed us to die, they would have taken us to a shelter, but we definitely endured what we could, we pushed it to the limits. We did everything we could to hide it from other people.

'I was very aware, not ashamed, but cautious about concealing the standard of living we had. In Canada, if you are not careful, the Children's Aid will take you away. The schools keep an eye on those sorts of things.'

The reality of the social services bogeymen was somewhat different. The teachers at Pinecrest seldom pried into family circumstances unless invited to. The root of the fear might have been that Jerry feared that, like so many Native children in the past, the boys would be sent away to special schools. On the surface the Twains presented a united front, their clothes were clean and mended, their passive behaviour never drew attention to the trouble at home. Those days taught Eileen how to dissemble, to hide in plain sight behind a polite smile. Pretending everything is fine on the surface when beneath all is raging turmoil is an essential skill for a nascent superstar.

While some doubts have been cast on just how poor the Twains were (most notably in Laurence Leamer's anti-Nashville polemic *Three Chords and the Truth*) there is no doubt that they suffered far tougher times than most of their contemporaries. Kenny Derasp, whose parents were divorced, often lived with Jerry and Sharon, whom he considers to be his second family. When he was eighteen he had a grant to go back to school, so paid them for board. 'I probably ate up what I paid them, they had a rough go of it. It was tough – one income and five children to clothe and feed – but they seemed to manage. Money was very, very tight. They spent a lot of time worrying about how they were going to pay the electricity bill in winter, they had house payments, then the car would break down. I used to fix Jerry's car a lot. I rode with Jerry to work in the morning and he had this really beat-up old Dodge. The gas gauge didn't work, so we used to carry a jerrycan in the trunk and a lot of times we just barely made it to the gas station. We'd be swerving all around the road to get the gas to swish around in the tank to get a little bit further. One time we ran out and we found a gallon of camp-stove gas in the trunk we had to put in, which got us to the gas station.

'We ate a lot of Kraft dinners – macaroni and cheese in a box, it was maybe twenty cents a box in those days. It's got a few noodles and some cheese you mix with milk. Add in a pound of hamburger and it stretched enough for everybody to have some.

'There was a lot of love in the house, for sure,' says Kenny. 'There was a lot of yelling too, it was a very loud household, very energetic. Everyone was noisy, kids coming in screaming, "Darryl did this . . . Mark took my toy." The house was in a highly excited state all the time, kids running around. Sometimes Sharon would just sit there in the kitchen and go, "Oh, my God," and panic.'

Although children are seldom aware of the bigger picture, all of Eilleen's friends recall odd incidents. When she was seven, Colette St Amande's family lived on Gravelle, just a block from Proulx Court. Her mother remembers 'a little Eilleen who lived a street over who used to come over and play, and I used to feed her all the time. She was always hungry.'

But it is the milk that jumps out of all their memories. To most kids, blue- and white-collar alike, there is always milk, it is omni-present, a constant in their lives from before they can talk. Nobody rations milk.

'I was aware enough to know that the Twains' house was different from mine,' says Colette. 'But the only thing that has really stuck in my mind was one time when Eilleen wanted something to drink she wasn't allowed to have milk. They only had so much milk, and that was saved for the boys.' When Laura Surch stayed over for the first time in 1979, she helped herself and drank the family's entire breakfast ration. 'I used too much milk and she had to tell me that in her house there wasn't cookies and pop and chips and enough milk to go around. She would actually come to school with no lunches. She didn't complain.'

There were days when Eilleen told Lynn, 'You can't come over tonight, it's not a good night.' Now Lynn knows it was because there wasn't enough food to go around one more plate. Once she was there for tea and the only food on offer was 'milk, sugar and bread. They kind of chunked up the bread, put it in the bowl, added milk and then sugar. I'd never tried it, but so what? Hey, some people have pancakes for supper or macaroni with butter. It was different and Eilleen never complained, so I thought it must be good.'

By history and circumstance the Twains were a dysfunctional family held together, despite the havoc that living below the poverty line brought, by Jerry's will, and Sharon's belief in her daughter's talent. 'To her parents Eilleen's career was everything,' recalls Laura, 'Everything. Any extra money was spent on her, on her singing lessons, her parents were very driven to make sure she succeeded.' They were prepared to sacrifice grocery money to pay for her singing lessons, for petrol money to get her to gigs, which in turn put extra pressure on the family.

The most acute damage was to Sharon's mental health. The incessant grind of poverty sapped her strength and led to fits of acute depression. 'When there wasn't anything to feed us for breakfast,' Shania has said, 'my mother didn't get out of bed. She didn't want to face that morning. And there were a lot of mornings like that. I think my mother's obsession for my music kept her going a lot of the time. We'd come home from school, she'd still be in bed. She would get very depressed. She would get up and want to hear my songs. Then she would get on the phone and start working out where I was going to sing. It was her saving grace.'

In 1978, things got even worse. Jill left home. She was only fourteen and why exactly she left no one will discuss, though she certainly chafed under Jerry's rule that there was to be no dating boys or wearing make-up until she was sixteen. (By the time she was sixteen she had Mandy, a daughter of her own). Ted Evans remembers Jill very well. 'She was a very sharp English student. I encouraged writing and Jill wrote a lot for me. I had a journal programme, which was of its nature personal. Although she never referred to her personal life, she did have insight into the human condition. Jill was – and Eilleen had some of this – an observer, they both stepped back and watched. Jill was tougher than Eilleen, she didn't have the softness that her sister could have. I often caught her, sitting watching. She had almost an adult perspective of the world and was a very strong writer. My impression, my instinct said that there was something hurting in her life, but I never got the details, nor did I pry.'

Once Jill had left the house, Eilleen was the oldest and was given a lot more responsibility. Laura remembers her taking control, making sure that everything continued to work. 'We were probably in the heart of our difficult times as a family,' she recalls. 'I had to take control and was really an anchor in keeping the family together. I ironed Dad's clothes and made porridge in the morning for the kids.'

Sharon's depression may have been exacerbated, because by 1979 Eilleen's career had stalled. While she was earning some money from her shows, it was often not enough to cover the costs of getting there. 'My mom was more of the stage parent,' said Shania, 'My dad was more practical. He made decisions about whether it made sense to drive somewhere to perform for free, or to pay the heating bill that week. Once, my father decided we couldn't afford to travel to a certain town to perform. After I went to bed that night, I snuck out of my window and my mom and I went anyway.'

Money drained out on demo tapes and travel, but the record companies never called. A cute little moppet had novelty value but a hesitant teenager did not. When Tanya Tucker sang 'Delta Dawn' and 'Would You Lay with Me (in a Field of Stone)', her appeal was jailbait raunch. Tanya knew she was sexy and played it to the hilt. Eilleen hated her body and tried to hide it. Eilleen developed breasts early. At eleven, her games were all outside – riding horses, running through the bush, climbing trees, ice skating – and suddenly her body had let her down. She kept on doing the same stuff and now boys stared at her in a different way, but she wasn't any different. Not in her head, anyway.

'I spent my whole youth hiding behind a tomboy image, trying to hide my figure,' she said later. 'I wanted to stay this tomboy, to stay flat-chested for ever. I didn't want the curves because of the attention it drew to me. It's like, the better shape you were in, and the more curves you had, the more you stood out. And you didn't want to stand out for that.'

'I liked boys,' laughs Colette St Amande (now Del Frate). 'I wasn't like

Eilleen, though, she was very, very developed. People think that she's gotten surgery, not so. She hid it, she wore baggy clothes, big sweatshirts. She was very modest and shy about it. She hated it when in Grade 9 she had to change for gym class in front of everybody. She didn't flaunt it, a lot of girls wore a lot of tight shirts and low-cut things, and she never dressed like that, never.'

By her own admission Colette was boy crazy, but too scared of the consequences to do much about it. Like Eilleen she was not allowed to be alone with a boy until she was sixteen but that did not stop them listening with open mouths to those girls in their class who went all the way – or at least bragged that they had. Eilleen might reciprocate if a boy was interested in her, as Lynn recalls: 'There was this boy, Mike Perrault, he was the cutie in the class, I had a really big crush on him, but he ended up liking her. She knew if a person was right for her or wasn't. She knew what she wanted. Then it was carry on, let's move on. But she never did the chasing.'

The teenage fashions of the late 1970s were not label-conscious. Girls seldom wore skirts and they were never short unless you wished to be considered tarty. They wore jeans with diamante studs stitched around the pockets and along the back, or bell-bottoms as wide as they could find them. Colette caused a stir with a pair of white super bell-bottoms wide enough to hide skates. They wore baggy work shirts or sweatshirts and 'runners' on their feet.

It was easier for Eilleen when she started to hang with Colette, for Colette liked the comfortable things in life – which meant passing the time at her house where there were milk and cookies aplenty, talking and dreaming about boys and sweaters, listening to records by the Alan Parsons Project and Meatloaf – until Colette's mother heard the lyrics to 'Bat Out of Hell' and it went straight into the garbage. Eilleen grounded Colette, showed her that being the richest kid in class wasn't that important, didn't have to be a barrier to making friends, while Eilleen got to escape the pressure of life in Proulx Court. In Ninth Grade they both bussed out fifteen minutes to Capreol High while Lynn went to the bigger Confed (Colette's folks were worried that there were drugs at Confed, while Jill had also gone to Capreol). Laura Surch was sitting in front of them and they all clicked.

Laura bonded so instantly with Eilleen that they became lifelong friends. Raised first by her grandmother and then by an aunt, Laura knew what a dysfunctional family was. She too had her dreams – mainly to get out of Hanmer. Laura saw behind Eilleen's mask, or maybe she let it slip on purpose, showed how much she hated school. Laura stayed over at Proulx a lot and saw her friend struggling to keep everything going. Says Laura, 'She'd eat at my place and I'd share my food and stuff but at home she'd give what food there was to the kids. Darryl and Mark didn't know what was going on. Her brothers were little brats. Always. Always brats. She didn't have much use for school other than having to go. She liked English, I liked Math. What did we like together? Nothing.'

Jerry's humour could not keep everything together for ever. Neither he nor Sharon were particularly physical in public. 'The whole family tends to be a little stand-offish,' Carrie Ann told *People* magazine. 'There wasn't a lot of hugging and grabbing between our parents.' During their last few years in Hanmer the Twains' relationship went close to foundering. The arguments got worse until Sharon left Jerry for a short time. 'Most times they just talked it out, but later on when Sharon got moody she'd come and see me,' says Karen. 'When they'd get angry at each other, they'd come visit and calm down.'

In Eilleen's first year at Capreol, Jerry realized that he had to do something. He had had enough of offices, paperwork and bureaucracy, of living on the 'bread goulash' line, of watching Sharon sink into depression and his family start to fragment. During the summer months, many of his family were involved in tree planting. Trees, he realized, were a natural but renewable resource and so, according to Karen, he started asking questions. One night he started asking her 'How many trees did you plant? How many hours were you out there?' That was when he got the idea to start his own company. His time in Indian Affairs came in useful, because he knew how to play the system at a time when the Canadian government was suffering from a major guilt trip over how it had treated the Natives.

Jerry got a grant to set up a tree-planting operation employing Native workers. Hanmer was too far south and the big concerns had already got it tied up. The business was all in the vicinity or to the north of Timmins. Timmins was their home town – returning there would certainly please Sharon and maybe help mend their marriage. He insisted that he needed her to get involved, to help run the business. The decision was made and the Twains moved into a small apartment on 137 Balsam Street South, just opposite a funeral home, in the summer of 1980.

The main casualty of the move was Eilleen's career. The extra distances made it impossible to do anything except the most important live shows. Secretly she was relieved. Perhaps she could become just another normal teenager.

CHAPTER FIVE

Blackflies and Brass Bands

E illeen loved the tree-planting business. 'We planted millions of trees every year,' she recalls wistfully. 'It was a wonderful life, there were no roads unless we made them ourselves, we were completely isolated, everyone we hired was Indian. That is another irony that lives strong in the mind of so many Indians: "We plant trees and they cut them down."

'I loved the whole feeling of being stranded. I'm not afraid of being in my own environment, being physical, working hard. I was very strong, I walked miles and miles every day, carried heavy loads of trees, it didn't matter what the weather was like. You can't shampoo, can't use soap, deodorant or make-up – nothing with any scent – you have to bathe and rinse your clothes in a lake because the bugs are so ferocious they can kill a moose. It was a very rugged existence. I wrote so many things, I was very creative then. I would sit alone in the forest with my dog and a guitar and just write songs.'

Financially Jerry Twain's reforestation business was to prove the family's salvation. The first two years establishing the business were tough. Although he got a government grant, Jerry still had to get a bank loan to buy extra equipment, and then he had to make contacts. One former employer, the Ministry of Natural Resources, issued some early contracts and as the business prospered more and more private lumber companies came on board. The business commenced operations in April 1981.

Tree-planting is a long established summer business across northern Ontario. After an area of forest is felled, the ground is cleared, prepared and seedlings planted, not in nature's haphazard manner but in straight lines that will make for easier logging in another decade. Tree-planting is a rite of passage for environmentally conscious students who every summer head north to discover that the forests are full of voracious insects, angry bears and unfriendly locals who despise their soft southern ways and tree-hugging habits. It is poorly paid, gruelling, back-breaking work in the summer heat, often miles from civilization. Seedlings have to be planted the regulation distance of three feet apart and at the right depth. If it is not done correctly, there is no pay. In the early 1980s the rate was 5–6 cents (3p) a tree. Karen Twain who 'was good for a woman, I guess' averaged 1,000 trees a day, earning her $50 for a working day that started before dawn and lasted between twelve and sixteen hours.

Jerry was well equipped to make a go of it: he was physically strong, totally at home in the bush and he knew how to motivate Native workers. His employees were primarily Cree and Ojibwe from Manitoulin Island or from Moose Factory and Moosonee up north on James Bay. Coming from communities where unemployment was endemic, the pay was reasonable for six months' work. They were divided into crews of six or seven, each under a crew boss.

Jerry planted trees all over northern Ontario. The gear would be driven up to a base town – Gogama, Matheson, Hearst, Moonbeam – where the tarmac ended and the crews would head out along the gravelled bush roads. The camps consisted of a couple of trailers containing supplies, fresh water and a portable kitchen; most of the workers slept in tents. It was a family affair – Sharon was heavily involved from the outset, Jerry's 23-year-old brother Tim was a crew boss, so was Karen when she wasn't back in Timmins minding the office, the house and the children, and getting lumbered with a mountain of dirty laundry every couple of weeks. Gerry and Selina did the cooking, so that when the crews staggered back into camp at seven and eight there was always hot food – 'beans, bread and tea in the morning, roast and steak at night, my brother made sure there was pretty good food for everybody' – waiting for them. Says Karen, 'The guys didn't mind being told what to do, because we pretty well hired the same crew every year. We were just one big happy family out there.'

Nobody was allowed to bring any alcohol or drugs into the bush. Anybody caught using was immediately fired and left to find their own way home. At the end of every plant there would be a party. Jerry, who did not drink much any more, brought in a few beers, though never more than two or three bottles, for each worker.

Conditions in the camp were Spartan. Washing was done in the lakes and if there was no local water supply they ran a hose out from one of the vans. The weather could turn nasty: torrential rain and sometimes, as late as August, hailstorms chucking down ice the size of pebbles. During summer, the insect life in the northern forests is particularly vicious. Mosquitoes can smell unnatural odours like shampoo or perfume from miles away and home in more effectively than smart Cruise missiles. Insect repellents only work sporadically and if there's a centimetre of bare skin the bugs find it and eat you alive. Worst of all was June and July – blackfly season. Blackflies are little wee flying sharks that operate in small clouds like some biblical plague. In the midsummer heat blackflies come in swarms so thick you can swallow them along with your lunch, millions upon millions of unrelenting bugs that take chunks out of the unwary and leave them bleeding. 'Imagine the world's worst weather, tremendous cold or oppressive heat, and you can't even come close to being eaten alive by blackflies,' says Canadian explorer Jeff MacInnis, who has planted trees in northern Ontario, 'At times I felt that if I lay down for just a minute they would slowly take my life away.'

By the summer of 1987, Jerry was employing seventy-five people. The crew bosses were John Rodrigues, Dave Rodrigues, Kim Spence, Tim and Karen Twain . . . and Eilleen and Carrie Ann. Eilleen had started out planting whenever she could and after she graduated high school in July 1983, she became a crew boss. The only concession made to the girls was that they slept in a trailer parked some distance away from the main camp so they could enjoy a little privacy. Her twelve-string guitar was always the first thing she brought and the sounds of her and Carrie Ann harmonizing echoed through the trees. On those evenings when she did not crash out early due to sheer exhaustion, Eilleen brought her guitar to the campfire to play and sing after dinner. The family joked – and not without reason – that Eilleen sang extra loud to scare off any curious bears in search of a snack.

In 1982, Kenny Derasp was with a band playing in Geraldton. 'About noon there was a knock on the door waking us up. It was Jerry, who was doing a tree-plant in the area,' he recalls. 'They came into the bar that night. Eilleen, who must have been sixteen, got up and sang a few songs dressed in her work boots and jeans.'

Out in the bush there was nothing feminine about Eilleen. There were no games to play, she could forget about being a sex object. Despite only being knee-high to a moose she was a tough cookie, who took no nonsense from her workers. She expected them to match up to her standards. 'Out there dating wasn't ever on my mind,' she says. 'There were a lot of four in the mornings when I did not feel like getting up to plant a tree. I was one of the guys, I really was. I worked as hard as any of them, if anything even harder. I was determined never to be outwalked or outworked and I gained tremendous respect from my workers. I would tell people how to do things a few times. If they didn't get it right then they would be let go. If they cheated, they would get fired and have to walk to the nearest road. It could take you a day to do that. Cheating lets other people down.'

The Twains always treated their Native workers with respect. When she was not out in the bush, Eilleen kept the books, so she regularly liaised with the CIBC bank and Zudel's Fresh Mart, a small convenience and grocery store at 49 Tisdale, just around the corner from the Twain home.

'Sharon and Jerry had a lot of Natives working for the planting business,' recalls Pam Kardas, who started work as Zudel's bookkeeper in 1982, 'and they were very good in extending credit for them. They'd come in and be allowed to buy groceries against their pay and Jerry would make sure we were paid for it. The account was always good, but when you are working on contract like that you have to have credit, because the money doesn't come in right away, so we would accommodate them. When somebody came in, I would have to check over the phone with Eilleen. Jerry and Sharon did not have a lot of money themselves – they were well below middle income, if not living in poverty – but there was never any finagling. They were poor but honest.' At times the Twains owed in excess of C$25,000 – which they always paid.

Paying their workers was a palaver. Most of them did not live in Timmins, some could barely read or write, nor did they have an active bank account or two forms of photo ID. On Friday afternoons, Eilleen regularly accompanied between five and fifteen employees to the CIBC bank on Pine and 3rd and stood on line to make sure they had enough money for the weekend. Before the days of ATM cash machines the queues were long and slow.

'Eilleen was very easy to notice,' recalls Carole Kiraga, who worked as a teller for CIBC in 1985. 'In order to accommodate them we allowed Eilleen to endorse the cheques. When anybody came up to the cashier, I would signal to Eilleen and she would come and introduce herself to the teller and say, "Hi, I'm Eilleen Twain, and my parents have an account here and I can guarantee that this is Mr John Doe."

'She was a little cutie, a tiny little girl, she had a ponytail, wore no make-up at all, didn't need any, she was always smiling, she had a very nice personality. She always had jeans on and a little jeans shirt and I used to chit-chat with her. It was neat that she came and did this for them. You could tell she had a little bit of control in the company and a lot of trust. I had no idea if it was a successful business, but there was always money to pay those cheques they were presenting. They were earning between C$600 and C$2,000, big cheques, especially in 1985.

'The Aboriginal workers wouldn't say much, but the guys had all due respect for her. I always find Natives to be very shy. They are very respectful and I could tell she was their leader. They were very pleased that she would do this for them they'd go, "Thank you, thank you," and when she'd done her duty she just kind of went her own way. And they went theirs until the next time.'

By the end of October, the onset of winter brought the tree-planting season to an end. During the winter, Jerry switched over to running a mining service company, cutting lines and staking claims. Timmins perpetually dreams of, exists on, the belief in another big strike. Claims are only valid for a short time, up to five years, when they have to be renewed. Staking a claim cannot be done in an office, it has to be done physically. Posts are erected at each of the four corners. A line is cut from corner to corner, then a tag is placed on each corner and the claim registered at the mining office. Jerry did not own the mineral rights to the land, because he was sub-contracting for Seymour Sears and companies as far afield as Wawa. Most times, Jerry left the actual staking to his Native employees; he would get them to the claim sites, some of which could only be reached by helicopter, snowmobile or snowshoe, and make sure everything was OK. During the winter, the stakers, who lived under canvas in temperatures up to fifty below zero, relied on Jerry to keep them supplied.

The business proved a welcome respite for Eilleen. Because Sharon was so involved, it took the pressure off, allowed her to have a normal teenage life at high school. If opportunities came up, they would take them, but Sudbury was three hours away and Toronto ten. Her star future was not abandoned, merely put on to simmer.

After Hanmer Timmins must have seemed a metropolis to a fifteen-year-old girl. Yet, in other ways it was like stepping back twenty years. There was only one pop, one country and one French radio station and just two channels on the TV (Much Music, Canada's answer to MTV, did not exist; MTV only started up in 1981). Some nights when the air was clearer, they could pick up WLS Chicago – real FM radio – full of new sounds, new bands and lots of Zeppelin. For teenagers there was not a lot to do. There was no Timmins Mall to hang in, no fast food outlets except the McDonald's opposite Hollinger Park. Fun was outdoors.

In summer, there was the skateboard park and the drive-in movie theatre. Freedom came with a car. Driving was essential. Once teens turned sixteen and copped a driving licence, they could go camping out by the lakes and rivers or drive up to Hilltop Rendezvous. That was one of the big things once school was out for summer. Drive up the hill to the radio station and make a selection from their musical menu – a choice of fifty rock, twenty country and ten French popular hits – and dedicate a song to your girl, or friends and relatives if there wasn't a girl, while everyone listened at home.

In winter, which lasted six months, there was hockey. Hockey has always been big in Timmins. The town has a long pedigree of siring tough, no-nonsense hockey stars like Steve Sullivan, the Mahovlich brothers, Frank and Peter, Allen Stanley, men capable of making the quantum leap from the farm teams to the NHL. There were hockey leagues of all levels for the guys and for the girls there was always . . . cheering hockey. The ski hill was twenty minutes down the road, or there was snowmobiling (you could get a permit at fifteen and pick up a lousy piece of machinery that still ran) and sliding parties, where everyone grabbed a sled or a bin bag and cascaded down the hills. At weekends there was always a house party somewhere, it just depended on how liberal the parents were, or whether they even knew about it.

Everyone drank beer long before they passed the legal age, for Timmins is a drinking town. That was a rite of passage in a conservative town. There were drugs, too, though they came late to Timmins. 'Even though we'd watched the Beatles invasion on TV we didn't get any rock and roll culture until Woodstock came to the cinema screen,' says John Emms. 'That was a real revelation. It started the drug era in Timmins, mainly pot and a little LSD. Until then, the music scene was old-style country. If there were fifteen bands in town eleven of them were country.'

The drug scene amongst teenagers was always more widespread than their parents cared to believe. 'I knew that that was black hash and that was blond,' Shania told *Rolling Stone*, 'but I was so high on music, and the music was so good – Supertramp and Rush and Pink Floyd. We're all going to see Pink Floyd, and I'm like, "You guys want to put a few things on your tongue, do acid, you just go ahead." Meanwhile, I probably looked high. I used to really rock out. I'd get people coming up to me saying, "Do you do drugs or what?" I never did, but I looked like I did.'

Although Eilleen kept well clear of drugs, she had her flirtations with alcohol, like any normal teenager. 'The first time,' she said, 'was when I was thirteen and my parents got me drunk because I was showing curiosity, you know, what does that taste like? And I think it was like a holiday of some kind and they were having a few drinks, 'cos they never drank normally, they never had liquor in the house. Maybe that's why I was so curious about it.

'So my dad, you know, being smart enough as he was, knowing that at thirteen kids start drinking. Experimenting and stuff. So he said, "Well, do you want to taste it?" And I said, "Yeah." So I tasted it and I said, "Hmm, that's good." And I didn't really like it, and he goes, "Oh, you want some more?" "Sure." So I don't know how much I had, not that much. But you know he wanted me to be drunk, he wanted me to feel terrible the next day. And it worked, it was good. And I was like singing, I remember so well, singing with my guitar and slurring my words and falling off the chair – I was drunk. I remember the feeling. And then I went to bed and [threw up] all over everything. And they knew, they waited for me, they came, cleaned me all up, treated me like the baby that I was. And then made great fun of me the next day.'

In 1982, the Twains bought a small house at 42 Montgomery Avenue. The upstairs apartment was rented out to help the mortgage payments. The front door was up three steps which opened straight into a small room with a battered upright piano to the left of the door. That led into a veritable warren of small, interconnecting rooms: a small sitting room/emergency bedroom led to Jerry and Sharon's bedroom and also to the kitchen. The back corridor led to the bathroom and a tiny bedroom which Jerry converted into an office. The stairs outside the kitchen led down into a semi-basement. The 'rec room' (about two by three metres) was mostly taken up by the boy's gear, ice-hockey equipment and Mark's drum kit. Off it were two bedrooms, the front shared by Mark and Darryl, the back by Eilleen and Carrie Ann. There was little spare space, so Eilleen kept all her songs in a cardboard box under her bed. (According to Laura Surch, a whole trunkload of her stuff – 'including a song she wrote about me' – was lost during the move back from Hanmer). At the back of the basement was the laundry room, which ended in a battered green door that opened to reveal an expanse of wall. The family called it 'the door to nowhere'.

Back in Timmins the rocky times that had threatened Jerry and Sharon's marriage in Hanmer vanished back beneath the waves. Those who knew them talk of them as if they were one person, 'Jerryandsharon'. They appeared to be together all the time. Unlike her first marriage, however, Sharon had no need to force her presence on Jerry, she stood by – and above – him by right. It was no longer a matter of possession.

'They were always close, I never seen one without the other,' says Lise Dubois, a half-Ojibway girl who worked for the Native Friendship Center in Timmins. 'They really stuck close together. You know how married couples drift this way, and that way? Not with them. Like, if their sons had to go to a hockey tournament, they both went to it. If Eilleen played music at the weekends, then both were there. They seemed a couple to me, very inseparable, they couldn't be split apart.'

Mark was still a lanky kid waiting to grow into his body while Darryl was shorter and tough as nails. Both were talented ice-hockey players, which was the only sport that counted. Although their team was sponsored by a local video store, equipment was not cheap and over a season the travelling expenses ran into a couple of thousand bucks. Just as they had done with Eilleen's music Sharon and Jerry found the money to pay for the boys' hockey.

'I would see Jerry supporting his kids, in the Native culture that's what they do, support their children, because we always say our children are the next generation. He taught them well,' says Lise, whose younger brother played in the same team as Mark. She and Carrie Ann often sat in the stands cheering the boys on. 'They didn't have much money, but I remember if they needed new pairs of skates or anything, they would always manage to get it. As far as I knew, the kids never asked for anything else. Mark used to come over at weekends and say stuff like, "Cool, you've got a video game," and "Does your dad always buy this much chips for us to come over?"'

If money was still tight the Twains were better off than they had been in Hanmer. In Timmins, outside of grocery stores, there was only one place where a fifteen-year-old could find part-time work – McDonald's. It was a popular teen hangout as well as an employment prospect, for Don's Pizzeria on Rea catered to an older crowd. Eilleen pulled on the blue polyester uniform with a white hat with a blue stripe around the side covering her hair and went to work on the cash desk. The pay was minimum wage – C\$2.30 an hour – but the shifts (11.30 a.m.–3.30 p.m. at weekends, 3.30–7 p.m. during the week) could be fitted around school and musical commitments in the evening. Eilleen appreciated her time at McDonald's, commenting later, 'I learned a work ethic, etiquette and discipline.'

'She was very fast and very friendly with the customers,' says Marjan Ilovar, who was working French fries at the time. 'I remember one time we had a crew incentive and she won Smile of the Week once. The only reward was you got your picture over the counter and a free meal.

'I knew that she was a singer, because she mentioned it during the six months she worked at McDonald's and Carrie Ann, who worked there for a lot longer, also mentioned it. Once, when she was playing with the band at the Escapade, I sneaked in to see her. Eilleen never stood out of the crowd. She wore plain ordinary jeans, a shirt and no make-up. She was beautiful to look at, but when she smiled it threw you off, as she had a huge gap between her teeth.'

Sharon knew that stars have to have a perfect smile. Once Eilleen was fully grown she had her teeth fixed. They embarrassed her. The problem was congenital, her laterals – the teeth between the front teeth and the eye teeth – never grew, which left four teeth struggling to fill a gap nature designed for six. Her Native status, which helped with basic dental work, did not run to cosmetic surgery. When she was sixteen the Twains found the money to fill the gap in her smile. 'Eilleen had to have a lot of orthodontic work done,' says Timmins dentist, Gerry Paquette. 'My colleague Dr Davis did some and also my study club, to help with costs, but it cost her a few thousand dollars to get everything done. I used a crown with a bridge to fill the missing gap but I know she's had it all done again since then.'

Timmins High and Vocational School, with 1,200 students, was daunting after cosy Capreol. In May 1981 at the end of Tenth Grade, the school moved to new premises off Theriault Boulevard. The facilities were a distinct improvement, with a fully equipped theatre and several well-appointed music rooms. As she had in Hanmer, Eilleen went through the motions, never giving the teachers any clue as to how much she despised going to school.

'She sang sometimes two or three nights a week and would come to class the next day,' says Maureen Yakabuski her Twelfth Grade English teacher. 'She would always make a point of getting the work done and hand it in. She was a conscientious student, although music was the love of her life much more than English literature was.'

Years of hiding her family circumstances had made her an accomplished dissembler. She was a rebel but never showed it. She skipped school a lot more than anybody realized, for she was smart enough to write fake sick notes from her mother to cover her absences. 'I felt invisible a lot,' she said. 'I actually wrote a song called "Feeling Invisible". I was athletic and into music and not really socializing, and I'm sure a lot of it was because I was introverted.' When she cut classes – especially history, which she thought irrelevant – she headed straight for the music rooms.

Her teachers recognized that she had a special ability. 'Her talent stood out even then,' says Tony Ciccone, who taught music in her final year. 'She already had the package, the voice, the delivery and the ability to project on stage. There are a lot of things you can't teach, like her innate ability to project and a way to touch people with her talent. We had a performance group, a wind band in which Eilleen played trumpet, but because she could sing so well, I did an arrangement of Pat Benatar's 'Hit Me with Your Best Shot' and left out the melody line. For the performance in the theatre we grouped the twenty people in the band around her; she stood in the middle of the circle and sang the words. She brought the house down.'

For a while, Eilleen was able to lose herself in the anonymity of the bigger school, but that was not enough. The adolescent advances of thirteen-year-olds are far more easily repelled than those of older boys. Eilleen enjoyed sports, she was on the track and field team and also played soccer. The problem was that it was her breasts that drew immediate attention, not her athletic abilities. While the boys admired her jiggling, she was embarrassed. 'I was very much into sports,' she said. 'So now I wasn't just running on the football team as one of the guys; I was running on the football team bouncing! They weren't seeing me as part of the team; they were seeing me as a girl, and I didn't like that.'

'Guys at that age, as you know, do tend to cross that line. They might grab your butt – they're not thinking – they're being impulsive,' she said. 'And that stuff really made me withdraw from wanting to be a girl. There was one girl at my school who didn't care. She had a figure very similar to mine. She was very curvy. We were in track and field together and she just let it fly. She didn't care. She was being natural. And I remember what people thought of her at the time. I would never have been caught being thought of in that way.'

'I was so confused about all that stuff, I did everything I could to hide what I had. I started wearing layers of clothing. I would always strap my breasts down so that when I was on the football field, the guys were watching me play, not watching me bounce.'

She wore baggy track pants and sweatshirts to school and sometimes two bras. 'I was a girl physically, but it didn't matter to me, I couldn't have cared less. I didn't think that's what it meant to be a girl. I resented the fact that there was a difference between men and women. I just wanted to be a person. On a hot summer day, I'd wear something over my bathing suit, and then when I'd get into the lake up to my knees, I'd thrown it off and dive in.' This natural shyness lasted for years and even in the superstar Shania there is still something of the gauche teenager uncomfortable in a body that has let her down. She never struts the walk of the physically and sexually confident.

Like any girl Eilleen enjoyed being fancied by boys, though she found their adolescent fumblings irritating and felt demeaned by the way their conversation was directed into her cleavage not her eyes.

Their small-town prejudices – the parents of one boy she was dating forbade him to see her any more once they discovered she was from a Native family – and ambitions irritated her too. In return she treated boys badly.

'In my teens I was as hard as a rock, I was so hard and so tough I wasn't very likeable,' she says. 'I was going to achieve whatever I wanted in life and nothing was going to stop me. I had little relationships with boys where I'd say right up front, "I want you to know I don't get too attached. My career comes first. If an opportunity comes up I'm gone." I'd make all these things clear up front. When you come from hardship you know what you don't want to repeat and I knew that if I was going to be independent, financially independent, I was never going to rely on anybody again ever, because there wasn't anybody in my life I could rely on.'

She was seventeen when she lost her virginity to Mike Chabot. She was much too sensible to take any risks. 'I'm kind of old-fashioned,' she told *FHM* magazine, 'so I was never really into the do-it-at-a-party-in-the-side-room thing. I wasn't drinking, it was well thought-out and I was like, "OK, now I'm gonna experiment." And it was enjoyable.'

Such an attitude to sex, plus her rejection of many of her suitors, gave Eileen the reputation of being aloof and stuck-up. She found it hard to make close girlfriends, whose primary interests, boys and clothes, did not appeal to her. She palled up with Cynthia Hagen, but her closest friendships were with boys – provided they never tried to put the moves on her.

'She wasn't shy but she was not the centre of attention either. She wasn't someone who, when she entered the room, everyone went quiet. I thought she was very pretty, though she wasn't flashy and she dressed fairly plain,' says Brian Hurst, who was one grade ahead. He first met Eileen in the drama class he was attending to pick up an extra credit. 'It was a fairly loose class. We did a lot of free-association stuff – pretend you're in an elevator stuff. She was already a performer, but it taught her how to improve her presence in front of people.'

Brian was also the lead trumpet in the brass band. Eileen was fourth trumpet, playing the typical high-school material, like movie themes, and massacring Beatles hits like 'Eight Days a Week'. 'She could make noise but she wasn't a lead player,' says Brian. 'She is a much better singer than a trumpet player.'

He knew that before they ever met. At Timmins High there were a couple of small practice rooms next to the main rehearsal room. 'One day during band practice,' says Brian, 'there was a lot of noise with people tuning instruments, and our conductor tapped on the stage to get us to pay attention to him . . . but when it was quiet we could hear Eilleen and Carrie Ann singing a country duet. Joe Belinkis, the music teacher, held up his finger and we listened a few minutes. Then he smiled and we started to play. There was everybody making a horrendous noise and there she was in the background making this beautiful music.'

Brian's best friend was Rick Thompson ('we met in the crib') who played tuba in the brass band but had ambitions beyond that. Both Rick and Eilleen also performed with the Timmins Youth Singers. Because of their mutual love for music Eilleen and the two boys became close friends, and none of them ever endangered this by throwing sex into the equation. Once she relaxed, Eilleen was a chatterbox just like her mother. She was, as Rick recalls, great company. 'There are some people that shine pretty bright and some that are pretty dim. She was always a lot more shiny than the rest of us. She loved to know exactly what was going on around her. If she started laughing, that was it, the whole room cracked up. She's got one of those infectious laughs and she loved to use it. She was an absolute howl. When she wanted to start speaking, she'd get all excited, go at a million miles an hour. She had a *joie de vivre*. She was passionate and enthusiastic about things. She wore her heart on her sleeve for us and we did the same for her. She called me her Big Bear, because we'd always have a big hug.

'She was one of the boys. One time, when she was about seventeen she insisted she wanted to party with us. "Come on, let's go over to Brian's place and have a couple of beers." We were seasoned northern Ontario beer drinkers at that point. She came over. She was always slight and skinny, well-proportioned and gorgeous, a great-looking girl but always a mate to us. Anyway, she had a couple of beers and that was it . . . she passed right out. She could not handle it at all. I tried to carry her, she must have weighed next to nothing but she was a dead weight, and I could not get her off the ground. So we both threw her in Brian's bed, closed the door both of us smiling at her and carried on our merry way, finishing off the rest of the case.'

Timmins High might have had the facilities but it could not provide enough to feed her yearning. Throughout her teen years music remained the focus of her life. She always knew what she was going to do as Vic Power, (Mayor of Timmins from 1983 to 2000), recalls: 'I was her guidance counsellor and it was my job to meet with students to discuss career or academic prospects. I was always impressed that she knew what she wanted and that she was going places even as a teenager. I didn't have to guide her at all, she always knew where she was going.'

'I hated high school,' she says. 'I would never do that again. All I ever wanted to do was music, so the last thing I wanted to do was waste my time in class, and I still look at it that way. When a child has a talent, let them concentrate on that, let them learn what they want, let them excel at that. I didn't want to be in school. I guess one thing it taught me was some kind of discipline.

'When I look back now I think, yes, I could have enjoyed my teen years much, much more. But at the time you could have never told me that because I was so passionate about music that that's all I cared about. I threw myself into music. All I wanted to be was in band practice or writing songs or singing. I loved being in the basement with the band, I loved writing music and that sort of thing but I didn't care to be the front person, as a matter of fact I didn't like it at all. I really had to grow into that, it took me a very long time. But music itself could consume me every hour of the day and I would have been content with that, not realizing what I was missing by not socializing with the other kids because most of the time the people I was playing with were much older. They weren't in school, they were adults. I did miss out a lot but I don't regret it.'

Eilleen's next major break came eighteen months after she moved back to Timmins. She desperately wanted to join a local rock band and had heard about these four young guys called Longshot. One winter night when she was working at McDonald's they came in after rehearsal . . . and gave her the kiss-off. 'We went to eat after rehearsal,' says Mike Chabot, 'and Eilleen was behind the counter serving us. She said, "You guys are in a band, aren't you?" Not knowing she had already done *The Tommy Hunter Show*, we just nodded and kind of ignored her.'

Her mother convinced her to appear on the annual telethon shown on the local CBC TV station. By coincidence, Longshot were taking a break from rehearsals and switched on the television 'to see which local bands were playing and who was making a fool of themselves. There was this girl singing,' says Dave Hartt, who did not recognize her from the burger bar, 'and she's got an incredible voice. I said, "guys we've got to get her to sing for us." '

CHAPTER SIX

Longshot

In the summer of 1981 Guy Martin had corralled four of his friends into the basement of Rick Dion's house on 371 Elm Street South, directly opposite Zudel's Fresh Mart. Guy's original plan was to record two songs as a birthday gift for a friend. He had already booked time at a recording studio down in Toronto in October. Rick played lead guitar, the quietly spoken Mike Mitchell bass, Tom Lauzon rhythm guitar, Mike Chabot drums while Guy, who, after toying with various stage names including Jonathan Devonshire, finally settled on David Hartt, played keyboards and sang. The rehearsals went so well that after the recording session was done the boys – with the exception of Tom – decided to stay together.

As bands do, they bickered over their name almost as long as they rehearsed and spun their fantasies of stardom. One night Dave grumbled, 'It's a long shot that anything will ever come out of this.' Mike Mitchell retorted, 'Well Longshot's a better name than anything else.' It stuck. Longshot did a few gigs as a quartet but mainly continued to rehearse at Rick's.

Although the band were stunned by Eilleen's voice on the telethon, nobody caught her name. They did hear the station announcer say she attended Timmins High. When Dave mentioned the girl to his friend Brian Hurst, he said he played trumpet with her in the school band. Brian gave Longshot's Toronto tape to Eilleen and a couple of months later she strolled round the corner from the Twain apartment on Balsam South, to meet with Dave, who thought his song 'Take My Hand' might work as a duet. He played the piano, she sang the first verse, he sang the second then they harmonized on the chorus. Upstairs Mike Mitchell, who had just walked in, heard Eilleen singing, ran down the stairs, almost tripping head first on his way. His first breathless words to her were, 'You're not going anywhere!'

'The band clicked musically from day one,' says Hartt, 'It only happens once in a lifetime that you really get that perfect mix. Everybody gets along, you're all friends . . . of course you always break up.'

During the early 1980s the mines were doing well so the town was booming. 'I could make C$35,000 mining in Timmins in 1980 and only C$20,000 in Toronto,' recalls John Emms, who has played in local rock bands since the early 1970s, 'and I got to play music in hotels at the weekend. Everybody's life revolved around the weekend. The hotels and bars were a way of life and all the twenty-odd bars in Timmins were packed. You would go from one to another. If you met anybody, it was at a bar. Everyone got polluted until the bars shut, then you'd go for a pizza at Don's or to somebody's house and continue the party until four, sleep late and start again on Saturday night. The bars were full for twenty years, it was a terrific scene . . . then satellite TV arrived and Timmins rejoined the rest of the world!'

On Friday nights everyone old enough to drink followed the same ritual. Back from work, a quick shower for the guys, a paint, daub and gossip session for the girls. Forget the movies, there were only two cinemas in town and they showed the same films for a month at a time. Then it was out to the bar playing the music of your choice. Most of the hotels featured country music but they were all packed out. If you wanted a table, you had to be there by half-eight as the band went on stage for the first of their four sets at nine. The bars closed at one so there was much serious drinking to be done. Shots of hard liquor with beer chasers were the order of the night and if you couldn't hold your drink until last call, you weren't a man.

The best bars were in a small six-block area south of Algonquin East. A major focus was the corner of Mountjoy and Wilson where the Escapade, the Rocking Tap and the more traditional Northern Star were but a short stumble apart. The younger crowd also frequented the Empire (the biggest gig in town). The 'Riv' (Riverview Hotel), the

Algoma Tavern, the GV Hotel, the South End Hotel and, for a major change of scenery, the Airport Hotel eight kilometres away in South Porcupine. Country fans preferred the Maple Leaf over on Balsam, still virtually unchanged from the days of Stompin' Tom or the Windsor. They were all small places, JP's Lounge could squeeze in two hundred if everyone breathed in at the same time, the Algoma could not fit a hundred.

Jean-Paul Aube was an entrepreneur before he was allowed to drink. At seventeen he was running his own club, putting on bands every weekend. He bought the Escapade Hotel with his brother Ben when he was twenty-five, kept on renting its rooms to construction workers on contract (though the bridal suite featured a round bed and a fur rug) and started a discotheque downstairs. It was not until J. P. canned the disco, rechristened the space 'JP's Lounge' and started booking live acts that he struck the pay-packet lode. The formula was simple and commercial: he hired in duos from southern Ontario who played easy listening top-forty hits. It worked. 'I could have had police directing traffic on Friday and Saturday nights,' he says.

Late one afternoon in early 1982 there was a timid knock on the door of J.P.'s office in the lobby of the Escapade. A sixteen-year-old girl he had never seen before asked nervously if she could come in. She was good-looking, not stunning, but there was something about her, a presence, something familiar, perhaps a quality he recognized from his own youth. That was why J.P. gave her the time of day.

'We have a group,' Eileen Twain told him – she didn't say 'I' – all business, very articulate, very focused and specific. 'We have been practising for a while and we're trying to get into a hotel because we want to play. I'll be upfront with you . . . I'm under-age, so nobody will give me a chance.' That all but finished the deal as far as J.P. was concerned. Hoteliers in Ontario had to abide by the rules otherwise the all-powerful LLBOA (Liquor License Board of Ontario) closed them down. Under-age drinkers were a definite no-no.

'If you are under-age you are not allowed in,' he said, 'Sorry . . .'

'No but you can,' she said so forcefully he stopped mid-sentence, 'the management have to provide me with a place where I can go between sets. I can be on the stage for my set but after that I have to be in a room.'

There were rooms upstairs at the Escapade, so that was not a problem. J.P. was intrigued by the girl's self-confidence in asking him to make an exception for her. She was certainly cute but could she sing? 'We'd like you to hear us first,' she said, as if she had been reading his mind. 'We practise most nights in the basement at 371 Elm Street South.'

J. P. discussed the girl with his brother, who had also been visited by Hartt and Chabot. They checked out the legal situation to find Eilleen was right and went to a rehearsal. 'As soon as they started playing and she started singing I knew,' says J. P. 'Just hearing the sound, the voice and the look. I'm not stupid. They were a top-forty band, better than I was getting from southern Ontario. It was more expensive than what we were paying the duos and I remember thinking "Do we want to do this?" but I looked at my brother. He agreed. They filled up the place pretty much from the first night on.'

J. P. and Ben gave the band a residency at JP's Lounge starting in May. They had only heard them play one song – which was fortunate. 'The date was twenty-seven days away,' says Hartt. 'We had to play four sets a night and we only knew five songs. We practised every night, marathon practises on weekends, going into the wee hours of Sunday morning. Sunday night, Monday night, every night we'd practise and by the first show we had forty-two songs.'

The pay was pretty good at a time when the minimum wage was C$2.30 an hour: C$1,200 for the first four-night residency at JP's, rising later to C$1,600. Within a few weeks they were booked solid until January. Some of the profit went into buying a small PA and to start with Eilleen – who didn't have to buy any gear – was asked to contribute. The other band members knew her family was poor and how much C$300 a week meant to them. Her deductions dropped from fifty bucks to twenty-five and then disappeared for good.

Longshot were such a good draw J. P. had to hire bouncers – after

9.30 nobody could get in. Much of Longshot's appeal was because they attracted the girls. 'They loved us, we had attendance records that stood for a long time,' says Hartt. 'It was simple. With a female lead singer, you attract women, men come into a bar, see lots of women, they stay, they buy the women drinks. Bars make a lot of money. We weren't cheap, we demanded a good price.'

'Longshot was not into drinking as much as Smuggler or Elmer Thudd or some of the other rock bands,' adds John Emms. 'These guys wanted to play it straighter so they had a larger audience of women. My wife would tell me, "Your band is terrible but these guys are great because they are playing the songs just like on the radio." '

'As a performer Eilleen was a mix of halting confidence but her personal attitude was great. She was kind of shy but she had to be the lead singer and at times she seemed forced into the role. She was good, she could hit all the high notes. Longshot were there to bang out the hits and they did that better than anybody else in town.'

On stage Eilleen never flaunted it. She hid her figure behind her Tacoma twelve-string guitar and played percussion when she was not singing. She dressed down, never too sexy, baggy sweatshirts over spandex tights and wool leggings – the *Flashdance* look – but no bare flesh on display. As she grew in confidence her clothes became a little tighter, she favoured black satin skin-tight pants with a matching top and headband – very Olivia Newton John – or black leather trousers. They all wore black satin tour jackets with the Longshot logo on the back. Although her hair was fine and thin she insisted that hairdresser Paul Cousineau give her regular perms. She wanted to wear it big, back-combed to *Dynasty* heights. There was one frizzy perm that was disastrous. Eilleen never wore too much make-up, no foundation or lipstick, just heavy black eye-liner.

To begin with, Eilleen never talked to the audience much, Hartt and Chabot took care of that, but her confidence grew steadily. She learnt to use the breaks between sets. Sharon, Jerry and the extended Twain clan were regulars, but she did not confine herself to family and friends, instead she learnt to work the room.

'I never saw her sleazy or flirting with guys, she was just very focused all the time,' says Cousineau, a friend of Mike Chabot's, who saw Longshot play all the time with his girlfriend. 'She would finish her first set and on her way offstage she would thank whoever was there for coming. She'd take a few minutes rest, get back up there, she'd play hard and the next thing you know she'd go through the audience on the second set, same on the third, and anyone she hadn't seen she'd go and say hello. She wasn't allowed to drink because of her age, but she was always the lady, she'd say hello to everybody on her way to the upstairs room.'

Longshot did not rely on original songs. They only did three David Hartt compositions: 'Thanks for the Good Times', 'Sandy' and the duet 'Take My Hand', which became an unofficial anthem at several local weddings. Eilleen sang over half the material with Hartt taking lead vocals on about forty per cent, leaving the two Mikes to sing three numbers between them. The material was miles from what Eilleen knew. Hartt loathed country and refused to touch anything with a twang. They concentrated on current hits by melodic hard rockers leavened with a sprinkling of classic cuts ('we didn't do "Hotel California" or "Stairway to Heaven", those were taboo songs,' says Hartt). The Beatles' 'Let It Be', Fleetwood Mac's 'Don't Stop', Creedence Clearwater Revival's 'Travelling Band' and Grand Funk Railroad's 'American Band'. Longshot covered hits by Canadian rockers Loverboy, Toronto and Bryan Adams as well as Bob Seger, Styx, REO Speedwagon and Journey, whose 'Don't Stop Believing' was a particular crowd-stopper, along with Survivor's 'Eye of the Tiger', Foreigner's 'Feels Like the First Time' (written and produced by one Robert John 'Mutt' Lange) and Orleans' 'Still the One' (which has nothing in common with the track on Shania's *Come On Over*). For ballads Eilleen convinced them to let her sing Linda Ronstadt's quivering version of 'Poor Poor Pitiful Me' and Sheena Easton's 'When He Shines'. Longshot never played any Pat Benatar numbers, although they did rehearse a couple.

All the band members knew that Eilleen wrote songs and they

wanted to tackle them, but she always demurred, insisting they weren't ready. Dave Hartt still has a tape of 'Stepping Stones' that he begged her to perform with them. 'Maybe she wasn't comfortable,' says Hartt, 'because when you put a song out before other people, you are standing pretty naked there. Also she was writing ballads which didn't fit with us so well. I remember her sitting on a stool at JP's Lounge singing this line: "the flickering fire on the wall made music that I found you". I looked across the bar and I could see her reflection in the mirror and I said, "That's great." She was really dedicated because while she was working at this, she was looking for the right words, putting it together.'

Although Eilleen was treated like one of the boys, they always took good care of her. Rick or Dave, who lived close by, generally walked her home after a gig. After a pool party during the summer the flirtatious looks she had been exchanging with Mike Chabot turned to kisses and they started going out together. She might have been three years younger than Mike but she was 'serious about my career and my life. Men were always secondary. I never put a man first, ever.'

'I'm not into how people look and she was a lot of fun to be with,' says Chabot. 'She had a great sense of humour, we clicked from that standpoint, we both liked music, played tennis a couple of times, then we hung out. It was nothing serious, a normal boyfriend-girlfriend thing, I bought a few things for her, but it only lasted a short time, just the summer. She was very, very energetic with regards to enjoying life; she knew what she wanted, that's for sure. Music was going to be her living, that was clear from day one. I've played hockey with guys in the NHL, I've worked in business with people who are very successful, but not like her. She is probably the most driven soul I've ever met.'

For her seventeenth birthday Mike gave her a present which she still has today. 'He gave me a black ledger and said, "You've gotta stop collecting all your songs on loose pieces of paper. You should put them where you're not going to lose anything." So I rewrote all of my songs into this ledger and I've kept that. I've been a little more organized from that point on.'

Eilleen soon emerged as one of the most forceful personalities in the band. If they made a mistake, she let them know, no holding back. During one show Chabot hit the cymbal wrong and the stand crashed over, missing Eilleen by half an inch. She never missed a beat, kept right on singing, until the guitar solo. Then she turned round and yelled at him. Just as the solo finished, she turned back and came in note-perfect, right on cue. The audience never saw a thing.

She got her own back in October on Chabot's birthday. As a treat they let him play a drum solo while they brought a cake on stage. Eilleen took the cake, went behind him and pushed it right in his face. That was the signal for a cake fight. 'We were not always the most professional,' laughs Hartt, 'but we liked to have fun.' Unlike some of their contemporaries, they did not drink much and did not smoke pot. After shows at JP's, they would repair over the road to the Cosy Corner Café to eat and discuss any problems.

When trouble broke out, which it often did when drink took over the crowd, the boys protected her. One night at the Riv a serious bar fight broke out just as the band launched into Toronto's 'Looking for Trouble'. Unlike the Deep South of the USA, where the stage is often surrounded by chicken wire, the band had no protection, so the guitarists stood in front of their singer, using their C$1,500 instruments as shields, and as the battle overflowed on to the stage pushed the brawlers off with their feet. They never stopped playing.

On New Year's Eve 1982, Eilleen's voice completely gave out, she could only manage two songs, one of which was 'Auld Lang Syne'. The boys went back to their oldest material, including some AC/DC songs, but nobody seemed to mind. By that stage it was already over for Longshot. They had decided to call it a day in the autumn but agreed to honour their commitments.

Longshot worked hard, perhaps too hard, for they seldom turned down a show. On the weekend of 1 July 1982, they picked up their gear from JP's, went down to Hollinger Park for a Battle of the Bands, returned to JP's. The next day they played at a friend's wedding barbecue and ended up back at the park in the early evening. They

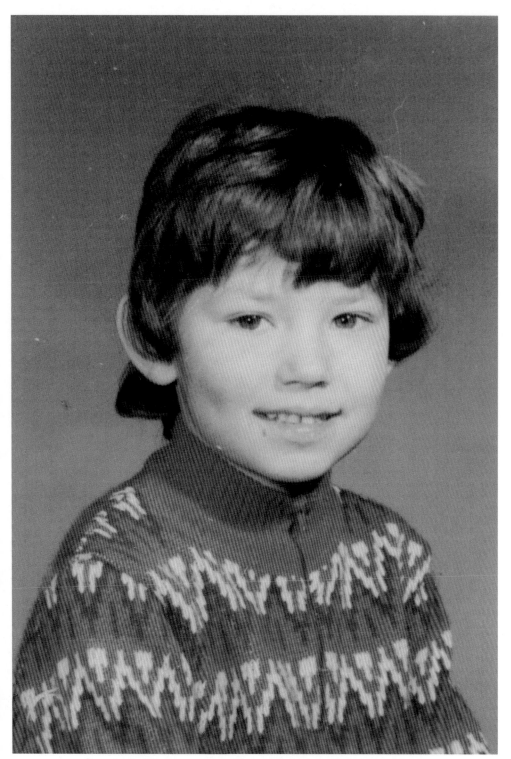

✳ Eilleen at six. Her first school photo. (*Don Fraser*)

✳ The Twains in 1973. Left to right: (back) Carrie Ann, Eileen, Jill, (front) Mark.
(*Don Fraser*)

✶ Grandma Eileen Morrison's house in Hoyle. Sharon and her daughters lived here after Clarence Edwards left. (*Robin Eggar*)

✶ Playing euchre on a camping trip to Halfway Lake Provincial Park with Pinecrest Public School, Hanmer, June 1979. (*Ted Evans*)

✷ Jerry and Sharon bought this house in Montgomery Avenue, Timmins, in 1981. The top floor was rented out. Eilleen and Carrie Ann slept in the basement. (*Robin Eggar*)

✷ Downtown Timmins. Wednesday night is still talent night in the Maple Leaf Hotel (left she even won. (*Robin Eggar*)

✳ Eilleen Twain's graduation photo in 1983. 'I knew she had something special even then,' says local photographer Claude Gagnon, who has been taking the pictures of Timmins High and Vocational school graduates for 25 years. (*Claude Gagnon*)

ack in the '80s, Eilleen Twain would bring her guitar and sing at the venue – sometimes

✶ Mary Bailey in her heyday as a Canadian country star. Mary first saw Eilleen sing when she was 11, and was to be her guide, mentor and support for many years. (*Redferns*)

✶ Viva Vegas. Eilleen singing at Deerhurst in 1988. (*Mike Taylor*)

✶ Eilleen with her then boyfriend Mike Taylor during a trip to Las Vegas, 1988. (*Mike Taylor*)

✶ 'I need bigger hair!' Eilleen in the bathroom of her house in Melissa, Christmas 1988. (*Mike Taylor*)

✳ Eilleen was not auditioning for a remake of *One Million Years BC*. The picture was shot as part of a planned campaign for the album she made with Harry Hinde in 1989. (*Denise Grant*)

played odd venues like a dance for a baseball team at La Ronde, the French cultural centre, and the occasional bummer like the GV Hotel, where they earned less than the waitresses.

The problem was that, while Longshot were good, there was nowhere for them to go. In the year they were gigging the furthest out of town they played was South Porcupine. It was a perennial problem, as John Emms recalls: 'Not many bands in town lasted more than two years. Playing three weekends out of four you didn't have time to change the set list so the audience got smaller and smaller. And if you went to Toronto you found out quick how you weren't as good as you thought you were. You would go see a band in a bar and these guys were schooled musicians and the drummer could play in time. That was an eye-opener.'

It didn't help that Eilleen was still at high school and that the next set of decent gigs were a three-hour drive away in Sudbury or North Bay. But that wasn't a real problem, as Sharon would drive her daughter to the ends of the earth if she thought it was a show up the ladder. They talked about going on the road once Eilleen got out of school but that was just talk. While the boys' ambitions ended at the city boundaries, Eilleen's did not. She was the one who left after a gig not in triumph but with the big black dog gnawing at her insides, 'walking home alone at 3 a.m. with a rock in my pocket'.

The experience of working in a rock band changed Eilleen's percep- tions, shifting them away from country. She learnt that there was more to performance than just singing. 'I couldn't hide behind my guitar,' she says. 'I sensed a freedom that I'd never sensed before.' It taught her how performance could be exhilarating, blow away the old fears but at the same time it made her yearn for more.

'In the summer we were all booked up so there was no point in leaving the area,' says Hartt. 'Why pay to go live somewhere else, when you can make better money at home? We talked to musicians that came in from out of town, making $120 for the whole band to eat for a week. That's not a lot of money, you're not going to buy instruments, put money away for retirement on that. I never wanted to take that big risk of leaving. In the end, Eilleen was a lot more dedicated than the rest of us. We lacked ambition but maybe because she went without when she was younger it didn't scare her to say, "I can leave all this behind and work on my music, because this is what I want to do." '

Longshot's final show at the Palmour Tavern on 14 January 1983 was not intended to be a permanent end. After eighteen months spending almost every night together the musicians needed a break, time apart. They settled into jobs and girlfriends and after a few months thought about starting up again. Hartt called Eilleen and asked if she wanted to come back. Even though the money would have been useful, Eilleen had seen them in their true colours. She said 'No.'

'We might have been the best band in Timmins but that was Timmins, man,' says Chabot, aptly summing up a band that might have done something. 'My dream was never North Bay or Sudbury. It was pure outright fun for me. I did think about making a living at it, but drummers are a dime a dozen. When the band broke up, I joined a band in southern Ontario, gave it a shot and it didn't work out. Eilleen went to a band down in Sudbury, but she was already looking beyond that.'

CHAPTER SEVEN

The Wilderness Years

After graduating from Timmins High in July 1983, Eilleen determined to expand her musical horizons. While Longshot had been a successful experiment, its ambition had been limited and she understood that no talent scout was going to discover her north of the Arctic watershed. For much of the next three years she spent her summers planting trees and her winters playing the Ontario club circuit, attempting to break into the business.

Musically she trod an uneasy path between country and rock. By the early 1980s country music's flirtation with cocaine and outlaws had evaporated. Strings and spangles had reasserted their conservative sway. The radical limit of Nashville's ambitions were to achieve pop crossovers like Kenny Rogers and Dolly Parton's excruciating 'Islands in the Stream'. In the USA, while the corporate rock of Journey and Foreigner was challenged by British bands like the Police, Eurythmics, Culture Club and Def Leppard, the real star of the era was Michael Jackson. Canada – and especially Timmins – was stuck firmly on the musical periphery. The advent of the video channel *Much Music* and FM radio showed just how much.

After the demise of Longshot, Eilleen was approached to join Flirt, a covers band operating out of Sudbury. Flirt's lead singer Diane Chase, who had decided to try her luck in the business down in Toronto, knew Eilleen from when they were children on the local talent circuit and recommended her for the job. Flirt travelled all over Ontario earning a reasonable way playing 'rock, R&B, top forty, whatever was making money at the time'. Eilleen missed her graduation ceremony because she was on the road with them. Laura Surch saw them at a hotel in Blind River. 'I managed to get my aunt to go into a hotel to see the band, which was a major deal,' she says, 'but it was just a job for Eilleen.'

By the autumn of 1984, Eilleen had attracted the interest of Toronto-based producer/DJ Stan Campbell. In a Canadian *Country Music News* article Campbell enthused about his latest protégée. 'Eilleen possesses a powerful voice with an impressive range. She has the necessary drive, ambition and positive attitude to achieve her goals.' Campbell was making an album with Tim Denis and drafted Eilleen in to sing backing vocals on 'Heavy on the Sunshine'. The following January, Campbell took her down to Nashville to record some demos.

The demo recordings cost C$10,000, which the Twains could ill afford. Sharon set about trying to raise some investment. 'She called encouraging me to invest in Eilleen's career,' says Jean-Paul Aube, with a rueful smile. 'She called more than once. She wanted money for Eilleen to live on while she got a portfolio together and developed contacts and connections. She didn't have an agent. I asked, "How much will you need?" and she said C$25,000. I told her, "I agree with you 1,000 per cent she has a lot of talent and she should be very successful. I'd love to be able to participate, but unfortunately I can't, as I've just taken on some fairly major commitments with McDonald's." '

Sharon turned to northern Ontario's brightest – and only – country star. Mary Bailey lived in Kirkland Lake, only a ninety-minute drive from Timmins. If Shania Twain's life can be likened to a modern Cinderella story, Mary is the Fairy Godmother – always there when she was needed. Mary had been successful in Canada, enjoying a run of country chart singles from 1976 and releasing two albums, *Mystery Girl* and *Think of Me*. She knew all about Eilleen.

'I was doing a show in Sudbury,' she says, 'and this little girl got up on the stage with a guitar, and absolutely blew me away. She sang two songs, Willie Nelson's "Blue Eyes Crying in the Rain" and Hank Williams' "I'm So Lonesome I Could Cry". Her voice reminded me of Tanya Tucker; it had strength and character to it, a lot of feeling. There was never a doubt in my mind that she had it; even at that young age she exuded a quiet confidence. Stars stand out.'

Mary knew what it was like to be a child with a voice. Her middle-class parents had pushed her too, woken her in the middle of the night to sing at their parties. They drove her to talent contests as far afield as Windsor and Toronto, where she sang numbers by Janette Macdonald, Nelson Eddy, Mario Lanza and the Ink Spots. She married young and had a family, but her ambitions did not wither with changing nappies. Her husband Bob Kasner 'was totally and only into country music. So I listened to it, it grew on me, I grew to love it.' Mary – or Eveline as she was then – was ambitious and smart with it. She bought advertising down-time from local TV stations for next to nothing and used it to promote her records. Pretty, vivacious and charming, Mary was an excellent networker who never forgot a face. She did well, but by 1985, her career was winding down and she was looking for a new challenge.

Sharon, ever mindful of her daughter's prospects, had kept in sporadic touch with Mary since '78. In the spring of 1985, she approached her again, ostensibly asking for advice on whether they had been overcharged for the Nashville demos. Mary listened to the tapes and told Sharon, 'Yes, it was too much money,' and how much they could have done it for, but all the while she spoke she was mesmerized by that reserved nineteen-year-old girl who sat in an armchair, silent while her mother did all the talking, but devouring every word.

'She sang a couple of songs that she had written,' says Mary, 'and I thought to myself, "This kid is like nineteen years old, where does she get this? This is from a person who's lived sixty years." Songs about being a woman in difficult situations, finding the best in a person, asking why are they staying in that relationship . . . pretty deep for a nineteen-year-old. No offence, but they haven't lived it and you don't believe that they think that deeply. But Eilleen could, she had an innate ability. She must have an old soul, for she always wrote beyond her years.'

While Mary was impressed by the girl's talent, Bob was visibly blown away. Eventually Sharon came to the crunch. Would Mary be interested in managing her daughter? 'I had never managed anybody in my life,' says Mary. 'I managed my own career out of necessity, not choice. Bob and I talked to each other, and he said, "She's a star, she deserves an opportunity." '

Mary bought out Eilleen's contract with Stan Campbell and Eilleen moved into the Kasner home, a well-appointed wooden chalet with a stunning view over Kenogami Lake. For nine months she became a surrogate daughter, connecting with Mary in a way her two sons never could. While she was there, Eilleen enjoyed a quick fling with Bobby Kasner, which they tried very hard to keep secret from his mother, if not the prying eyes of his little brother. She was given her own room and helped around the house and kitchen. Mostly she played guitar and sang. She practised every day for hours.

'She wouldn't just let her voice do it for her,' says Mary. 'You may be born with a talent to be able to sing but ninety-five per cent of us get by on that. She didn't, she perfected her craft. She listened to all her influences, especially Karen Carpenter. If you really listened to Karen she had this total control. Eilleen worked on that, learnt to be able to control, how to use certain intonations to take the song further. She understood that the voice was an instrument, and how well she learnt to play that instrument was how good her chances were. It's very rare finding people like that. Everybody wants to be a star but very few people want to do what's required . . . but she did it, in everything.'

Just as Eveline Kasner was not the right name for a country singer, Mary knew Eilleen Twain did not cut it either. They discussed names for hours and eventually Mary suggested 'Sophyah'. She sent tapes to her contacts south of the border, including Ken Kragen, the manager of Kenny Rogers and Lionel Richie. The answers all came back the same: 'Thanks, but no thanks.' Mary and Bob never lost faith.

Towards the end of 1985, Mary took Eilleen down to Nashville to stay with her friend, record producer Tony Migliore. Fellow Canadian Kelita Haverland was cutting an album at Chelsea Studios and Tony drafted Eilleen in to sing back-up. (When the album was released by RCA the title track, 'Too Hard to Handle', became a minor hit.) She wrote and demoed songs with songwriter Cyril Rawson, but after five months nobody had shown any interest, so she returned to Kirkland Lake to stay in the Kasner house. In order to raise extra money to finance the project Mary went back to work, releasing a couple more singles.

There was a more fundamental problem. In 1985, country was so far from cool as to be beyond tepid. Eilleen did not want to sing country, she wanted to be a rocker. They began to argue, but Eilleen was not frightened of confronting her manager. After years of subsistence living, Eilleen had tasted middle-class luxury at Kirkland Lake, and while she liked it, that was not enough. Eilleen was not frightened of being poor. She had survived on mustard sandwiches in the past and, if she had to, would do so again. Once her mind was made up, the girl had a will of steel: she did not bend, she did not break and she would not compromise. Convinced that country was not the right route forward, Eilleen convinced Mary to let her front a rock band.

In September 1986, Rick Thompson had decided it was time to go to college to study music. The week before his audition with Humber College in Toronto, Eilleen called him up. 'Listen, Big Bear, I've got a project going. I've got some musicians and we're going to get together in Kirkland Lake and I'd like you to come and play bass for me.' Rick didn't hesitate for a moment.

The musical mainstay was keyboard player Eric Lambier, who, with his hair past his shoulders, looked like 'a complete metal head'. Eric had two glass eyes – the result of a gunshot accident when he was a kid – but aside from needing some help to get behind his equipment, his handicap went unnoticed. The line-up was completed by Tom on guitar and Randy on drums (neither Rick nor Mary Bailey can remember their last names), both of whom had worked with Eric down in Toronto.

Eilleen lived with Mary while the band were in a second-floor flat in downtown Kirkland Lake, two blocks from the rehearsal studio, a converted changing room next to the hockey rinks. There was no wage, but Mary paid for rent, food and the rehearsal space. Rick and Eric got up at 5.30 in the morning six days a week, even if it was forty below outside, grabbed some breakfast and headed for the studio. When

Eilleen walked in, the band were always ready to go. The music was a continuation of what Eilleen had been doing with Longshot and Flirt – production rock with a lot of top-forty influence, nothing more experimental or out on the edge than a dance groove – except it was all original material. The core of the songs originated from Eilleen, who threw ideas at Eric, which they then bounced back and forth. 'They had a pretty good writing chemistry together,' says Rick. 'Because she is a singer, she likes to write with somebody who knows what they are doing with their instrument. She loves the tension of throwing ideas at people.

'There were times she'd run helter-skelter, she'd want to do so many things at one time. We'd go, "Hang on, look at this, make it simpler," but when she was running we couldn't pull her down if we wanted to. Harmonically Eric would have more idea and say, "That doesn't work." She'd have to think about that for a little, so she'd clam up and put her pensive face on, I loved it when that would happen and she'd come around after a while or she'd say, "No, I want to try it my way." Eilleen was the boss, she ran the show. She wasn't tough because we worked our asses off. It was one of the most productive times in my life. We came close to working up twenty tunes we could have played on stage – but we never got the chance.'

After her brief dalliance with Bobby Kasner, Eilleen took up with Randy. 'Eilleen was always cool with her boyfriends. She didn't change her "one of the boys" attitude,' says Rick. 'Randy asked the rest of us in the group if it was OK if they had a relationship, which I thought was a very cool thing to do. He also said it didn't matter a hoot if we said, "No way," but they thought they'd be considerate and ask anyway.' The band rapport was good. They enjoyed several parties in the flat. Rick remembers everybody watching the movie *Spinal Tap*; the band all fell about laughing, while the non-musicians sat there bemused, saying, 'It's kinda funny, but we don't really get it.'

After three chilly months in Kirkland Lake, Mary suggested the band move back down south and get ready to do some recording. In January, they moved to Orono, thirty kilometres east of Toronto, where Eric's mother had a tobacco farm, and set up their equipment in one of the drying rooms. They continued to rehearse and play for the odd visitor Eilleen or Mary invited out. They recorded a song 'The City', for a contest sponsored by Q107, the big local rock station. It made the final top twenty-five. Soon afterwards, everything went pear-shaped.

The band hoped a record deal was imminent and kept asking about it. When nothing materialised they felt they were kept in the dark about what was going on. The band seethed away until Randy announced, 'That's it, it's finished.' 'We tried to keep the band going as a four-piece,' says Rick, 'but I kept getting "Rick you sing all right, but you are no Eilleen Twain." I absolutely didn't understand why the whole thing fell through, wasn't given much of an explanation, so I stayed angry at Eilleen for a while after that.'

One of the reasons that no record deal materialized was that, by the end of the stay in Kirkland Lake, Mary and Eilleen were arguing constantly. 'Eilleen and I always had little shouts,' says Mary, 'Some days we'd be diamonds, some days we'd be stones, it doesn't mean that we didn't love each other. She knew what she wanted, and worked towards it. I couldn't bring to the table where she wanted it to go, I was trying to make inroads in country, she was steering one way, I was steering another.' Finally, after one argument, an exasperated Mary snapped, 'If you don't want to sing country, what the hell can I do for you?' Eilleen left for Toronto and after the band imploded, they did not speak for nearly two years.

She had already found the man who was going to be instrumental in the next stage of her career. In the late summer of 1986, Mary engineered a meeting between Eilleen and John Kim Bell, a half-Mohawk, half-American conductor. After a glittering career split between conducting Broadway musicals, symphonies and ballets (he was the first Native to conduct a symphony orchestra), Bell had rediscovered his roots. He settled in Toronto and founded the Canadian Native Arts Foundation (soon renamed the National Aboriginal Achievement Foundation). The foundation was formed to help young Native people get a start in the arts. Mary was a friend of Gordon

Burnett, a former president of the Canadian Country Music Association whose Métis wife Suzanne was on John Kim's board of directors. After a couple of firm steers, John Kim drove down to the Burnett's house in Welland, near to Niagara Falls to meet Eilleen.

'She had some sheet music for some pop tunes, so I played piano while she sang,' says Bell. 'I noticed that she had a very clear and strong voice, she had good control over it, very nice tone, and an extremely large range. She could sing Broadway torch songs, really sell a song, and she is capable of singing much more technically difficult, artistically difficult and flamboyantly interesting songs than she now does for a living.'

What also struck Bell was the girl's looks. 'She was a very attractive young woman, not immediately sexy, because she was kind of small. She was very pretty, a natural beauty who didn't wear a lot of make-up. She had big poofy light strawberry hair, that flew all over the place.'

Bell was thirty-four, a big-city sophisticate whose tastes ran to high culture, good wine and fancy foods. Here was this country girl from the forests of the frozen north, barely twenty-one, a jeans and sweats kid with no formal education to speak of. Not his type at all. Except he couldn't get her out of his head. He knew she had talent but he did not know what he could do for her. His foundation was starting up and had no money and even less clout, yet Suzanne and Mary kept on phoning him, demanding, 'What can we do to help Eilleen?' Eilleen, too, refused to take maybe for an answer and kept sending Bell the songs she was recording in Kirkland Lake.

After she fell out with Mary, Eilleen needed the help. She and Laura Surch, her old friend from Hanmer who was studying business administration, were living in a high-rise on Jane and Finch on the northwest side of Toronto. It was a dangerous part of town, a predominantly black slum area complete with shootings, prostitutes, drug dealers and a plague of cockroaches. The girls were so broke they had no furniture. Eilleen slept on a mattress on the floor. Partly because he felt sorry for her – but mainly because he fancied her – Bell went to see her rehearse.

'I drove out to a barn out in the country east of Toronto to see her in some grunge band,' he says of his trip to the tobacco farm in Orono. 'She was never really satisfied with the bands, she was always very precise, picky about everything. But I observed that she was a good singer, the best thing there. Of course, all the time I was going out to see her I was developing a relationship. I was obviously attracted to her and she liked me too.'

It helped when the girls moved to the slightly more salubrious area of High Park on the corner of Indian Road and Howard Park, one block from Bell's home at 27 Indian Grove. She worked as a cashier in a little Zellars store in the nearby shopping centre. A month later, she moved in. All the time she lived with John Kim she always had part-time jobs; she took a course at a computer school who promptly hired her, she worked in a dry cleaners – anything to help pay her way. The rest of the time she worked on her career. She never stopped hustling. Professionally she started to use the name Sophyah Twain.

It was an attraction of opposites. From the outside, it seemed a modern Pygmalion. He was Professor Henry Higgins to her Eliza Doolittle. From this northern waif he could create a five-star performer, and an elegant addition to any salon. John Kim was a 'New York downtown kinda guy'. She was a hard-cussin', tough-talking bush-woman from a blue-collar culture where you chain-smoked and drank your pay cheque away on Friday nights (except Eilleen did not smoke and hardly drank, save for sharing the odd bottle of wine). At home they listened to a lot of classical music, jazz and mainstream pop artists like David Foster, as well as black performers like Earth, Wind & Fire and Whitney Houston.

To her family she was always 'Leeni'. John Kim preferred the pet names 'Boobooeski, Boo or Booboo', though he cannot remember where they came from. John Kim sometimes describes her as a 'plucky kid', making her sound like some freckled brat from *The Little House on the Prairie*.

Not that there was any doubt that Eilleen was beautiful, but you could see her roots in the way she walked: real fast, as if she were in a perpetual hurry to reach her destination, striding out at a bushman's pace, her arms swinging tight into her sides. A tough guy's walk, nothing feminine about it. Her buttocks never shimmied, never undulated with that Vegas strut which attracts men's gazes like hypnotized rabbits. There was nothing sophisticated about Eilleen or her wardrobe. She didn't have a lot of money, so tended towards the grunge look – velour pullovers, track pants, or jeans and heavy work shirts with tennis shoes in winter, shorts and T-shirts in summer. 'She always wore pants rather than dresses,' says Bell, 'because her legs were short. High heels and nylons were not her style. When she dressed up she'd put on black pants, flats and some nice sweater.'

Her hair was always bushy, almost unkempt, and she had this habit of running her hands through it and shaking her head like a dog trying to shed fleas. John Kim found that funny and endearing. Men were drawn to her but not because she was sensuous. She never flirted, appeared to have no concept of how sexy she could be.

'She had a perfectly shaped body with a flat washboard stomach,' says Bell. 'Yet there was always this reserve about her. Her sister Jill was older, kind of a sex kitten, attractive and effusive with her sensuality, the opposite to Eilleen, who suppressed it. She was quite well-endowed as a young woman, and because of that she was self-conscious. She didn't want guys ogling her breasts all the time, so she always wore things to try to minimize that. She wasn't shy and self-conscious in our relationship. We had a normal life that way, but as a person she was understated, shy and innocent. She was very bright, able and opinionated, she had thoughts about things. OK, she wasn't going to discuss philosophy and Mahler, but she had insight into humanity, she was naturally a bright person.'

However, try as they might, Eilleen and John Kim found it difficult to adapt to each other's lifestyles. Never comfortable in the city, she yearned for the forests and lakes. His idea of a vacation was visiting Italy or a Caribbean island; hers was to go to the bush. 'One time we went up north of Timmins and rented a cabin, no TV, no running water,' says John Kim. 'She took me out into the bush to pick blueberries and I was hoping we weren't going to bump into a bear, as we couldn't outrun it. I had very expensive running shoes on, but the terrain was so tough with the rocks that jut out and point everywhere that my shoes were ruined. So that was our vacation, walking around out in the wilderness picking wild blueberries.' John Kim did get to take her to Acapulco, where she was introduced to a major concert promoter from St Louis. (Years later, Bell was able to tell his friend, 'Do you remember Eilleen? Well, she's Shania Twain.') She turned down a trip to the Big Apple in favour of driving through Vermont to Cape Cod.

In January 1987, Selina Twain sent a box of frozen moose meat to Toronto. John Kim was not a big fan of moose, which is too chewy and rubbery for his palate. Eilleen stared out of the window for an hour. Then she went out into the back yard, where it was twenty below zero, cleared away the snow and built a fire. Despite the freezing cold, she stuck the moose meat on a pointed stick, squatted down on her haunches 'just like an Indian' and stayed there for the next two hours slowly rotating the meat.

One evening, they were dining out with John Kim's brother Kevin, a lawyer who lived upstairs, and his girlfriend. The conversation got increasingly loud and lively, which upset a customer on the next table. The man started mouthing abuse and eventually stomped over to their table. John Kim stood up to remonstrate. He only got as far as saying, 'Excuse . . .' when the man picked up a glass of water and threw it. It missed him but hit Eilleen full in the face. Soaked and furious she was stunned that her boyfriend did not immediately deck her assailant. Back home the bastard would have been spitting out teeth. 'Aren't you going to do anything about that?' she demanded.

Eilleen was no doormat. She had a fiery temper and when things did not live up to her exacting standards she let the world know in no uncertain terms. Her emotional guard was always up, and if she loved John Kim, she could never quite come out and say it. In his turn John Kim talks of their affair with a wistful, regretful air, as if their relationship existed in different dimensions. She owns a little piece in his heart but he wonders, because he does not know, what, if any, place he has in hers.

'She was a sweet, warm-hearted kid,' he says. 'We had moments of tenderness. She had a sincerity about her, she could be scrappy but she had a kind, soft side. There was also a rough edge around her. If she wanted something done a certain way and she didn't get it, she could become angry. I knew that side of her very well. She could be insistent, she could fly off the handle, she wanted what she wanted.'

While it was the National Aboriginal Achievement Foundation that had brought them together, their Native roots were a mutual illusion. Although he was half-Mohawk, John Kim was brought up in a predominantly white middle-class value system. While Eileen, who was at most an eighth Native, and certainly did not look it, had a legal card and personal experience of Ojibway traditions.

While Bell learnt that Jerry was not her real dad, he chose not to question the assumption that her natural father was also Native. 'She wanted me to believe that, as I was a Native person running a Native organization trying to promote young Natives. She was legally Native, culturally she was Native and Native people accepted her. I guess she was sensitive about it, as the racism from the Native community towards whites can be horrible too.

'We talked a lot about what I was trying to do. We exchanged views about what Nativeness was, what it should be, where we were going, and what we should do. We talked about how the culture was pretty dysfunctional and hurt, and it was going to be hard to ever fix it. Her view was different – "I know them, I worked with them," she'd say to me.'

In the beginning, Eileen kept her relationship with Bell secret from her parents. To excuse her frequent presence at Indian Grove she claimed she'd dropped by to use the phone. When the truth leaked out, Sharon and Jerry were not at all happy. Bell in turn was wary of Jerry, who seldom came to the city. In time, he got on pretty well with the family, especially the boys Mark and Darryl (who still keep in touch). Jill's daughter Mandy would come to visit and be treated to the movies and lunches at the Spaghetti Factory.

Sharon was not convinced. She telephoned every day and visited

Toronto regularly to push her daughter along. 'Her mother thought that her living with me meant she was not pursuing her singing career,' admits Bell. 'She thought that, while I was helpful in a sense of refining her, I had no regard for her becoming a pop artist. That was all Sharon ever wanted. She was the driving force.'

Sharon regularly phoned Mary Bailey, giving her updates and detailing her concerns over Eilleen's relationship with Bell. 'To my mind, John believed more in himself than in her,' says Mary, 'and that's what bothered me when she was with him. He was a classical artist and if he had taken her into his environment, then I would have been fine with it. I think his intention was honourable, but it had to be under his conditions. He was the star of the show. And that frustrated me no end.'

Certainly it would have been a big boost for Bell's foundation if he could discover a Native star. However, in 1987, he was the one with the career and the connections, the one who knew Leonard Bernstein and the people who made Broadway hum. OK, so he was playing Pygmalion, but who was getting the benefit? Eilleen Twain. For her part, some of his friends dared suggest that she was using him as a meal ticket and a chance to shin up the ladder. 'That's been the subject of speculation over time,' he concedes, 'She was seeking out people who could make her career and I was there at the right time.'

Bell gave Eilleen opportunities to escape from the country straitjacket she felt her mother and Mary were pushing her into. She wanted to be a mainstream pop singer first, but if that failed, she told John Kim, 'I'll get into country, and once I make it in there, I'll move into pop.' It was a mutually convenient alliance. Bell did several things to push her career along. In a CBC documentary of 1986 he was filmed in his apartment playing the piano while she sang. There were no signs that she lived in the place and it looked as if he was just helping out a struggling young Native performer. Bell was hired to put on a Native talent show for Chief Walter Twinn's – a wealthy Native who later became a senator – fiftieth birthday party in Alberta. They rented an old fort in a suburb of Edmonton – real cowboy country – and Eilleen and John Kim flew out in the chief's private jet, where she did an hour's show wearing a tight leather outfit.

He did give her her biggest break to date when he staged his first big fund-raiser for the National Aboriginal Achievement Foundation at the Roy Thomson Hall in Toronto on 8 February 1987. John hired Bernadette Peters, the movie and Broadway star, to sing with the Toronto Symphony Orchestra. He also put Eilleen and Miq'maq jazz guitarist Don Ross on the bill. Don and Eilleen did a duet, and then Eilleen performed with the Toronto Symphony.

'I had a nice dress made for her,' says Bell. 'We had a big wig made for her, so she had this big hair that went all the way down her back. She looked like Crystal Gayle. She only got a mild response; she sang very well, but she wasn't a performer. She didn't look at or talk to the audience because she was so scared.' The newspaper reviewer for the *Toronto Star* was not so kind. Eilleen was furious, complaining to John Kim, 'God damn it, look what he's saying here, I'll kick his ass!'

In one essential way Mary's concerns about John Kim Bell were spot-on. While he recognized her ability, fundamentally he despised pop music and would have preferred Eilleen to perform torch songs. He dismissed pop as unworthy of her talents and by association his. 'Eilleen wanted to be a pop star and I was a serious musician,' he concedes. 'I have always felt pop stars get disproportionately paid for the talent they have. So while I wanted her to be successful, I didn't admire her goal.'

While John Kim supported her and respected her efforts, he had seen hundreds of hopefuls queuing to be on the chorus lines of Broadway. He knew the odds. In the back of his mind was the ever-present thought: 'Honey, how are you going to become a downtown Whitney Houston?' He did not believe in her chosen career path. One thing Eilleen has always demanded is that people close to her believe in her as much as she does.

By the autumn of 1987, the passion had seeped from their relationship and the differences that had once seemed so endearing were now widening the gap. 'I enjoyed her company, we had some great times, I cared for her, I think she cared for me, but we were heading in two different directions,' he concedes. He felt uncomfortable about the age difference and hovering unspoken was the knowledge that, when she was ready, Eilleen would up and leave. And his ego insisted that he had to be the one to make the break.

Fate dealt a tragic hand first. On the evening of Sunday 1 November 1987 the phone rang. It was the first of the two phone calls that changed the course of Eilleen Twain's life.

CHAPTER EIGHT

A World Turned Upside-down

It was just another normal Sunday evening in Indian Grove. Winter had not yet come to Toronto but the thermometer was dropping fast. Inside it was safe, cosy and comfortable with a big fire that both lit and warmed the spacious first-floor sitting room. It had to be large to take the Steinway grand piano. There was a roll-top desk in the other corner, and a pair of couches flanking the fireplace.

John Kim and Eilleen were having a quiet night in watching television. The routine was always the same, long ago they'd reached a compromise. Both watched *60 Minutes* and then *Murder She Wrote* – Eilleen was a big fan of Angela Lansbury's detective show. She was curled up on a couch, snug in her sweat pants and baggy sweater. At moments like that she could forget the fissures in their relationship, pretend they did not exist for a few hours. When you have had nothing for so long, sometimes it was hard not to luxuriate in comfort like a cat.

The telephone rang. John Kim picked it up.

'You're John Kim Bell?' said a voice he didn't recognize.

'Yes.'

'This is Selina Twain, Eilleen's grandmother,' she continued in the same odd, stilted tones. A pause. 'I'm calling to tell you that Sharon and Jerry have perished in an automobile accident.'

Perhaps it was the formal way she spoke, but the blood drained out of John Kim's cheeks, the shock punching into his heart, sucking the heat out of the room. He stammered out, 'Could you say that for me once again, please? I'm not sure I heard you correctly.'

Over on the couch Eilleen snapped upright, sensing something appalling and called out 'What is it?'

'Sharon and Jerry have just perished in a car accident,' repeated the

voice. All Bell could do was ask, 'Could you give me some more details?'
as if knowing the facts could somehow make them recede back into the
dream time. Eilleen was on her feet, standing by the phone, mouthing
furiously, 'What is it? What's happening?'

So he told her. He stood there with the receiver dangling useless in
his hand, like a gun that had already fired its fatal charge and had no
more use in it, told her both her parents were dead. She picked up the
receiver in a daze, her grandmother talked but all she heard were the
voices in the background. Up in Timmins, Darryl, who had just come
in, was having the news broken to him by his sister. The reaction slowly
sinking in, how her present had been shattered into the past, that in the
future she was alone.

When she put the phone down John Kim tried to comfort her, but
she was beyond comforting. She ran into the bedroom crying hysteri-
cally, 'Oh my God, my God,' screaming from the depths of her soul.
Eventually, she let him hold her as the tears that she never normally
shed came pouring down. All night other calls came in from Timmins.
One by one. All wanting to know what to do, sure that Leeni could
somehow make it right again.

During the calls she was strong, regaining her composure because
somebody had to. But once they ended she crumpled again. Tears and
screams. Kevin's girlfriend, who Eilleen hardly knew, came down to
help. For hours she made endless cups of tea and rubbed the sobbing
girl's back. Rubbing her back because she was beyond words. The night
passed like that, shudders, sobs, then screams as all the absolute
certainties of Eilleen's life were dashed away. Jerry, the only father she
had ever known, the one on whom they all relied. Gone. Her mother,
who believed in her so unconditionally as to inspire belief in others.
Gone. Lost in the pit of her despair, Eilleen Twain made her decision.
There was no hiding from it. Deep inside she found and grasped the
steel core at the centre of her being.

When morning came she took back control. From now on she was
to be the rock on which the family rested. She had just turned
twenty-two.

The snows of 1987 had come early to northern Ontario. It was frustrating for Jerry Twain. The tree-planting business was going well, he had new government contracts in the bag and plans to expand, to move the office out of Montgomery Avenue. Winter made it progressively harder to supply the claim-staking camps.

On that Sunday morning, Jerry had to transport two of his Native workers beyond Wawa, where they would meet a helicopter that would drop them into the bush. As always, Sharon sat in the front of their Chevrolet Suburban, a nine-seater station wagon, to keep him company. Mark, fourteen, scrambled into the back with the two Native workers. Darryl was supposed to go too but he had vanished. With time running out, Jerry asked his mother to make sure the boy was fed.

The last thing Jerry heard was the horn. He was driving along a bush road when they collided head-on with a logging truck. The Chevy was demolished. Jerry and Sharon were killed instantly. The two Natives were knocked out and Mark was thrown clear out of the back window, landing unconscious in a snow drift. He would have frozen to death if one of the workers had not regained consciousness in the ambulance and asked, 'Hey, where's Mark?'

'What do you mean Mark?' replied the paramedic before explaining the Twains were dead. The ambulance turned back to the scene of the accident, and after a frantic search in the gathering dusk they found the boy. Mark survived but he was traumatized by the accident. The 'lanky, friendly, innocent boy' who John Kim Bell knew died in the crash.

But for a recent change in the law which restricted Sunday trucking on the highways of Ontario the truck would never have been barrelling along a narrow, untarmacked back road. 'It shouldn't have happened' is what Shania has said in interviews. But it did and nothing was ever the same again.

The family went into a fugue state. 'I called her,' said Carrie Ann, who was about to turn twenty and was working in McDonald's. 'I just remember pretty much saying what happened and hanging up the phone, and the next thing, it seemed that she was sort of there.'

Down in Toronto Eilleen knew she had to get back to Timmins. She had stepped out of herself and had to regain control. 'I was in shock,' she said. 'The whole night I just cried, I was out of control, I was numb. I managed to get to my home town for the funeral and once I was with my family, it made it a lot easier. But we were all lost. It was a terrible time.'

Getting home was not easy. John Kim Bell had just bought a new Oldsmobile. The transmission went and he had to get it towed to a garage and hire another car. On the eight-hour trip north Eilleen said little and wept more, but inside where the numbness lay she began to wrest power over her emotions, preparing to bury them deep. The family needed her. Carrie Ann was the happy one, the one who never thought anything bad could happen. Jill had been gone ten years already, she had Mandy, a marriage on the cards and she wore her emotions like a push-up bra. Mark was in hospital. He was going to be OK but God knows what the shock would do and Darryl, poor confused Darryl, just thirteen, who had gone missing just before the family took off and had been fielded by his aunt Karen. He'd been damaged enough before he joined the family. Eilleen had been the leader, the one who held it together when Sharon had been too depressed to get out of bed. She knew she could do it again but to do it she had to face sacrificing her dead mother's most cherished ambition, the one thing she had spent her whole life building. Her career.

By the time she reached Timmins, Eilleen had made the decision. It was, she recalls, surprisingly easy. 'After the accident happened I had to consider quitting altogether. I was young, focused on the fact that I was going to be a singer, I was going to keep going until I had enough success so that I never had to worry about where my grocery money was coming from. When something like that happens to you, you don't have time to stop and think about it. It was so drastic that at the time I didn't care if I never sang again.'

Once back home, Eilleen took charge. She organized the funeral within a few days, told everybody, 'OK, this is what we're going to do.' She called Mary Bailey for the first time in two years. 'Hello, it's Eilleen,' she said, 'my mom and dad are dead.' Mary went to Timmins for the funeral, did all she could to help, but what could she do? What could anyone do?

Jerry and Sharon were buried in Timmins cemetery, their tombstone nothing fancy, reading simply 'Together Forever', one of many similar small memorials that line the graveyard. In Timmins it was a three-day tragedy, for the Twains were not that well known. Helene Bolduc read about it in the *Daily Press* and thought, 'Isn't it awful . . . the whole family, poor kids being orphaned.' Dave Hartt did not attend the funeral, for he had just started a new job in the hospital and his boss refused to give him time off.

When the mourners had left, John Kim asked Eilleen what her plans were. 'I'm going to stay and run my dad's company.' She moved her stuff back home and within a few weeks of the funeral Bell ended their relationship. It had been on the wane for months but the accident accelerated its demise. He tried to be calm and sensitive, telling her things weren't what they were, that maybe it was time for a change but there can never be a right way of dumping your girlfriend after she has just been orphaned. There were no tears, just a cold anger in the way she took the news.

'Maybe she did feel that I was forsaking her when she didn't have any parents,' he admits. 'When I was breaking up she had an edge about it, an anger . . . I have always felt she never really forgave me for it.'

Eilleen set about sorting out her parents' estate. Jerry had left much of his equipment in the bush ready for the next planting season. She kept Karen on to fulfil all the winter mining contracts. Kenny Derasp quit his road band and hurried to Timmins; arriving a week after the funeral he helped run supplies out to the camps, for Gerry and Tim could not drive and were in shock. 'I thought about keeping the business going,' says Karen, 'but I am only one person. I needed someone to go out in the bush and I couldn't handle it all by myself.' The new tree-planting contracts were voided by Jerry's death and passed on to the next company in line. When she realized there was nothing left to keep going, Eilleen sold the business and all the equipment.

There was no will, so the family had to sort out the estate, which took time. Don Fraser and Jill went to Zudels and asked if the Twains owed any money there. The staff were already devastated by the news and Paul Zudel told them everything was all paid up and then added, 'That is one couple I'd have lent C$50,000 to any time.'

The process took its emotional toll on Eilleen. 'For a time I wasn't even there any more,' she said. 'Then slowly I found myself again. The fighter that I am, I was able to come to terms with what had happened, it was a saving grace which distracted me from grieving or feeling sorry for myself or being angry. I am good at moving on and forward and really meaning it, not burying it. I indulged myself in responsibility as opposed to grief. I was miserable but there was nothing I could do about it, so I didn't allow myself to grieve for almost a year. Before that, I went through some hard times.'

For eight months after the accident she was the leaning post just as Jerry had been, coping with all the responsibility, believing, pretend-ing she could handle everything the world threw at her. For solace Eilleen drove out into the bush and trekked through the trees, remembering her parents breathing in the stillness, hoping it might heal her. Sometimes she sang to herself. One plaintive melody came back time and time again. 'I would go for long walks in the bush by myself with this song swimming around in my head,' she said. 'It was different. There was no chorus, no verse, just a thought.' She sang it unaccompanied, a requiem for her parents. It was called 'God Bless the Child'.

One morning she woke up and the certainty had gone. With nobody else to turn to, she called Mary Bailey again. 'She said she didn't know what she was going to do,' says Mary. 'I told her, "I know damn well what you're going to do, you're going to do what God gave you, and that's sing."'

CHAPTER NINE

Viva Las Vegas (Muskoka style)

'I can't do it,' replied Eilleen, a break in her voice, 'I've got responsibilities. I can't just go around getting gigs here or there or writing when I feel like it.'

Mary promised to help her find work. She was doing some business at Deerhurst, a resort hotel in Huntsville, 220 kilometres north of Toronto, and suggested Eilleen come along for the ride. When they got there, she convinced the musical director Brian Ayres to give her protégée an audition. Auditions for the revue were usually held at night. Hilda Montgomery, half of Cherokee Rose, who were performing in the Green Room, had just taken her eleven o'clock break when she heard this voice emanating from the ballroom. 'I just snuck in. I remember seeing this small person with a huge, beautiful voice singing a country song. She looked just really normal, relaxed, but I could tell she knew what she was doing. We would get so many singers who would come in and not be very good. Brian snapped her up and she started working almost immediately.'

Fortunately, one of the two featured singers had just quit, so Eilleen was able to negotiate a contract that gave her enough to live on and support her family. She drove the 400 kilometres north to Timmins, sold the house in Montgomery Avenue and moved everybody down to Huntsville in June 1988. The family stayed in a condo on the property – Bill Waterhouse hated to see his entertainers homeless – until she found a small, run-down bungalow to rent out on Porcupine, 24 kilometres from Huntsville, and bought a battered truck. Carrie Ann went to work at the Shoppers Drug Mart in town.

Their family life returned to a semblance of normality. They were not so happy, when the well ran dry. 'She would bring these big jugs of drinking water from Deerhurst,' said Carrie Ann. 'We would all jump in her [truck] and go down to the river to bathe. We hated it.' At the river they filled five-gallon jugs to get enough water to flush the toilets, and do the washing-up; laundry was sometimes down in the river.

Eilleen found a new boyfriend. Mike Taylor was a 25-year-old accountant living in Mississauga, a suburb of Toronto. As he preferred the outside to the office, he had a cottage up in Burk's Falls. In late June he was out on Horn Lake when he was introduced to Eilleen by a friend who worked at Deerhurst. Instantly smitten, he went to see her perform in the revue and then left a note on the windshield of her Jimmy pick-up truck. They went out together for the next eight months, though their relationship was always overshadowed by the needs of the family.

Eilleen tried to be both mother and father – she insisted on screening Carrie Ann's boyfriends – but she wasn't Jerry. 'She was really strict with us,' says Mark Twain. 'She was scared.'

'Eilleen was forced to be a mother,' says Mike. 'Carrie Ann was very easy-going, never been a problem, the most level-headed of the entire family. It was difficult with the boys. She has a low tolerance level but under the circumstances she did an excellent job just being prepared to shack up with them all. I remember getting up in the morning and saying, "What are we going to do today Eilleen?" We'd look across the hall and there would be mountains of laundry and she would say, "You know what I'm doing." They were your typical teenagers. She did everything for them, cleaned the house, they didn't do any of their chores and she did all of them, at twenty-two years old. She could have a lot of fun and kick back too but she didn't have a lot of patience for the teenage way of life.'

After the first shock of their parents death and the move to Huntsville had worn off, Mark and Darryl started to spiral out of control. Eilleen realized that she could not do everything. Working nights six days a week was hard enough, but once she factored in rehearsals for a new show and demo time for her songs, there were scarcely enough hours left to run the household, let alone to give the boys any time.

'They were devastated,' she candidly admitted. 'I had so much sympathy for them I grieved more for them than I did for myself. We didn't fight, it was very emotional, a tough, tragic time for all of us. Picking up the clothes in their rooms was the least of my worries. I was more worried about other things . . . drugs, alcohol, AIDS, pregnancy. I know I didn't do a great job but I put every effort I had into it. If my parents had been alive and the boys had got into trouble, my parents would have been there to help. Big sister doesn't have the same impact. It's not the same.'

Darryl had always had problems at school, now magnified by the sudden death of his adoptive parents. Eilleen was in a dilemma, for Carrie Ann could not be expected to baby-sit two teenage boys six nights a week. She decided to send Darryl to the Robert Land Academy in Wellandport (half an hour from Niagara Falls) at the beginning of the school year, while Mark went to Huntsville High. 'It was a surprising move,' says Mike, 'It was all Eilleen's idea and it did make great sense. Eilleen knew she couldn't be a proper mother for a potentially delinquent kid. The idea is you put these troubled kids into a very strict environment where they are forced to come around and march to the beat of a different drum.'

In Canada boarding schools do not have the same social cachet as in England. Founded in 1978, the Robert Land Academy is a small (less than 150 pupils) single-sex boarding school run on military lines. For many parents it is the institution of last resort. The school claims to have 'a record of making bad boys good. Virtually every cadet at Robert Land Academy has been in trouble with school authorities or the law; has a drug or alcohol problem; or is uncontrollable at home.' The school wasn't cheap (fees are currently C$27,000 a year) and at Deerhurst people wondered how Eilleen could afford the fees on her salary. Mike insists Eilleen used money left from her parents' estate and the insurance settlement from the logging truck company in the hope it was going to turn Darryl around.

Celia Finley, who worked in the wardrobe department, believes some of the fees were paid by the government. 'Eilleen mentioned to me once that she tried to send them to military school and got Indian Affairs to pay for their tuition. She was an orphan with Native status who accessed all the resources she could from all levels of government. Through her relationship with Indian and Northern Affairs, she knew that there were within any large organization policies and procedures and funds available. She was a girl who always had a plan.

'She certainly gave me to understand that she was Native-born, she never mentioned anything about being adopted. I don't think she was consciously trying to hide anything. It was hard to hide anything with those two little buggers getting in her way. They were never anything but trouble.'

To begin with, military school worked. 'Darryl showed up after two weeks with his uniform on and his buzz cut,' says Mike. 'He was incredibly proud of what he was doing, he was getting good marks at the school. Mark thought, "That looks cool, I want to try it," and decided he wanted to go too. It was his own decision.'

Mark joined Robert Land the following September. His commitment level did not last much longer than his brother's, who had only survived six months. Darryl quickly fell foul of the school's harsh regime, refused to settle and ran away. Mike remembers 'picking him up several times in the middle of the night when he had run away from school'. (He was fortunate. In 1998, two boys running away from the academy were killed by a train.) Early in 1989, Eilleen gave up the unequal struggle and Darryl went to live with Jill in New Liskeard. Mark's school career followed suit. The boys' behaviour got no better.

'I got into trouble joy-riding in cars and ended up in a group home for troubled teenagers,' Darryl told the *National Enquirer*.

'The two boys were trouble-makers and Eilleen had to deal with that,' says Dean Malton. They were actually sweet kids, they just turned out a little bad because they lacked attention, and they had to deal with their parents' death. They'd get away with anything they possibly could behind her back, but in her presence they seemed to have pretty good respect for her, though I remember a few instances where she would tell them get ready for bed, and they wouldn't do it.'

Late in 1988, using the rest of her parents' legacy, Eilleen bought a three-bedroomed house in Melissa, a small hamlet eight kilometres out of Huntsville. It cost C$80,000 but she had to spend C$12,000 digging a new well and when she sold it four years later the property market had declined and she just about broke even. She looked long and hard at another house way out in the bush, complete with barn and horse, but there were just too many potential problems. The house had a small apartment in the basement she could rent out for added income. Eilleen was happiest out in the bush. Mike gave her a trailer hitch for her birthday so she could tow a boat with her truck and occasionally she used the Jimmy as a deadly weapon: 'She would run down a partridge, throw it in the back and take it home and cook it up for supper.'

Her life was full of odd contrasts, one night all glitz and feathers the next tramping through the snow in the dead of winter, gathering sticks and making a fire, while Sadie, the family German Shepherd, dashed about. Eilleen loved Sadie – she'd leave the back door of the house open and the dog would come and go as she pleased. She had another dog, Roman, but he was killed by a neighbour's car. It must have seemed that trucks and winter took everything she loved but by the time Mike came up at the weekend the dog was buried. She might have hurt inside but she never showed a flicker of emotion, just got on with life.

There was a lighter side to Eilleen. Christmas '88 was a hoot with all the family and Mike having a wild time out at the Melissa house. Sometimes on Saturday nights when the show was finished, she'd leap into her truck and head for Toronto. 'She loved the idea of dressing up, of going out for dinner. I took her to a couple of Christmas parties, which she loved. We went to Vegas together, where she loved going to the shows. There was a little theatre we went to where they have this thing when they shine the light on people and make them sing along to a song. They hit on her and she got up there and amazed the audience.

'One time she had a party at her house. There she was running around singing all over the place, having a big party dancing and carrying on. She'd had a couple of drinks – though she never was a big drinker or into drugs or smoking, I don't ever remember her drunk – and then I saw the reality hit home . . . that she had these kids and the laundry to do the next day.'

Mike and Eilleen split early in 1989. 'We were certainly in love for a while,' he says, before admitting, 'There were times when things were fine, but she was tough. No question there. In the end we were going in different directions. She wasn't ready to settle, she had her career going and she had to deal with the death of her parents. Eilleen basically tied herself up, forced herself to get on with life and never had a chance to grieve properly. There wasn't a lot of sitting around the house crying. The reality is that teenagers at that age aren't thinking about their parents much anyway. Certainly they were upset, but it was not something that was talked about a lot. It wasn't something that was taboo, but they knew they had to get on with life.'

In the Shania Twain legend Deerhurst and its musical revue has been portrayed as a glittering Canadian clone of a Las Vegas resort hotel. Today that may be the case, but in 1988 Deerhurst was a very different animal, caught in the throes of change but still at its heart hokey, charming and laid-back – occasionally to the point of insensibility.

Back in 1884, Charles Waterhouse, the son of a Yorkshire lawyer, answered a newspaper advertisement that promised opportunities farming in northern Ontario. It was a classic con. Young English gentlemen, scions of wealthy families who had more than their share of landowners, soldiers and clergymen, were sent out to the dominions to create a new squirearchy. Except in Muskoka there were trees as far as you could train a telescope, lakes everywhere else, voracious bugs and the land was mainly rock on which no crop could grow. It was, however, stunningly beautiful.

As far back as the 1870s people, mainly Americans, had been coming up to the Lake of Bays by train and steamer boat to idle away their summers, hunting, fishing or swimming. Charles Waterhouse bought four acres on Peninsula Lake for $100 and, in 1896, built the Lodge, a wooden summer house of eighteen bedrooms, a dining room, a smoking lounge and a veranda stretching its entire length. The investment was funded from the £5,000 his fiancée Hilda brought out from England, hidden in her corsets.

The hotel was a tremendous success; extra wooden bungalows were added and it was fully booked every summer, even through the depression years (helped by the tourist phenomenon created by the birth of the Dionne quintuplets up near North Bay). Charles was a genial host, behaving with perfect courtesy as if he were the lord of some grand English manor. Every winter, the Waterhouses headed back home, returning in early summer with their English cook, nanny and servants. Their sons Gilbert and Maurice went to public school back home.

In 1925, Maurice took over (his brother had been killed in the Great War) and the business continued to tick over for the next four decades. Yet so much of it was keeping up appearances. Most years, they had to pawn the family silver to get enough cash to stock up with supplies for the summer. By 1972, Maurice's son Bill, the first to have been educated in Canada, might have been the heir to a delightful, if rather run-down hotel, but in the words of a local resident he 'didn't have a pot to piss in'. Until 1972 there were only two phones at the resort and all the cooking was done on a huge wood-burning stove, dubbed the 'Queen Mary' by the staff.

Bill was pretty canny. Prior to taking over Deerhurst Resort from his father, he had helped develop the Hidden Valley Ski Club. Recognizing that, in order to survive, Deerhurst had to become a year-round resort, Bill and his parents completely refurbished and winterized the Lodge. One of his dreams was to have proper entertainment and, in 1980, he set about redesigning the Lodge, adding a wing with a ballroom and connecting to the Four Winds Cottage, which was converted into a discotheque. Wintering down in Florida with his parents, he convinced Brian Ayres, a Canadian who was working on a hotel show, to come north and run a musical variety entertainment show in the summer. It went over so well that he asked Brian to stay on and keep the show going all year round. Originally the manager of a rock band and a bass player who didn't know anything about theatre, Ayres became Director of Entertainment at Deerhurst.

The Lodge was the musical hub. Ayres worked his musicians hard, making them jump from room to room until last call. The ballroom became the permanent home for the revue, *Viva Vegas*. The Cypress Lounge – also known as the Green Room – had nightly entertainers performing four sets a night ranging from the pop R&B of Cherokee Rose to the country of Silver and Degazio. On weekends, the Four Winds featured a nine-piece rock band belting out the standards of the day.

The *Viva Vegas* show was a wonderful illusion. The McIntyre Theatre at Timmins High had infinitely better facilities. The ballroom was no theatre, its acoustics were limited and the guests sat on long metal and pine trestle tables, craning their heads to see the action. The stage – once it had seven musicians and a half a dozen dancers on it – was cramped. The girls' dressing room was so crowded that some performers preferred to change in the ladies bathroom; the boys had a curtained-off alcove at stage left. Everything about it – the music, the costumes, the dance routines – should have been much too tacky for the clientele.

It never was. The show transcended the penny-pinching production values with its exuberance. The musicians and singers were top-notch, the dancers gorgeous and together. In the darkness nobody seemed to notice the carpet or the high-school-gym layout. The show was as intimate as the resort. People loved it.

So did the performers, although the pay was not that great. Featured singers pulled in C$600–800 a week, while dancers were lucky if they made C$500. In 1985, the cast of the first *Vegas* review had walked out en masse after a pay dispute. Mike Taylor remembers Eileen earning about C$45,000 a year (C$850 a week). The whole show was done on the cheap. Celia Finley, a local housewife with limited theatre experience and an ability to sew, was hired to design and make the costumes.

'Brian had all these ideas from the Vegas shows he'd seen and he wanted them translated into reality, but I never had a budget,' laughs Celia. 'We were talking shoestring here. Because he didn't come from a theatre background, he didn't at first understand the need for a wardrobe mistress, costume storage, weekly cleaning. He'd bring back all these brochures from Vegas with all these ridiculous things on. I'd been to Vegas, I knew what these girls did: they came on, they strutted, they walked off; they didn't dance in the goddamned things. I had to guess about the costumes. He never told me they would be doing the splits or turn upside-down . . . and so the first night their tits would fall out.'

The 1980s were great times for the staff at Deerhurst. Unlike most hotels there were no rules about hanging out with the guests. 'Here was this group of kids – mainly college and high-school drop-outs – who'd found a reason to stay up here most of the year so they could ski, snowmobile and booze cruise all year along,' says Celia. 'It went from endless summer to endless night. It was pretty lively. At the Four Winds the band would play rock and roll until one in the morning and everybody would sit around and drink as much as they could until last call, when they ordered three drinks at once and sat there for another hour. After the bar closed they moved off to the *maître d*'s house in Hidden Valley until dawn. It was all pretty innocent until the cocaine era in the late 1980s, when a few people ran out of control.'

For young performers the *Vegas* revue offered the opportunity to stretch their talents and to try out new ideas. 'If you had a good idea, Brian would use it,' recalls Hilda Montgomery. 'I grew up in the Bahamas idolizing Diana Ross and Brian said, "OK, we will do a Diana Ross section," and it was wonderful. He worked with people and their talent and tried to bring the best out of them.' The show lasted two hours, including a thirty-minute break, running Monday to Saturday, when there were two shows (except in weeks including holiday week-ends, when it ran seven nights straight). Showtime was 8 p.m., but the dressing room would be crowded from 6.30.

From the day she arrived at Deerhurst, Eilleen understood that this was her finishing school, a place she could fill in the gaps of her stage education. She knew she could sing but, despite Longshot, performance still unnerved her. Those years of singing in smoky bars to drunks had left her nervous of moving anywhere except behind the mike stand. Here she had to dance alongside girls who had been at dance class since they could put both legs into a leotard without falling over. She had to confront her long-standing shyness about her body and bared her navel for the first time – playing the Indian in the revue's Village People tribute.

'Her singing was so natural and free she was almost cavalier about it, it was a treat to sing with her,' says Gilles Lanthier, who played keyboards, rhythm guitar and sang. 'The other aspects – the blocking, how many steps do you take, which foot do you start on and partner work – she had to work harder on. When she first came here she was almost awkward – which is a kind word.'

When she sang 'Over the Rainbow', wearing a green dress so tight she could barely get in and out of it, it blew the audience away. 'She sang the balls off that song,' says John Kim Bell. 'It is such a tremendous torch song, it really showed her talent, and you'd think, what's a kid like this doing here in this tacky little resort?' She and Gilles, who in those days looked uncannily like Lionel Richie, slipped into red satin catsuits for a blistering Motown medley – including Marvin Gaye's and Tammi Terrell's 'Ain't Nothin' Like the Real Thing' and 'It Takes Two'.

Although she could not dance as well as Lynn Hill, Karen Carrette or Sherrie Higgins, Eilleen was determined to show off her best assets. Her hair had to be the way she wanted it and her clothes figure-hugging. 'She was very particular to show off her great little figure,' says Celia Finley. 'She needed to offset the fact that she was short and it was easy to get lost in that sea of tall dancers. She had to stand out and insisted that everything had to be skin-tight and showed lots of décolletage. I remember making the alterations so they would be tight, tight, tight. You could never tell her that too tight was as bad as too loose.'

On Friday and Saturday nights after the revue finished, she would join the rock band crowded on to the stage of the Four Winds. One of her stand-out numbers was Def Leppard's 'Pour Some Sugar on Me'. 'She was a rock and roller when she was here,' says Gilles. 'We were a hot band and she sang stuff like Heart's 'Barracuda', which is testing your vocal prowess.'

By 1988, Deerhurst had grown from a small family operation to a huge employer running an enormous property – initially without a personnel officer. 'It was a human resources nightmare,' says Celia, who found a wardrobe mistress who was a hippy relic from the Pacific Northwest of the US who had somehow scammed herself full Canadian social security benefits. She often refused to help the girls fix their costumes unless they bought her a drink. One of the most powerful men in the resort was Michael Walker. Nominally the *maître d'* he became Bill Waterhouse's *de facto* second in command. He hand-picked the staff that worked in the resort. Naturally they were very loyal to Michael.

'He was like a living god or something,' says Celia, who does not mince her words. 'The first time I had lunch with the cast I poked fun at him. One of them whispered to me, "You mustn't ever criticize Michael." He was a head waiter for Christ's sakes. Once new partners had bought in and wanted the hotel to be run differently, the party era was over.'

Such chaos was not for Eilleen Twain. Solitary by nature, now further confined by responsibility, she was not a party animal. Drugs did not interest her and she drank only to appear social. While to many Deerhurst was their life, a comfortable place to stay or to land up at the end of a career, to her it was just a staging post. For the first time in her life there was nobody there to back her up. She saw all this potential around her just being wasted. So she went for it . . . and upset a lot of people in the process.

'Dressing rooms,' says Celia Finley, 'are inherently stressful places to be. Being cooped up in a small room with seven bitchy women, all of whom had egos the size of houses but barely a brain to click together between them . . . well that was stressful.'

The cosy bitchery of the dressing room was not for Eilleen. She played golf with Gilles and the girls a few times, as she was enthusiastic about learning it (the golf course, as men know, is an excellent place to do business). Deerhurst was only ever going to be a pit-stop for Eilleen, a place to regroup until the boys were old enough to legally offend for themselves. Friendly and non-judgemental Lynn Hill and Karen Carrette became friends, but they had little in common. Eilleen's home situation and her ambitions made it hard to sit around with the other girls watching videos and gossiping. Particularly as, if she wasn't there, she was inevitably the subject of the gossip.

Eilleen made one early mistake that coloured much of her two-year stay in Deerhurst. She had a fling with drummer Pierre le Gendre. Unfortunately, Pierre was also involved with Sherrie Higgins, one of the dancers. Higgins claims she came home early after a two-week vacation to surprise her boyfriend.

'When I opened the door,' she told the *National Enquirer*, 'my boy-friend and Shania were naked on the couch making love. And the horrible situation was made much worse because my mom was with me. Shania jumped up and grabbed a wrap – she was just crimson with embarrassment. I couldn't believe it. Here was the man I loved, naked with Eilleen. The house was in an uproar. I was crying my eyes out and my mom was screaming at my boyfriend and punching him. I called off our relationship right then and there.'

When the allegations surfaced Shania's only official retort was, 'It has nothing to do with reality as I know it.' Whatever the exact truth – the love lives of the Deerhurst entertainers could be as tangled as any episode of *Melrose Place* – Eilleen and Pierre soon split up. Because she had crossed some of the unwritten rules of the resort, wittingly or not, Eilleen found herself ostracized.

In March 1989, Dean Malton arrived at Deerhurst to work as a sound technician. Although Dean was the son of comedian Wayne Malton, who headlined the show with his partner Mike Hamilton, he knew nothing about the internal politics. He came with no baggage. One night at 11.30, a week before he was to start work, there was a knock at his door. Eilleen was standing there with a bag of popcorn and a couple of movies she had rented. 'Hey, how are you doing?' she asked. Dean, thinking, 'God I have this gorgeous woman standing at my door,' invited her in.

They never got round to watching the movies, they just talked about music until dawn. Dean loved the Pretenders' *Get Closer* album, Eilleen hated Chrissie Hinde, complaining, 'How can you listen to her, she can't sing?' She admired Mariah Carey, indeed anyone with a good voice, as if she already knew they were her competition for the future. It was the beginning of a close friendship. For the next eighteen months, whenever she wrote a new song, she'd call Dean, he'd demand to hear it and record it.

'Shortly after Eilleen and I started hanging out, one of the dancers came up to me and warned me, "Dean, don't get involved with her, don't; you're going to get hurt." That obviously had something to do with that whole fling that had happened with Pierre, but I didn't know that at the time.

'She was a very great girl, really, she's just very driven,' says Dean, who was never one of the party crowd at Deerhurst. 'At the time a lot of people had something against her, probably because she had tunnel vision, she knew where she wanted to go, she knew that Deerhurst was not where she wanted to be in ten years, and that was taken as arrogance and ruthlessness.

'She wasn't into dolling herself up. She'd walk through the mall with her shoes untied. All the other girls would be coming into work with their make-up on, looking beautiful before they even got there. Eilleen would pull up with a bag over her shoulder, and walk in with her hair up, no make-up, nothing, she didn't really care what anybody else thought.

'She was fun, very family-oriented, she loved her animals. A perfect evening for Eilleen was to get home from work put on her track pants, a big bulky sweater and stand around the bonfire in the backyard with an acoustic guitar, singing songs or talking or whatever. She was very much a country girl, but when it comes to her music, and her lifestyle in general, she's certainly not this flower for everybody to just pick . . . she's not a prima donna in any way, but she's very driven and very focused, and what comes into her mind is what she says.

'I always felt that she was unhappy, somewhat jaded, by the fact that she was forced to come home and take care of her siblings. But she was never one to complain about anything, always kept it inside. If something was bothering her, she might say one sentence and then stop, or change the subject.

'When we sat around and talked, dreaming about being successful in the business, she'd get lost in another world thinking about it, yet her reality was stagnant. The fact that she was recording her songs was probably the only thing that kept her sane. The sadness I got from her came from a lot of different things; all she really wanted to do was to be liked by everybody and yet she wasn't, probably because her looks and her talent led a lot of people being envious of her. And so she would spout off, but only in defence. Her parents dying made her that much more driven. All she ever wanted was to make it, to show her parents: "Look, I did good". So I don't think she felt she had to answer to anybody.

'I know I got wrapped up with her for a little bit,' continues Dean, 'how could I not be attracted to her? But it was that much more fired-up because we were being creative together. We were hanging out a good three months, nothing going on between us, and all of a sudden Paul was there. I never knew about Paul until he moved to town. Paul and Eilleen lived out at the house, and my girlfriend Julie Frick and I, we used to spend quite a bit of time up there, sit around the campfires listening to rock and roll.'

Eilleen had turned to a handsome construction worker from her home town. Paul Bolduc, a tall, dark French Canadian four years her junior, first met her in the bar of the Mattagami Hotel – the same bar where she used to perform when she was just eight – in February 1988, when she was at home sorting out her parents' estate. After splitting from John Kim she needed a friend, and he offered to help in any way he could. He was struck enough to take her home to meet his mother, Helene, and as far as Helene was concerned that was it. A while later, Paul headed down to Huntsville to find work – including a stint as a bellhop at Deerhurst.

Eilleen's relationship with Paul worked very well. Sometimes in private she would refer to him as her 'toy boy', but he was stable and loyal, a down-to-earth, beer-drinking, hard-working guy, intelligent but taciturn – just like Jerry had been. 'Truly, I think she loved Paul,' says Dean. 'They made a great couple. He didn't talk a lot. She was in charge of the relationship and Paul was somewhat of a yes-man to her. He was not into confrontation, so if she was having one of her moods, Paul was not the one to start a fight, he'd just go along with whatever she was saying. She was moody, I can't lie about that. When she was off, she was off. If she was in a sniff, look out. But what woman doesn't? She was like every other woman I've ever known – they have days when they're kind of pissy and some days when they're not.'

The other appeal Paul had was his family, which allowed Eilleen to be part of a secure, loving environment. Christmas and holidays reminded her of the old days. The Bolducs were a link to Timmins, to her roots. Eilleen struck up an instant and enduring friendship with Helene Bolduc, a clerical worker at Timmins Hospital. 'We just seemed to have a lot to talk about,' says Helene, 'and we could go on in conversation for, you know, hours and hours. We would go for long walks. We always had good parties during the holidays – I have a sister that plays piano and guitar, and we just like to have a good time, a French Canadian good time. And my husband would make jokes, and he would say to Eilleen, "One day when you become that superstar, I'll go drive your bus." '

In the tight-knit community of Deerhurst it was easy to upset people. The senior member of the *Viva Vegas* cast was Sammy Kelso, whose wife Mia worked the door of the ballroom. One night after she had been told not to let anybody else in to see the show, Paul Bolduc rushed in at the last moment, and Mia told him he could not come in. Paul just snapped, 'Don't be ridiculous,' and walked past her. Mia got upset, Sammy yelled at Paul which led to Eilleen losing her temper, and a major scene. Kelso never forgave her and has not had anything nice to say about her days at Deerhurst ever since.

For once, Eilleen's timing was spot-on. She had arrived on the cusp of a major change at Deerhurst. The storm clouds were gathering and she was able to take full advantage. In 1988, Bill Waterhouse finally sold out to Apotex, a major pharmaceutical company run by Dr Barry Sherman, who invested $100 million in the resort, expanding it to 800 acres with two golf courses. In a radical departure from the rustic wooden charm they also embarked on an ambitious condo-building programme, all marble and mod cons. They built a new pavilion which would house a bigger, more lavish entertainment. Apotex installed John Kotowski as the new general manager at Deerhurst. Born in Poland, Kotowski was an accountant in his mid-fifties who had been responsible for brokering the deal with Waterhouse. He was responsible for overseeing all the new building and development.

'Kotowski loved the entertainers,' says Gilles Lanthier. 'The two years he was there were the only times we got Christmas bonuses and we were the only ones who got them in the resort.' He especially adored pretty girl-singers who flattered and flirted with him. Kotowski was no oil painting, sitting there at his table in the ballroom, short and squat, a benevolent bullfrog with a coronet of white hair talking with a thick Peter Lorre accent. He had a wide, homely face, blue eyes that existed only to twinkle and a perennial beguiling smile. He was an old-fashioned charmer, a compulsive flirt, whose appeal was enhanced by the Polish fracture at the edge of his English.

Kotowski had a vision he was determined to carry through. There was talent at Deerhurst. Everyone said so. There were quality musicians on site, choreographers and different stages on which to perform. What better place to groom stars? What better atmosphere to wine and dine record companies? Using an American sports analogy, it could become a farm club, spotting potential stars; developing, managing and record-ing talent for the major leagues.

The man Kotowski brought in to get his fledglings out of the Huntsville snow was producer Harry Hinde. Hinde, who started his career in Detroit as Motown's only white record plugger, had enjoyed a reasonable level of success producing country artists like Ronnie Milsap. He had also found a girl called Phyllis Boats, changed her name to Charity Brown and made a successful album for A&M. There is something faintly tragic about Harry. Like the hero of the Woody Allen movie *Broadway Danny Rose*, he can spot the talent but is never able to capitalize before it turns to mist and slips out of his hands.

Silver and Degazio became the first artists on the Deerhurst Entertainment roster. Mike's singing partner Rhonda Silver – though they couldn't stand each other – was the first to spot the potential in Kotowski. She was not the last. Michelle Marie Beer, the other featured singer in *Viva Vegas*, also danced attendance. Kotowski held the purse strings. Rhonda was the first to have John's ear; then it was Eilleen.

Eilleen recognized where the power lay and set about charming Kotowski. With youth, beauty and talent on her side, she soon had his attention. To onlookers the three singers resembled the Witches of Eastwick, except that in this coven each was out for herself. 'They were all trying to get out of Kotowski what they could,' says Dean Malton. 'And the fact that Eilleen got out of him what she could, and they didn't, had plenty to do with the animosity between the three of them.'

'There were three of them,' recalls Mike Degazio. He might have been a beer and spuds local lad but he ran a construction business during the day and he, too, realized there were other advantages to gain from cosying up to nice Mr Kotowski. 'He asked me if I would start contracting, because he felt other companies coming in were gouging him. I remember being in a studio down in Toronto recording with Rhonda and he came in and said he was all excited because he'd just sold five buildings to some Hong Kong money. I was fairly close to him on the business side, so I did end up spending quite a bit of time with him.

'Rhonda, Shania and Michelle, all three of them were always around him . . . he'd buy them dinner, sit and chat, he was always chuckling and laughing, having a good time, there were rumours, of course . . . but I think he was harmless, he felt good about sitting out in public and having a talented, beautiful girl sitting down and having a glass of wine with him.'

After Eilleen won over Kotowski, the rumour factory at Deerhurst went into overdrive. 'She has a full-time condo on the property with a connecting door to his.' 'Her picture is on his bedside table.' 'He paid to have her teeth fixed.' ('My husband paid to have her teeth done – he gave her a Hollywood smile,' Mona Kotowski claimed in the *National Enquirer*.) Charges Shania Twain denies absolutely.

'There are stories of him spending money on her and other women as well,' says Marg Reid, who worked in wardrobe. 'There were all sorts of rumours about her new kitchen and her new well and the brother's school fees.' The rumour that Kotowski had bought Eilleen her truck started because the licence plates on the brand new vans that he bought for the property were only one number different from Eilleen's Jimmy. Such gossip always follows the same formula. Old man with money/ power plus pretty/ambitious young girl times innuendo must equal SEX.

Many who worked in Deerhurst back then say the same thing: 'I heard she was sleeping with him, but . . .' and the 'but' is that they have no evidence, no proof at all. For sure, after the show, she would come and sit at his table, chatting and flirting with him and his guests. So did the other girls, but nobody bitches about an also-ran the same way they do about an international superstar.

Although he has heard the stories, Mike Taylor does not believe them for a minute. He met Kotowski when he picked up Eilleen from his house in Mississauga to take her to buy some clothes for the show. 'She was very open, didn't hide anything from me, and unless I was incredibly blind there was nothing happening that I was aware of,' he says. 'Kotowski had a lot of money and she knew it. She was friendly with him because he did a lot of stuff for her to help get her career going. Nothing more than that. The gossip didn't annoy me, because I understood it . . . everybody loves to talk.'

John Kotowski is not an easy man to find. He spends much of the year absent on business in Poland. He has had his share of harassment from the tabloids and is wary of saying anything about Eilleen Twain. His recall of events is not always accurate. He says he worked with her for four and a half years (when she only spent twenty-seven months at Deerhurst and he has not seen her since he left in March 1990), and that he fixed her an appearance on *The Tommy Hunter Show* (which never happened). He says the answer is straightforward – he paid her more money because she was worth it. He points out that Eilleen was friends with his wife and daughters, so there could be nothing improper in their relationship.

'I didn't have any scandals with her and vice-versa and that is the way it is. Our relationship was strictly business,' he says. 'I singled out Eilleen because of her talent, I did see the future in her. Sure, I paid her more, and that's where the friction primarily was, because she was making more, much more, than anybody else. That's how I took care of things, paid her enough so she could support her two brothers and have a decent life. I took care of her because I saw an asset, I wanted her to be dressed beautifully, look beautiful . . . that is showbusiness. I don't want to give any impression that I was doing something improperly or vice-versa. I invested in talent.'

Kotowski will not discuss the allegation that he paid for her to have her teeth fixed (though a former Deerhurst employee recalls him signing the payment off). 'I was no sugar daddy,' he insists. 'She was an employee of Deerhurst like Rhonda Silver and Mike Degazio. She was not satisfied when Rhonda got recorded first. I was paying her; the dresses I bought her, these things are part of the maintenance in recognition of her potential. I don't think she used me.'

Lots of talented men, not just Mike Degazio and John Kim Bell, hung on Kotowski's words, laughed at his jokes and got work out of him. But that was OK. Guys can do that sort of thing. It was business. Eilleen Twain was doing business, too.

CHAPTER TEN

A Taste of Stardom

As part of its new expansion Apotex decided to build the Pavilion, a huge complex with indoor tennis courts, a health spa and a swimming pool. It also contained a big palladium show room, complete with terraced marble floors, and a pool in front of the stage, which was the size of a downtown theatre. They needed a spectacular show to complement the space. Kotowski was not sure Brian Ayres was capable of putting it together.

Eilleen saw her opportunity and grabbed it with both hands. She told Kotowski: 'I know somebody who will come up here, kick their ass and make things happen.'

John Kim Bell had the perfect credentials to impress Kotowski. He had started working on Broadway at eighteen, had conducted *A Chorus Line* and *On Your Toes*, collaborated with Gene Kelly, Vincent Price, Carol Lawrence, Sonny Bono and the Bee Gees, and knew Leonard Bernstein. He had conducted the New York Philharmonic, the Toronto Symphony; and the Royal Philharmonic in London. Eilleen knew that he had grand plans for staging the National Aboriginal Achievement Awards on TV (which were first broadcast in 1994 and have since become an annual event), for they had talked about his ambitions many times. Above all he was a professional who really understood production values. Eilleen was fed up with cheese-paring.

Eilleen and Kotowski took John Kim out to dinner and gave him the pitch. For him it was a no-brainer. How often do you get a chance to create a show from scratch with no apparent financial restrictions? OK so it went without saying who was going to be the star, but he knew she had the voice and he could fix any problems. It was a no-lose situation for Eilleen. She knew John would take the gig and that he would create a show that would make her shine. It was also a fair payback for the times he had supported her in Toronto. Sure she enjoyed the reversal in the balance of power, but Eilleen has always honoured her debts. 'She was friendly and nice to me,' says Bell. 'Considering the way I broke up with her she could have said "piss off", but she thought of me. It was very clever, because I really did take care to protect her and help her.'

Bell's arrival in the summer of 1989 was akin to a giant meteorite crashing into Peninsula Lake. The fallout created a lot of bad feeling. Brian Ayres left and his assistant Lynn Foster resigned in disgust (though she came back a year later). For all his idiosyncrasies Brian had been a popular guy. Because she had suggested John Kim, Eilleen was held responsible for his departure. 'Of course, there were whispers and rumours,' says Celia Finley. 'To me, Eilleen always acted in a completely professional way. Sure she was looking out for number one, but when you are focused you have to be ruthless. This girl had a career she was serious about, so she wasn't going to drag her feet in the mud. Why wouldn't you take advantage of an opportunity like that, when you can see that all others around you are losing their heads, and if you keep yours it might pay off?

'Did she step over bodies? Absolutely. I was sorry for Brian because he had spent ten years building up an entertainment department . . . but he was a big boy and should have seen it coming. Brian's time was up. It was inevitable.

'Shania understood that the show needed to go to another level and helped convince the management to make her the star. Millions of dollars were being invested. That was a business decision. All these little twits in the dressing room can talk all they want, but the fact is any one of them would quite gladly have changed places with her.'

Rehearsals for A Touch of Broadway started in July 1989, ten months before opening. The new cast members were on full wages but only required to work in the day. As the old revue continued to play in the ballroom, those working in both were in effect pulling double shifts with no overtime. One day in August 1989, Eilleen was rehearsing 'La Vie en Rose' with Gilles Lanthier in a school out in Dwight. 'Our producer wanted her to do it both in French and English, so we had to translate the French lyrics into English and I am fluent in both,' says Gilles. 'It was a beautiful summer day, we were sitting out back on the tennis courts with our guitars and I was in stitches, we came up with so many rhymes for rose – nose, panty hose and every other possible idea – we were just having so much fun. She looked me in the eye that day and she said, "Some day, I'm going to be there." I didn't have any doubt . . . the only things that surprised me were how big and how quickly.'

Viva Vegas employed up to seven musicians, eight dancers and four principal performers, three technical people and a dresser/wardrobe mistress. The new show had a cast and crew of forty including thirteen dancers. One of the new employees was wardrobe assistant Marg Reid, who soon found herself working on the *Vegas* revue. Perhaps because of their shared love of the bush – Marg's husband now runs the largest dog sledding operation in Canada – or because she was a newcomer, she became friendly with Eilleen.

'She kept herself distanced from other people,' says Marg. 'I assumed that it was to do with what had gone on, the feeling people had about Brian leaving, but I think there is more to it than that. She did not make close friends because she's not a person to show her emotions. She was very quiet about things, she had her life and her direction.'

Dancing and moving on stage were always the biggest problems Eilleen had at Deerhurst. Bell solved the problem by bringing in Sammy Vivarito, a former dancer and choreographer, to sort out the dance routines and give Eilleen some 'real skills in moving'. Sammy was only able to come up for a short period and Bell needed someone full-time, because 'the kids had no discipline whatsoever, they weren't doing the same steps together'. In came Aileen Sugano – another friend from Broadway – as the dance captain and resident choreographer. The tiny Japanese woman and Eileen became fast friends and she set about turning the singer into an accomplished dancer.

By the autumn of 1989, Eilleen's schedule was shattering. In addition to giving seven shows a week, rehearsing *A Touch of Broadway* and learning how to move and dance on stage, she was also preparing to demo songs for her first album. Even before he started recording Silver and Degazio, Harry knew that his next project must be Eileen Twain. His wife saw her twice and announced she would be a superstar. He knew it too. 'She had no fear, she had total confidence. She wasn't a great singer, she wasn't Barbara Streisand, Edith Piaf or anything like. But she didn't sound like anybody else, she had her own style. I already saw the big star . . . I was crazy about her, the way she was there on that little stage . . . she was ready.'

There were disagreements on the direction to take. 'Off-stage she was very quiet,' says Harry. 'If she didn't like something, she could give you a look, make a face. If you told her you were going to do something, and you didn't do it then . . . Look out. With me she never screamed and yelled, we disagreed on things, and we would discuss it to the point that sometimes we needed to take a breather, but that didn't last, in two hours everything would be OK again.

'She played me some ideas for songs; she had great ideas, great hooks, or ideas close to being a great hook. I wanted to take her pop-country with a little bit of edge on it, but she wanted to be a rocker. She told me she did country as a kid and at that time she didn't feel like doing it. I wanted to give her the benefit of the doubt and try those things. I was going to suggest bringing in Bob Ezrin but I didn't think Bob would be receptive to the project. I didn't hear it going rock, really hard rock. It didn't feel right.'

Eventually Harry agreed to follow Eileen's wishes and record rock songs. If those did not work out, they would go back and do it his way. He asked Paul Sabu, a talented young guitarist – 'a cross between the guy from Kiss and Clapton, plus he had a little bit of punk' – to come up and write with Eileen. They had first met in 1975 through R. Dean Taylor (who sang the hit *There's a Ghost in My House*) and engineer Don Gootch. His plan was to 'go down this path and change it gradually, and hopefully I would be able to get the type of songs and the direction I wanted'.

'He [Harry] thought he could get a deal with A&M with her,' says Paul Sabu. 'I met her in Toronto and went up with her to the middle of nowhere. It kind of progressed. She was great and A&M really liked her and wanted to do a record. She had a lot of people kind of hanging on her I'm pretty sure she didn't want around. She had some pretty good reasons to really try. I'm just glad she did.'

Sabu and Eilleen hit it off right away. He was all California cool, swanning around in a full-length black leather coat, but he knew his stuff. 'They got along,' says Hinde. 'They laughed a lot, the chemistry did work. They did enjoy each other's company, they definitely found a relationship together . . . but as far as I know, it was a working relationship.' Kotowski mistrusted the flashy Sabu and complained to Harry Hinde that he would stab them in the back. Harry just thought he was jealous.

Sabu, who was paid C$15,000 for his time, remembers Eilleen as being a sweet, ambitious, talented girl desperate to break out of her small-town life and succeed at music. 'It wasn't a Hollywood kind of recording studio,' he said. 'We had a cabin in the middle of nowhere. We were taking these eight-track tapes and carrying them around in the snow. It was way above the call of duty for that kind of stuff, but it was fun. I had never done that kind of stuff before.'

The songwriting partnership worked with ideas batted back and forth. Eilleen might come up with an idea, or a theme, and Paul would shorten the hook and make it grab the listener. When Paul came up with hooks, she'd either tell him, 'I don't like that', or 'Yes, that's cool.' Paul definitely added things, contributed a great deal. Most of the lyrics came from Eilleen, but her major problem was always in putting everything together musically.

Sabu flew up to Canada several times in the winter of 1989. As she was still doing the show at Deerhurst, he was given the use of a wooden cabin on the property (complete with all mod cons). Harry would drive up, drop by and record the demos on a boom box. Some of the vocals were recorded in the sauna up by the Lodge by Dean Malton. If someone was using the lavatory she couldn't record because of the background tinkle. They recorded the masters in Toronto at Gord Hein's appartment and two recording studios, Wellersley Sound and

McClare Place and bounced some of the sixteen-track tapes up to 24- and 32-track.

Throughout the rehearsals for *A Touch of Broadway*, the relations between Eilleen and Michelle Marie were fraught. Recalls Dean Malton, who was doing the lights, 'Michelle was always a little jaded because Eilleen had the torch songs, and she had to do the Ethel Merman numbers . . . and she was equally as good a singer. I remember her coming off and saying to Eilleen, "Top that!" They were very professional. They would come out the door, big smiles on their faces, but as soon as they got off the stage it was pretty ugly. They were so at each other.'

With two months to go, Michelle Marie was succeeded by Joni Wilson, a younger but equally feisty girl. Joni and Eilleen got on a bit better, but not much. John Kim gave Eilleen ballads and Joni the more comedic numbers – wise as Eilleen had no sense of comedy – which infuriated her. 'Joni,' says Bell, 'danced really well. There was this rivalry between them, tension all the time. And while Eilleen was a tough kid, if there was another tough one, it would hurt her feelings and she would shy away a little bit.'

'There were diva conflicts, but none of it ever showed up on stage,' agrees Gilles Lanthier. 'In Eilleen's defence, Joni could be very difficult. It takes two to tango; it is not one person who is responsible for the problems and the conflict.'

There were the odd nights when Eilleen, like any performer, missed shows, which meant the revue had to be rearranged. This led to more dressing-room bitching. Once, when they heard she was sick, one dancer cracked, 'What she got, a hangnail?' Another night Eilleen rushed in with two minutes to go, as she had been in Toronto recording and the traffic had been bad.

Eilleen also clashed with Mike Degazio in the Cyprus Lounge. As Degazio also played a rock and roll set in Steamers restaurant a mile away on the edge of the property, he always left his amplifier pre-set so he could walk in, plug in and play. One night he came in to find Eilleen singing and playing the guitar, using his amp. He complained that she had used it without asking. 'OK,' she said, 'sorry.' Degazio's story is that a few nights later in he came and there she was doing the same thing. So he walked up and unplugged her.

'Maybe that's why when I asked her out to dinner one time she said no,' says Degazio. 'I never really got to know her that well, sometimes people's personalities clash. I have a hard time dealing with women being too dominant and thinking they can just say, "Do this, do that." '

While a few of the girls might have had problems with Eilleen, the musicians and the support staff seldom did. 'I really liked her, she never did anything to me,' says Marg. 'I sat right beside her and I fixed her clothes. Some people can be mean, but I never found her high and mighty, she was always very appreciative of anything I would do.'

With a budget of C$2 million, no expense was spared on *A Touch of Broadway*, quickly christened by Dean 'A Touch of Bankruptcy' – a joke that stuck. The room looked fabulous, windows reaching up towards the sky almost to the ceilings, seating on terraced marble tiers, but it had not been designed as a theatre. The acoustics never matched the ambience. C$50,000 went on the costumes – including C$5,000 on a sequin dress for Eilleen's opening number. She made a show-stopping entrance at the back of the room, singing Bette Midler's 'Wind Beneath My Wings' walking slowly past the tables down the steps on to the stage. There were Stephen Sondheim numbers, Lionel Richie songs and standards like 'Over the Rainbow'. Bell had two comedians write a skit on *Cats*. It was called *Dogs* and Eilleen played the French poodle. She sang 'La Vie en Rose' with a microphone concealed in the rose in her hand.

'This show was very important for Eilleen for two reasons,' says Bell. 'One, it gave her a chance to refine her ability. I saw her go from the country bumpkin, always a great singer, to a kid who could look at you and flirt with you; that was more seductive, more sultry . . . and she learned how to dance. We gave her ambitious choreography, given that she was not a dancer at all. It wasn't just step to step, she was doing stuff all over the stage. We had her doing Gloria Estefan numbers, guys picked her up and carried her across the stage, and then she danced in formation, and she really came out, she grew as a performer. She had to work out. And she did because she was serious about it.'

Nobody who saw *A Touch of Broadway* could doubt it. Eilleen Twain was a star. Except that, just as it seemed she had finally made it, everything fell apart.

While her songs were being demoed Hinde had set about getting the other parts of the business sorted. Eilleen signed a producer's agreement with him on 18 October 1989. Photo sessions were commissioned and shot, including one with her posing in a deerskin bikini. Unlike Raquel Welch in *One Million Years BC*, she looks uncomfortable and forced. She also needed management. Ann Murray's manager, Leonard Rambeaux, was invited to the resort for a weekend with his family and was suitably impressed by her performance. Leonard agreed to manage her – provided she had a record deal.

That proved to be the sticking point. A&M were heavily courted, especially after the Silver and Degazio album did well enough to be nominated for a Juno. In March 1990 at the Juno awards show, Kotowski met Gary Hubbard, the record company's Vice President of Finance, and invited him to have dinner and see the show the next time he was visiting his cottage in Huntsville. When he did, Eilleen sat down at the table and had dessert. 'Harry had told me all about Eilleen Twain. She was a talent even in those days,' he says. While Gary liked what he saw, the record company's A&R men were less impressed (talent scouts hate being pointed in the right direction by bean counters). 'Granted she sang Broadway numbers, but they couldn't see beyond that,' says Hubbard. 'They didn't like the tracks Harry did with her either. A&M don't like to be reminded that Eilleen Twain and Shania Twain are all the same.'

The demos were indeed worlds apart from the sequinned sophistica- tion of Deerhurst. The best song was 'Send It With Love' about the death of her parents, in which the anguish in the vocal is all too apparent. The other songs are in the main raw and raucous, with Eilleen's voice fighting the guitar, not surfing over it. She had grown up on Dolly Parton, Stevie Wonder, Karen Carpenter and Elton John, not on Janis Joplin and Grace Slick . . . and it showed. The sound was also out of date, harking back to the early 1980s. Tastes had changed. Pat Benatar's career was long on the slide, Heart had peaked. Mariah Carey and Whitney Houston were what record companies wanted to hear. Eilleen singing 'Wild and Wicked' was not.

Even though the rejection slips started to pile up, Harry was not too worried. He hoped he could get Kotowski to pay for the demos next time and maybe the girl would listen and they could do some country-pop. Unfortunately, Deerhurst was tumbling into a financial black hole. In the context of a C$100 million development and C$2 million on *A Touch of Broadway*, Kotowski's plans to spend C$50,000 launching the career of a girl singer was no big deal. However the massive cost overruns on the Pavilion – budgeted at C$8 million, it ended up costing three times that – coincided with some serious changes in the economy. Deerhurst was hit by a sharp left and right. Cash flow and recession. By May 1990, when *A Touch of Broadway* premiered, the resort was in considerable financial difficulty.

At the time, building the Pavilion was a black comedy. When the walls were all up it was discovered that a huge crane had been left in the middle of the showroom. For some reason, perhaps because it looked good on paper, it was decided to double up the new showroom by having the pool in front of the stage. John Kim Bell ordered a fly system and moving lights from Italy. That was the easy part. The stage, though 20 metres wide, was not nearly deep enough to accommodate the sets and props. So a hydraulic stage had to be installed. It rolled majestically out over the pool and snapped up into place. This took forty minutes and it weighed tons. There was no loading dock to bring in sets of any size. When Bell announced he needed to cut a hole in the wall, John Kotowski went crazy.

'How am I going to get things in and out?' demanded Bell.

'We'll take them in the front door.'

'You can't take in a thirty-foot-high Statue of Liberty through a pedestrian door. It's got to be loaded in, and you've got to have hydraulics.'

'I'll be goddamned it you're going to cut a hole in that wall.' A week later, Bell told a crew to cut the hole he needed and never informed Kotowski about it.

The condo developments which had seemed such a good idea suddenly ran into bureaucratic problems. 'It was a hot potato seller,' says Mike Degazio. 'Everybody wanted one. All you had to do was put ten per cent down and Deerhurst would build you a condo. As soon as you were issued an MCC (Muskoka Condominium Corporation) number, you had to pay the balance.' The Ontario government was so stretched in issuing the MCC numbers that a massive backlog built up. Having built dozens of condos, the resort was unable to get the balance owing to them, but still had to pay interest on outstanding loans.

In March, Kotowski pulled the plug on Eilleen. There was no more money to spend on recording sessions and making videos. Naturally, she went ballistic, stormed into his office and was there for forty minutes. This was betrayal. What about all those promises? But there was nothing he could do. Kotowski acknowledges that the last time he saw Eilleen, 'we parted in a cold way'. Apotex brought in Canadian Pacific Hotels to run Deerhurst. Shortly after the new management was brought in, Kotowski moved on. He left the resort and the country because he 'got involved with medicine in Poland'.

Eilleen turned to one person who had never let her down. Mary Bailey had told Eilleen that if and when she wanted to make a country record, Mary would do whatever it took, pay whatever it cost, to make it happen. 'Out of the blue she called me and said that she'd given a lot of thought to it, she was ready to make records and do country music. Was I interested in helping her out?' says Mary. 'I really struggled with it. But I also knew that she's a great talent. So I had no choice.'

Mary swung into action. Once again, she bailed Eilleen out. She bought back the publishing, management and recording contracts from Deerhurst Entertainment for C$5,000. Harry Hinde called Craig Baxter, the Financial Controller of Apotex, begging him not to sell her contract. Baxter told him, 'Harry, you're just whistling in the wind. Forget this girl, you know we've got to cut our losses and run.' Harry had invested a great deal of his time and money in the recordings. He had paid Sabu C$15,000 and spent a further C$16,000 on recording studio bills, and was left with tapes that he couldn't get arrested with. Eilleen called him once, four weeks after it fell apart. The next thing he heard she was in Nashville. The big one had got away.

Canadian Pacific, who knew how to run a resort hotel, wanted to use the Pavilion showroom for conferences and business functions. After discussions to take *A Touch of Broadway* to a Toronto theatre foundered, they decided to close it down at the end of the summer season. It had been brave – or rash – to believe that the resort could expect to fill a 500-seater showroom 300 nights a year. The show only ran for five months.

'The show was good, the location was wrong,' says Gilles. 'The room was beautiful but acoustically terrible. Too much marble and brass, the ceilings were way too high. It was very high-tech with posh, elaborate sets and a huge budget, but it was Muskoka and a tourist area. In the city it would have been a hit.'

Many of the dancers and musicians, including Gilles and Lynn Hill, went back to the ballroom in the Lodge and quickly pulled together a new revue which is running to this day. Others, including Rhonda and Eilleen, did not have their contracts renewed. Mike Degazio stayed on singing with Christina Taylor (now his wife and a successful gospel songwriter). During that last summer Eilleen sometimes sang with them as part of a trio in the Green Room. 'It always was a fun room, it was so jammed, I don't know why the floor didn't cave in,' says Mike. 'We did some country stuff, three-part vocals, it was just brilliant. Essentially they wanted Chris and I to back up what Eilleen was doing, which was fine, though what we ended up doing was I got to sing the lead vocal while they did the harmonies. Those two dealt with each other the most, so there was never really any friction there, because my wife is so easy-going. Eilleen was the boss, Chris was the one holding it all together musically. I just kinda floated along, playing acoustic guitar.'

To have the cup of stardom so close to their lips that they can taste it and then dashed away is a blow from which some performers never recover. Not Eilleen. She never was a quitter.

In many ways her last few months at Deerhurst were her happiest. The boys had finished with school and there was nothing left she could do to keep them off their chosen paths. Her contract with the resort was coming to an end, and with it her responsibilities. For the first time in years she was free to concentrate on what she had to do. The experiment in rock had failed, so it was time to let Mary have her head. Finally, Eilleen had the perfect showcase. She looked exquisite and she sounded exquisite. Throughout the summer, Mary was inviting record companies to come and see her.

She left the resort in September 1990. After her last performance on a Saturday night, she asked Marg Reid if she'd come to brunch the next morning. 'I turned up,' says Marg, 'and it was just she and I. She'd been there two years and I felt bad that I was the only one she'd invited. I still feel sad about that today.'

Eilleen didn't. This time she knew she was going places. In those last weeks, a big fish from Nashville had seen her . . . and bitten.

And she had found her new name.

CHAPTER ELEVEN

State of the Country

Dick Frank has been an attorney in Nashville 'for ever', if not quite as long as his family have been in Tennessee. One ancestor fought under Andrew 'Old Hickory' Jackson, giving the British army a bloody nose at New Orleans in January 1815. He is an old-fashioned gentleman lawyer, reeking of Southern courtesy, behind which hides a sharp, no-nonsense business brain, who does not like the way lawyers shop for record deals in the modern business. His credentials are golden. He was at the first board meeting of the CMA (Country Music Association) back in 1958, when they spent the whole time arguing exactly what country music was (he says, 'I know there is one unbreakable rule in the Country Music Association, it was adopted at the second board meeting – no one will try to define country music') and has represented Roy Orbison, Acuff Rose, Don Williams and Don Everly.

Dick never charged Mary Bailey for his first job, a minor dispute over the ownership of some master tapes. She appreciated his efforts and used to call in to see him whenever she was passing through town. In the summer of 1990, she phoned, inviting Dick up to Canada to see Rhonda Silver and Eilleen perform.

'I thought it was a really good trip for my wife and I, someone to pay our way and bring us up to Ontario,' says Dick. 'I've always liked Toronto, so we flew up for the weekend in August, had dinner at the first night, listened to one of the acts, very talented club singer. Lovely girl, nice voice, but lacked in my judgement that little magic ingredient. So the next day we drove up to Deerhurst.'

At that point Dick had not heard any of Eilleen's tapes. That Saturday night he went to see the late show of *A Touch of Broadway*.

'When she stepped out on stage she owned it,' he says. 'I've seen that on a very few occasions – Nat Cole could do it, Lena Horne could do it, Sinatra could do it – and I have trouble of thinking of any other artist that projected a personality through an entire venue. For one of her numbers she came out in a black dress with a red rose, singing in faultless French. You know what a dinner theatre is at eleven o'clock at night – dishes clashing, drunks talking. You could have heard a feather fall. So after the show we got together and on due consideration I said yes, I would like very much to work with her, because she had more natural talent than I had ever personally experienced before.'

Dean Malton, who wanted to be a record producer, was recruited to demo some country songs. When it came to making music away from the show a lot of the rivalries were forgotten. Dean has an 'album's worth of stuff that I did with Rhonda that Eilleen sang background on' and another tape with Joni singing Eilleen's songs. 'Eilleen was always very open with her advice, she wasn't the type to keep it all in, and not share any of her ideas with anybody. I was dabbling in singing when I first met her. She told me, "Whenever I'm in the car, whenever I'm listening to the radio, I never sing the melody, I always try to harmonize with it, and that's how you get good at singing harmony." I started doing that, and to this day I still do.'

The first three country songs were recorded one Sunday evening when the Pavilion was dark. The musicians (Dean on bass, Pierre le Gendre on drums, Glenn Bladon on guitars and Pete Pereira on piano) set up the band room while Eilleen was miked up in a 'really great sounding stairwell'. They sat down, arranged and recorded three songs live: 'Diamond in the Dark' and 'Love in My Pocket' were simple, no-frills country weepies, while 'Go and Be Gone' was rockier. Eilleen's voice rings with a sincerity that was lacking in many of the sessions she did with Harry and Paul Sabu. Mary obviously liked what she heard, because Dean was then paid a couple of hundred dollars to record four more tracks. Retiring to his basement with a drum machine, Glenn and keyboard player George Guerrette, he produced 'Lay Down Your Arms', 'I've Seen Better Days' (lyrically a real kitchen-sink melodrama with added vibrato), the jaunty 'If I Were You' and 'I Thought I Left the Storm'. The songs may appear somewhat clichéd, but in country if the heart rings true all is forgiven. The way things turned out, none of the basement tapes would have disgraced Eilleen's first Nashville album.

Satisfied that she was heading in the right direction Mary set about investing in her protégée. 'My dad was making his money and my mom was spending it on this dream,' says her son, Robert Kasner. Everything had to be perfect before she went out with Shania.'

Back in Nashville Dick played the basement tape to Norro Wilson, whom he had known since the producer had worked in the mailroom at Acuff Rose. Wilson has played most of the roles available on Music Row, performer, songwriter (he co-wrote Charlie Rich's international hit '(Did You Happen to See) The Most Beautiful Girl in the World' with Billy Sherrill), record company executive (head of A&R for Warner Brothers) and producer. A genial warm bear of a man with a dry, self-deprecating humour, he has proved capable of straddling the changes in Nashville style and fortune. He has produced veterans like George Jones and Tammy Wynette as successfully as new country divas like Sara Evans and Mindy McCready. In 1991, he was co-producing Sammy Kershaw with Mercury Records A&R executive Buddy Cannon.

Dick wanted to sign Eilleen to Mercury, who were a subsidiary of the Dutch multinational Polygram. Mercury were on a roll with artists like the Kentucky Headhunters but they were seriously short on superstars. Dick reasoned that, while they had great distribution and a far better international set-up than most US companies, they needed Eilleen as much as she needed them.

'Dick Frank called me over to his office. I listened to this tape she'd done in a basement in Canada and I could hear her voice texture. Then he showed me a picture – and she is *so* ugly,' jokes Wilson. Eilleen flew down to Nashville and immediately hit it off with the producer. They went into Fireside Studios and demoed three songs. Eilleen was acutely nervous, faced with a recording session that could prove to be her last chance, but as ever she kept her feelings hidden. Sensing her anxiety, Wilson determined to relax her and set about cracking jokes, the way Jerry used to.

'She has a great sense of humour, she likes jokes and laughs and laughs – whether they are clean or dirty,' he recalls. 'I told her, "I already know you're good. I can hear that. I want to try a few things with you, see what suits you best." I only had a budget of $1,500 and we did three songs, including 'You Lay a Whole Lotta Love on Me', which I'd recorded with Con Hunley when I was at Warners. On that budget I didn't have time to nit-pick, but the feel was great.'

Looking for feedback, Wilson played the tape to Buddy Cannon, who loved it and immediately took it off to his boss, Harold Shedd. Shedd liked what he heard so much that when Eilleen met him he flipped, thumped himself on the chest and announced 'I want.'

'I thought she was a star when I heard her,' says Shedd. 'She wasn't the greatest singer I'd ever heard but she had a uniqueness about what she did. I've produced twelve of the biggest acts in country music, so I kind of felt she might be one of those acts.'

The deal Dick negotiated was pretty standard for the time: five albums at a royalty rate rising to fourteen per cent. 'It had a number of special provisions, but it was not what I would call a monster contract.' Harold Shedd made two further suggestions: That he should produce her debut album and that she should find another name. Eilleen Twain simply did not cut it.

Eilleen and Mary had discussed a better stage name many times. The singer was determined to stick with Twain to honour the memory of her parents and she already knew what she wanted to be called. *A Touch of Broadway* had employed a head wardrobe mistress and four more dressers. One of the dressers who worked for Eilleen and Joni Wilson was called Shania (neither Marg, Joni nor John Kim Bell can remember her last name). The girl told them she was an Ojibway who had been adopted soon after her birth and that her name meant 'on my way'. Marg Reid, who worked alongside her, is not so sure about that. 'I believe it might not have been a Native name at all.'

(There is confusion about what 'Shania' means and if indeed it is an Ojibway word. The language is dying out, not helped by the many different dialects and regional words. Mary Bailey did some research and came up with the alternative meaning 'silver', while 'zhu-ni-ya', an Ojibway word from northern Minnesota, best translates as 'money'.)

The name entranced Eilleen. Marg says, 'As soon as Eilleen heard it, she went, "Shania . . . isn't that a great name. I'd like to use that name," and this went on for several months. She kept going on about it.'

So Eilleen became Shania Twain. It was a good choice, easy to remember, both exotic and instantly familiar. Shania hinted at the exotic, showed the Native Canadian in her and it trips off the tongue easily in a chant. Twain had a resonance all its own. Mark Twain was the pseudonym of writer Samuel Clemens, who, in his masterpieces *The Adventures of Tom Sawyer* and its sequel *The Adventures of Huckleberry Finn*, had chronicled nineteenth-century Southern life both exquisitely and humorously. Shania Twain is the sort of name a country singer should have.

Country and western music is as American as apple pie, woven deep into the fabric of the nation's mythology. It is also a totally artificial creation. During the 1930s, two distinct musical forms, Appalachian mountain music and western swing, were melded together by Hollywood, neatly sanitized and packaged with a cowboy hat sitting on top, a maraschino cherry with a wide brim. That cornpone image made by the movies has meant that country music has always been a bit of a joke to the rest of the world, its musical value confined to a ghetto – if a ghetto can consist of wide-open spaces. Outside of its core market country was never cool for more than ten minutes. How can redneck be cool contrasted with a jive-talking, hip-waggling dude from Harlem?

What is often forgotten under a sea of bad jokes about Trigger and Dolly Parton's breasts is that country and the blues woven together created rock and roll. 'It's the backbone of American music – blues and country, 'cos country and western and blues are right there together, just that close, and gospel. Everything else comes from that,' says soul singer Rufus Thomas in Peter Guralnick's seminal book *Lost Highway*.

The traditional home of hillbilly and bluegrass music lay in the Great Smoky Mountains of Tennessee and North Carolina and the Blue Ridge range. Both are part of the Appalachians, a natural barrier separating the East Coast of the United States from the fertile plains of the Midwest. In 1750, the Cumberland Gap was discovered and Scots labourers, Irish weavers, runaway slaves and indentured servants (both black and white) poured through the natural gateway to settle the cheap land available in Kentucky and Tennessee. The whites carried their fiddles, mandolins, lutes, their Celtic jigs and reels and songs dating back to Elizabethan England. The blacks brought their five-string banjos, adapted from the long necked lutes of West Africa. The two cultures swapped musical ideas back and forth and the geographical and cultural isolation of the mountain hillbillies spawned a unique fiddle and banjo sound.

Although their records sold from day one, the music industry regarded both white and black country music with ill-disguised contempt. The blues, slave music from the plantations of the south, was labelled 'race music' while the white string bands were 'hillbilly' – an implied slur that still stands today. In his 1979 biography of Jimmie Rodgers, Nolan Porterfield memorably describes how the New York-centric business viewed country as 'a sort of backward, ugly, show-biz step-child that refused to go to school, and learn from its betters, but could not be locked up in the back room.' In many ways its attitude was not very different in 1990.

In 1925, the North Carolina Ramblers sold 100,000 copies of 'Don't Let Your Deal Go Down' while Vernon Dalhart, a failed light-opera singer, sold a million copies of 'The Prisoner Song/The Wreck of the Old '97'. Those songs are still country standards. The original string bands concentrated on fast and furious instrumentals. The Carter Family changed that. A. P. Carter was a fiddle player from Virginia who soaked up traditional Appalachian songs at his mother's knee and spent his life searching out new material. His wife Sara played banjo and autoharp, while her cousin Maybelle (who married AP's brother Ezra) developed a unique guitar style. However, it was not instrumental prowess that turned them into major stars, but their blend of tight harmonies. Vocal harmonies have been an essential ingredient of country ever since. By the end of the 1920s the Carter Family were a major act, creating a dynasty that, notwithstanding multiple divorces, has spanned three generations. Maybelle's daughter June married the original man in black, Johnny Cash, while June's daughter from her first marriage is Carlene Carter.

The first country superstar was Jimmie Rodgers – also known as the Singing Brakeman and the Blue Yodeller. Diagnosed with tuberculosis, his disease exacerbated by poverty and the itinerant life, Jimmie cut just 110 sides in less than five years before literally drowning in his own blood in 1933. In his lifetime he sold twelve million records, an incredible figure considering his brief career spanned the years of the Great Depression. Nolan Porterfield wrote of Rodgers that he 'couldn't read a note, keep time, play the "right" chords or write lyrics that fit. All he could do was to reach the hearts of millions of people around the world and lift them up. They listened and understood.'

When Rodgers was recording, there were few musical barriers. Louis Armstrong played trumpet on 'Blue Yodel No. 9'. And Jimmie was one of the first to use a Hawaiian guitar. The Hawaiians played their guitars seated with the instrument laid horizontally, the strings raised with no frets so they could run a steel bar rather than fingers up and down the neck. The instrument was later electrified and in the 1950s pedals were added to create the pedal steel guitar, which, along with the dobro, gave country its most distinctive instrumental sound, the melodic sob, the catch in the throat that all but mimics the human voice crying.

Western swing originated further south and further west, pioneered by the much married, never fully reformed boozer and fiddle player Bob Wills. His Texas Playboys were a big band (from twelve to twenty-two strong) featuring brass in addition to banjos, fiddles and guitars, playing good-time dance music, Texas two-steps punctuated by Wills' high-pitched shouts of 'Ah haaa' when they were really cooking, alongside songs like 'San Antonio Rose' and 'Faded Love'. Although he recorded some bluegrass and yodelling numbers, Wills always insisted his band were closer to Dixieland and the big-band jazz of Glenn Miller and Benny Goodman than to country, sometimes fighting with the audience to prove his point.

Inspired by the commercial success of Rodgers and Wills, the movie business fell in love with the image of the Wild West. Hollywood turned Gene Autry, Tex Ritter and Roy Rogers, who had begun their careers as Jimmie copycats, into Singing Cowboys. They dressed in glittery suits, run up by Nudie's of Hollywood, that would have lasted about a minute out on the range. The magic of the movies spread the cowboy image and the syrupy songs they sang worldwide.

Radio, the other boom mass media, saw the appeal of country early. WLS Chicago put their *National Barn Dance* on the airwaves in 1924. A year later, WSM Nashville came up with the *Grand Ole Opry*, a weekly live concert, which has been running ever since (though the venues have got bigger). As the home of the Opry, Nashville soon appropriated for itself the position of the *de facto* HQ of country music. It has been setting the agenda ever since. Acting out of the purest commercial motives, Nashville became an anchor on country music, a self-appointed censor of what is acceptable and what is not, channelling once rebellious music into vinyl jars labelled 'prude plus added family values' or 'for God-fearing folk only'. Fortunately, while the contents are often filled with sanctimonious bullshit leavened with hypocrisy (country singers are just as prone to sup to excess at the table of stardom as their pop colleagues), every so often they turn out to contain pure moonshine. The greatest stars have been those who broke the mould and fought against the respectable straitjacket of Nashville.

Country's greatest rebel, a legend in his own lifetime, was Hank Williams. He drank and pilled himself to death at twenty-nine, leaving a legacy of 170 songs, including classics like 'I'm So Lonesome I Could Cry', 'Jambalaya', 'You Win Again' and 'Your Cheatin' Heart'. Born in poverty in rural Alabama with a spine defect that left him in constant pain, Williams sang songs which reflected the realities of working-class life. Hank's Joes survived in dead-end jobs, waiting to drink the weekly pay packet away, lived their lives down the honky tonks and bars, full of petty infidelities and discarded dreams. His concerts were rambling, lethal affairs, pumped along by his band the Drifting Cowboys, who had no need of a drummer. To the establishment Williams was a serious threat. They despised his thick hillbilly accent and his contempt for money, the fact that he drank too much, swallowed pills by the handful, played with guns, destroyed hotel rooms and threw dollar bills out of the car window at passers-by. Williams was in conflict with life itself, enjoying rock and roll excess while Aerosmith were still in nappies. He wowed the audiences on the Opry – being called back for six encores on his first appearance – but eventually they told him to come back once he was sober. He never did.

Williams focused country songwriting back at its core audience, telling tales they could understand. Lyrics have always been much more important in country music. It allowed Kitty Wells, the first, and for a long time only, female country star to tear off her apron and tell the guys to stop crying in their beer. The 1950s were a boom time for country – half of Decca's and Columbia's sales were rooted in country music. Singers like Hank Thompson, Eddy Arnold and the Louvin Brothers toured constantly, building up a solid circuit that financed careers for the next four decades. Slim Whitman, a second-rate yodeller, became a bigger star outside the USA than in it.

The advent of rock and roll changed country. Rockabilly and skiffle borrowed from it but catered to a new group. Teenagers do not exist in country music, where you are a man with attendant responsibilities – workin', cheatin' and drinkin' – or you are a woman who falls in love, has to look after the kids, and then worry about her husband's cheatin' and drinkin'. Faced with the Red Indians of rock, country circled the wagons and retreated behind them, cutting off the exchange of musical ideas with outsiders and breeding only with its own. Occasionally, bright stars like Patsy Cline might shoot up before – if they survived – falling back carefully to the hayride and country fair circuit.

Country songs worked in the pop world but not if they were perceived as country. The song that allowed Tom Jones to make the great leap to international stardom was not 'Its Not Unusual' but 'Green Green Grass of Home', a classic country weepy. His manager, Gordon Mills, understood that you could take country songs, arrange the hell out of them, sell millions, but you must never admit where they came from. Country music's greatest strength has always lain in the songs – and maybe the high lonesome wail of a pedal steel in full flow – and the connection that the songs give to their listeners. Rock stars like Gram Parsons understood that, so did the Eagles and Linda Ronstadt, but to stay country was just not cool.

The genre has produced stellar talents. Songwriters like Dolly Parton plus underrated geniuses like Guy Clark, Billie Joe Shaver and Townes Van Zandt; great voices like George Jones, Tammy Wynette and Loretta Lynn; dark, brooding characters in Merle Haggard and Johnny Cash. There were bursts of beards and dope credibility in the late 1970s fronted by Waylon Jennings' and Willie Nelson's Outlaw movement, but in general Nashville's attitudes to women and blacks were perceived as Neanderthal and its political views to the right of conservative. But there was money to be made and a machine to be fed. A singer who joined the treadmill, worked hard and paid their dues could see a twenty-year career beckoning. Country music was profitable for the multinational record companies – and the stars who made it – because the market was defined. Recording budgets were set low and touring was expected. It did not cost a great deal to launch an artist. This did allow for careers to be built slowly.

By the mid-1980s country music appeared to be in a parlous state, its traditions corrupted by the electronic age, turned to saccharine by an overdose of strings and sequins. In 1985, the *New York Times* declared the traditional Nashville sound virtually dead – at about the same time as Hollywood decreed the western movie a defunct art form. (Hollywood's attempt to cash in on the Urban Cowboy boom of the early 1980s was a disaster.) Both forgot that country, like the cowboy, is an integral part of American mythology. Those were the dark years before the dawn.

Seven years later, the sales of one country singer accounted for nine per cent of EMI Music's $2 billion global turnover. Garth Brooks spearheaded a national resurgence in country music. In two years he sold over 35 million albums, outstripping Michael Jackson, Madonna and Whitney Houston. His second and third albums – *No Fences* and *Ropin' the Wind* both sold over 10 million copies, phenomenal figures for any artist but unprecedented for a country act.

Garth Brooks was a most unlikely superstar. He was podgy, with a tendency to over-indulge in junk food; he always wore a cowboy hat, primarily to hide his thinning hair. But he could communicate direct to the heartland. Sure, he had a voice that could reach deep inside but he wasn't a grab-you-by-the-heart-and-squeeze-until-you-can't-cry-another-tear communicator like Jimmie or Hank. Garth was a marketing genius. He understood how the business worked.

By copying George Strait's cowboy image, whether by accident or deliberate design, Garth placed himself in the centre of a conservative musical tradition and its attendant audience to which he added a mixture of natural charisma coupled with rock showmanship. Initially rejected by every label in town, Brooks' eponymous debut album, released in April 1989 was no overnight success. His first single 'Much Too Young (to Feel This Damn Old)' scraped into the top ten, after Garth and his manager Bob Doyle had driven his battered pick-up truck to promote it at any radio station that would let them in the front door. The next three singles were all country number ones.

Garth worked hard to keep his success (his album sales now exceed 100 million). And once he made it, he did not cut himself off from the fans who put him there. One night in Texas the show finished at eleven and he was still there at 6.30 in the morning, signing autographs and talking to the fans. One of his most endearing qualities, along with his impeccable Southern manners, was a seemingly compulsive desire to reveal his personal life, whether it be telling the world about his infidelities or outing his sister on prime-time television. As ever with Garth there was another more calculated side to it. 'I made a conscious decision to tell the truth,' he said, 'for what the media finds out is ten times worse than what you tell them.'

It was in his live shows that Brooks broke most radically with Nashville traditions. A fanatical Kiss fan in his teenage years, he imported standard ideas from rock concerts – wireless microphones and instruments, pyrotechnics, varilights – and gave high-energy performances that rivalled Bruce Springsteen at his peak. Garth possessed that unique ability – much coveted by political demagogues and preachers – to mould the mundane into something very special, to absorb the energy of the crowd and throw it back at them tenfold. New converts to country were impressed.

By the time he released *No Fences* in 1990, Brooks was one of Nashville's leading lights. What nobody expected was that the album would crash into the pop charts at number one, instantly placing Garth in the national spotlight. He was fortunate in that the *Billboard* charts had just gone over to SoundScan, a system that for the first time reflected real record sales. For a long time country had been selling more records than were showing up in the charts; SoundScan counted more accurate sales figures from mass-merchandise stores in non-urban parts of the US – the equivalent of counting in sales from W.H. Smith in Doncaster as well as HMV in Oxford Street. WalMart stores in the Midwest and South had always sold a lot of country records, but for the first time the media realized how many.

Nashville's boom was aided because American pop music had temporarily lost its centre. By fragmenting into sub-genres like rap, heavy metal and grunge, radio had created a generation gap which effectively alienated the baby boomers, the one audience with money to spend. They had grown up listening to melodic rock, exemplified by the singer-songwriters and California sound of the Eagles, and found it again on country stations, listening to new stars like Garth, Clint Black, Randy Travis, Wynona Judd and Reba McEntire. They could hear the words, it was well sung, played and produced, and with families to feed, they were also prepared to buy into the stability it promised.

'If it's the role of alternative music to be breaking the boundaries, to challenge the status quo, Nashville represented a contrasting force,' said

Bernie Leadon, a founder member of the Eagles turned Nashville record producer. 'My thirteen-year-old son liked rap: it's angry, it's a voice crying out, "We don't give a shit, there is no hope, so we're going to burn it all down." Country also talks about societal breakdown, always has done, but it upholds family values, is supportive of centrist policies, about people who have the guts to get up and go to work. They'll buy a car because they expect to keep up the payments. Both rap and country are handling reality, but country does buy into the American dream, coupled with the work ethic. Life's hard but life's good.'

Nashville became a boom town, with record companies and song-writers sprinting in from LA, signing up the office space and anything that sang in a cowboy hat. In 1992, country acts accounted for some twenty per cent of all record sales in the USA, $4 billion worth. In 1985, only sixteen country albums went gold (over 500,000 copies). In 1991, thirty-three went gold and another thirty-five platinum (over 1 million copies).

In the first flush of its Garth Brooks-driven success, with new country radio stations opening up in Northern cities like Boston, country music appeared to have the world at its mercy. Instead of becoming more daring, encouraging artists who wanted to break boundaries, who sought success across the ocean rather than north of the Mason-Dixon line, Nashville turned in on itself. 'There is a tendency with money in the air to go straight for the format,' said Bernie Leadon sadly. 'The new labels came in and said "Give me a Brooks, an Alan Jackson, a George Strait," they were more worried about covering bases with existing proven acts than developing new ones.'

To break new acts, Nashville found itself in thrall to country radio programmers, just as the corporate rock of the 1980s had been to FM radio where the unspoken commandment was 'Thou shalt play Led Zeppelin, preferably 'Stairway to Heaven', once every hour.' Radio stations have never been in the business of selling music. They sell advertising and to do that, they want more listeners than anyone else in town. They find a niche and – as long as it's working – stick with it. They do not like change. The power of country radio over record sales meant that country artists had to first break through radio by sounding like someone else, sell tons of albums and only then develop a distinctive sound. While a premium was placed on talent, a general lack of offensiveness to 2,600 radio programmers was equally important.

This is the opposite of pop and rock, where artists break through by being different, even visionary. This may involve being offensive, as with the Sex Pistols and Eminem, but the rock business long ago realized that upsetting Mum and Dad is a sure fire route to success – provided the world knows how upset Mum and Dad are. Country had taken the opposite tack, being deliberately folksy, down-home and cosy. Its very appeal could also become very boring very quickly.

MTV had broken the rock radio stranglehold. By the mid-1980s the video channel had redefined rock and roll, brought in a whole tranche of new acts where the look counted as much as the music. The two country music video channels – CMT and TNT – had not had the visual impact of MTV. Their programming was conservative. Visually, new country was just old country sung by younger guys in bigger hats and tighter jeans. Shania Twain was to change that.

CHAPTER TWELVE

Music Rows

aving Harold Shedd produce her debut album should have been a great move for Shania Twain. It was a fairly common practice in Nashville, allowing the executive a bonus, in the form of producer's points, if the record was a hit. Having the boss behind the desk meant he should really get behind it with marketing and promotion. Harold had a proven track record. He had produced Alabama's ground-breaking crossover hits, albums that sold in the millions where previously a country hit notched up only 200,000 sales. He had enjoyed great success with songwriter K.T. Oslin. And he was on a run at Mercury, having signed the Headhunters, Sammy Kershaw and Toby Keith. Just prior to going into the studio with Shania, he finished the biggest hit of his career – Billy Ray Cyrus 'Achy Breaky Heart' and its accompanying album, *Some Gave All*, which went on to sell 10 million copies. Because Shania had struck up such a good rapport with Norro Wilson, it was agreed that he and Shedd were to share the production duties and the points.

A year after leaving Deerhurst, Eilleen had a new name and an American contract with a happening Nashville label (considered very prestigious in Canada). Her debut album was about to be recorded by two of Music Row's most successful producers. She moved to Tennessee with Paul Bolduc, rented a small apartment in the Landings off Elliston Place, bought an old banger and started to hone her best songs in preparation for the record. Next stop Hitsville.

Unfortunately, Nashville does not work like fairytales, where talent and beauty will eventually be recognized wherever they hide. It is packed full of great singers, red-hot musicians and accomplished songwriters who have never had a break and may never get one. Like any entertainment industry Mecca, it is ridden with gossip, jealousy, half-forgotten feuds and the exploitation of the wannabes by the kingpins. It is a town where music is a commodity, a product that can and will be manufactured and moulded to suit the demands of the consumer. The country music establishment had ways of doing things, rules to be obeyed and dues to be paid. Shania knew none of them.

'I had no perception of what Nashville was all about. I'd been there a few times, but I'm a Canadian from northern Ontario, what do I know?' said Shania. 'I didn't understand the structure that existed in Nashville. I have realized that it is a very successful structure, since it works very well for a lot of people. But I questioned it for myself and it wasn't for me. I was a square peg in a round hole.'

It was the musical assembly line that really got to her. Writers scheduled sessions like doctor's appointments, got together from 9 to 5 with a break for lunch to write songs tailored for country radio. She did forge a partnership of sorts with Kent Robbins, who had written dozens of hits for the Judds, John Anderson and Ronnie Milsap. Together they wrote 'God Ain't Gonna Getcha for That', but it was a professional not a magical relationship.

'I wrote with a few people, but it didn't work out, so the songs I came to Nashville with ended up on *The Woman in Me*. I let myself be a product,' admits Shania, 'but I questioned everything – I was a hick from the sticks with not a hell of a lot of diplomacy. I didn't fit. I would stay up all night, eat junk food, write songs, get on the microphone. They didn't want to know about my songs. They weren't really taken seriously, because I was a nobody and I was new in town. I knew that I had better keep my ears and eyes open and learn and I planned on basically evolving over time.'

As Shedd and Wilson prepped the recording sessions – the budget was around $125,000, standard for a country debut – they shopped around Music Row for songs, corralling material from established writers like Gretchen Peters, Skip Ewing, Mike Reid, Kent Robbins and hit upon Tony Haselden and Stan Munsey's 'What Made You Say That'. Shania soon realized that they were not interested in recording any of her material. Mary rushed into action like a bear defending her cub. 'I was determined to get them to record her songs,' she says, 'because I knew she had something. Even if it was getting a writer to help tweak them, she deserved that, she had worked hard for it.' She pushed so hard that on several occasions it was Shania who reined her in, saying, 'Mary, forget it, let's just get out of here.' Mary was rocking the boat and in Nashville that was not what women did.

'Most people don't know how it worked in Nashville. The people who ran the record label chose the songs,' says Norro Wilson, who eventually agreed to let her cut 'God Ain't Gonna Getcha for That'. 'Her songs were not bad and most singers who come to town their songs aren't worth a flip. We didn't show enough attention to her songs, as we were looking for what we thought was right for the label.'

Harold Shedd is both more defensive and certain. 'She didn't have anything song-wise that would contribute to an album. She didn't have them finished. We did what we thought were the most commercial songs that related to that first project. We cut a couple of her songs, but she was not the writer that she is now, and she would not have been that writer had she not met Mutt Lange.'

The recording sessions at Music Mill Studios were not especially comfortable for Shania. 'I would have preferred Norro to do more of the album, because he and Eilleen had a real good chemistry, which was not entirely true of Harold,' says Dick Frank.

Shedd was a Georgia boy, born right on the Alabama state line. He might have had the ears, but with his success came a certainty that he was right. In the studio he was the boss, a physical person who was quite touchy-feely. This was anathema to Shania, who was not prepared to reciprocate.

'She knew how to keep people at arm's length when they needed to be, but didn't offend them; she's very cool like that,' says Wilson, who had done his best to make sure Shania had settled in town. He phoned her regularly and took her, as his guest, to the annual BMI country awards dinner.

Two of the songs on Wilson's demo tape, including 'You Lay a Whole

Lotta on Me', were upgraded for the album. For the rest it was primarily Shedd's call and Shania soon learnt it was best to stay out of the studio except when she was needed to sing. The producers tried everything to make a radio-friendly record. The musicians were top-notch – drummer Larrie Londin had played with Elvis, the Everlys and Chet Atkins; guitarist Reggie Young with Waylon Jennings, Jimmy Buffett and Johnny Cash. The material incorporated all the usual Nashville elements, up-tempo numbers, contrasted with ballads, all suffused with a pop-country sheen, showcasing Shania's vocal skills.

As the recording sessions were underway, Mercury Nashville underwent serious restructuring. Out shopping for labels – a sure-fire way to boost market share – Polygram had bought Motown and A&M Records. As country music was booming, A&M decided to establish a presence in Nashville. Harold Shedd was to head up A&M, while Luke Lewis came in as President of Mercury Nashville. The idea came from Polygram boss Alain Levy to pair a record man (Lewis) with a creative force (Shedd). The formula had worked well in the past – but not in this case. The situation was complicated because, although Lewis was the president of the label, Harold Shedd did not have to answer to him.

When the news came through, Shania and Mary were worried. New brooms often ignore their predecessor's projects. In fact, the appointment of Luke Lewis was one of the most important events in Shania's Nashville career. 'The making of that record was troubling for her in a lot of different ways, some musical, some personal – which I'd rather not speak to because I wasn't there,' says Lewis diplomatically. 'She and Harold clashed, especially during the recording process. We had some pretty straight-up conversations about the political climate. She wasn't pissing me off and she sensed that right away.' The upshot was that the trio forged the start of a close working relationship.

Like Shania, Lewis was a Nashville outsider. He loved country music passionately but understood that the world did not end at Highway 40. Born and raised in south Florida, Luke's teenage buddy was country rock legend Gram Parsons. 'I loved him,' says Lewis. 'Musically he took me here. I wouldn't have ended up here without him. Like a lot of artists, he had to embellish; he'd sing Scottish folk ballads and claim he wrote them, puff-yourself-up shit, when he actually had it anyway.' Luke can recall the first record he bought (Guy Mitchell's 1956 hit 'Singin' the Blues') and was once the only white face at a James Brown concert. After serving as an army journalist in Vietnam, Luke worked for a Tennessee record distributor and then an editor on *Record World* magazine before landing a job in sales, promotion and marketing with CBS, helping acts like Michael Jackson, Bruce Springsteen, Cyndi Lauper and Men At Work to rule the charts. He ended up as New England regional manager, before being poached by MCA in Los Angeles as Vice President of Sales and Marketing in 1988. Two years later, he was promoted to be VP and general manager of its Uni Distribution at a time when Bobby Brown, Tom Petty and the Fine Young Cannibals were at their peak.

Although his experience was in the nuts and bolts of the industry, Lewis yearned to run his own label. When he was offered the opportunity at Mercury Nashville, he leapt at it. What he brought to the table was the knowledge of how to maximize marketing and sales on a national, not just a regional, basis. He thought big and he thought outside the box. If Michael Jackson, a black artist, could sell over 40 million copies of *Thriller*, why couldn't a country act? Luke also had a different philosophy about recording – he believed the artist should be able to choose, not the head-office hats.

'Mercury changed quite a bit with Luke, and that was fortunate for everybody there, because he gave Shania freedom,' says John Grady, Senior VP of Sales, Marketing and Promotion. 'At that point I don't believe any of the other companies in town would have done that. He had the vision and the guts to do that, to say, "Go make your record and bring it back and we'll listen to it and we'll take it from there." '

Unfortunately, that attitude was too late to help *Shania Twain*, which was released in April 1993. It is easy to judge it against what was to come, but the truth is there was nothing special about it. It sounded OK, a bit bland and obvious, but the songs were flabby, missing any killer hooks, and the vocals, though technically fine, are lacking in self-belief. Lyrically the songs were equally predictable. A cheated, put-upon wife in 'When He Leaves You', a lament about the decline in good ole country values ('There Goes the Neighborhood'), lots of 'lyin'' and/or 'cryin'' set next to 'Oh my God, I'm so lucky that this wonderful guy walked into my life' themes. At least in 'God Ain't Gonna Getcha for That' Shania broke the mould by buying the beer and delivering the pick-up lines. The best song, by a mile, was the bouncy opener 'What Made You Say That'. *Shania Twain* was not a bad record, it just wasn't very good. Worse, it was boring.

Perversely, although the songs on her debut offered little insight into what was going on inside Shania's head, the original album sleeve is a stunning photograph that really does capture her very essence. The photograph shows her standing in the snow, on a chill day where the deep blue of the sky diffuses over the snow. She is dressed in a fringed buckskin jacket with a fur collar and fur moccasins – a deliberate visual play on her Native heritage. To her left, standing motionless, is Cane, a large grey timber wolf. A fire smoulders in front, but they both look straight ahead, two pairs of bright unblinking eyes staring into some future that only they know. It is a most unlikely image for a country singer and the stronger for it. It really is her, the great outdoors, the fire . . . and the wolf. Both aloof, both alone, but standing together, alert and aware. She is the wolf, and the wolf is her. Her very soul manifested in animal form. This is not an entirely fanciful notion.

'She's always been different,' says Mary Bailey. 'I'd sit and look at her and she always reminded me of a wolf, always very aware of everything, but always standing back. A wolf stays back among the trees and never gets right into it and she's like that, always aware, always back. There is an aloofness, a shyness about her, but she is always totally aware.'

In Timmins the shooting of the album cover was a big deal – local girl makes an album for an American record label. The session was shot out near Kamiskoka. Shania was in her element; she trekked out to scout the location wearing her grandfather's old snow shoes, and built the fire herself. The Native Canadian/woodland warrior theme was continued in her first record company biography.

What now seems strange was how the video for her first single, 'What Made You Say That', completely contradicted the intrepid snow maiden image. Mercury had reservations about shooting a video at all, arguing that CMT (Country Music Television) did not affect sales, but Mary convinced them to fund it. Shania sat down with director Steven Goldman and came up with a script that involved her cavorting around a Florida beach with a bare-chested male model. The tenuous musical link was that the song contained steel drums.

'I thought I was going to have the freedom to be myself,' she said, 'to have control over my image and the way I portrayed myself and my music. It didn't turn out to be that way, but I was sort of, like, well, if I can't have any control, then what am I doing here at all? I felt I should be myself, ignore the warnings and go with it.'

The video cost $40,000, a mid-range budget at the time, which required Montreal-born Goldman to scout the locations, take her shopping and even pin her clothes. Both he and Shania were determined to get away from the expected image. There was to be no dressing in a Daisy Duke ensemble. Shania had a very clear idea of how she wanted to represent herself, contemporary and modern, because that was the way she saw her image heading. The radical move was when she danced around showing her bare stomach. Wearing a bare-midriff outfit – though no belly button could be glimpsed – and going braless under a tight evening gown was, she contends, the bravest thing she had ever done. Although very tame by what was to come later, in 1993 female country singers did not behave in such a wanton manner. The video raised a few eyebrows.

'I was warned by my label there might be repercussions. They didn't come out and say, "No, you can't." It was more like, "We're kind of advising against that. This could be the end of your career. It might not work." And I didn't care, really.'

'That video was Eilleen's idea,' says Mary, 'and Steven Goldman allowed her the opportunity of being who she was. It was great. It wasn't bold, it was just sensuous, and that's what she is. Do you know what it did? It excited people. They were saying, "Hey, Nashville isn't the bales of hay and the straw, it's not that tarty look." It turned her into a 90s woman.'

Although the video attracted media interest, CMT initially refused to play it and the song stalled in the country charts at fifty-five. Mary was furious, berating the record company. 'It was a hit song, it got up the charts. Why didn't it fly? But they [Mercury] had other irons in the fire, they couldn't commit to making that song what it should have been. I was very unhappy, because I think it deserved more.'

Luke Lewis agrees: 'We put the record out and we actually had a hit — that we missed. Faulty promotion, I call it. It became a top ten record in about half a dozen cities. It was a bit white bread, but so is most country, and hits have broken out of there before. It was a hit record, but we couldn't get it through the system. It was bad timing, faulty planning. I wasn't paying attention to radio, when they tightened their playlist, I put the record out right in the middle of it. I didn't know what the fuck I was doing.'

Touring has long been considered the mainstay of country music, so much so that an entire twenty-year career can be spun off a couple of hits. It costs a lot of money to tour, money which the record company have to provide. For a newcomer the established route was to start as the opening act and work your way up the bill. The difficulty was, to get the opening slot, you had to bring something to the party — like interest from radio. If you couldn't get on radio . . . you couldn't get on the tours. Vicious circle.

Another of Lewis' bright ideas to break out of Nashville thinking was the Triple Play Tour. It was conceived during a brainstorming with Ron Baird of CAA (Creative Artists Agency), who had just opened the Nashville branch of the most powerful agency in Hollywood and was looking to make his mark. (He signed Shania in 1992, saying, 'Mary brought Shania into my office, and she had the characteristics and attributes of a star.') The idea was to give live exposure to young acts, thus forcing radio to pay attention.

With three new acts they wanted to push – Toby Keith, John Brannen and Shania – Mercury agreed to underwrite the costs. Baird booked a sixteen-date tour in markets (Louisville, Dallas) where they had significant country radio stations. The gigs were in small clubs with a $10 ceiling on the ticket price. Each act did a twenty-minute set and had to use Toby Keith's backing band. The theory had worked in the rock market, but Triple Play died. 'It was one of the hardest projects we'd done because nobody had heard of any of these acts, and nobody cared,' says Baird. 'So we had to kind of push and jam and cram. We didn't even take a commission on it, there was so little money.'

The situation was further complicated when Keith's 'Should've Been a Cowboy' was a bona fide radio hit, eventually reaching number one. The tour did nothing for Brannen, while Shania held her own. 'It gave me a vision of her potential,' says Baird. 'She was fine given the circumstances, working with a band that wasn't hers. She did very respectably and everyone liked her. She made a good impression on the audience and on the radio people.' Which, as radio were not all over her songs like a rash, means it achieved almost nothing. 'I think the video has more to do with her success than the tour did,' adds Baird. 'The video aspect of that first album was probably more significant than anything else. It established her sexiness, and beauty, and it clearly established her belly button! It was unheard-of in country music. Sexiness was discouraged because women fans would be intimidated.'

The video for 'What Made You Say That' proved to Shania that being young, sassy and sexy worked, that she did not have to conform to Nashville's ideas of the correct feminine image. In sharp contrast to their Nashville bosses, CMT Europe loved the clip and showed it so much that for a couple of weeks it was their number one high-rotation play. It was different enough that it attracted attention from major players who were not country fans. The first was actor-director, sometime Hollywood bad boy and the first Mr Madonna, Sean Penn.

Sean Penn had just branched out into directing movies and wanted to expand his skills in videos. He had completed one for David Crosby and his agent suggested he look at two other CAA clients, Susie

Bogguss and Shania Twain. Choosing Shania was easy. His agent contacted Mary, suggesting that he direct Shania's second video. Shania was literally 'jumping up and down' when she heard the news. One Sunday night she called Retta Harvey at home and said, 'Sean Penn's in town, and you've got to come and meet us at the office.' The three all looked at his showreel, discussed his ideas, then they went out for a drink.

'We closed the bar,' says Retta, now Senior Director of Video Production. 'Shania was drinking, but not to excess, but he was quite drunk. Sean was very quiet and reserved until he had a couple of cocktails and then he was like your best friend. By the end of the evening he was telling everyone in the bar jokes and doing imitations and was just a very entertaining man.'

At one point in the evening, when Shania had gone to the bathroom, Sean, who at the time was separated from actress Robin Wright (whom he later married), leant over and asked, 'So, is she serious with this guy?'

'Well she's been living with him for years, I think it's pretty serious,' said Retta. 'Anyway, I don't know if that's an appropriate situation for us to be talking about here. I think that's between you and Shania.' Any half-hearted flirting Sean did that evening was ignored by Shania, who showed no interest. Or perhaps she did not notice, because later, when Retta told her the story, she gasped, 'What, he said what?' and burst out laughing.

All the time Shania lived in Nashville industry bigwigs hit on her with three-chord regularity. Many artists in her position would have leapt at the chance of a dalliance, however brief, with a member of the Hollywood elite. Penn certainly had connections. The stakes were the highest she had ever played for, yet she turned them all down. What, one wonders, would the Deerhurst gossips have made of that?

'Dance With the One That Brought You' was shot in May. Penn brought burly character actor Charles Durning, a veteran of countless movies including *Tootsie* and *The Sting*, in to play the character of Good-time Charlie. Set in an old-fashioned barn dance, the video reeked of nostalgia. Penn was impressed enough by Shania to suggest she try acting. Despite being much more traditional, the song made it no higher in the charts. The final single, 'You Lay a Whole Lot of Love on Me', featured a straightforward big-hair video, but by that stage the album was dead.

First time out, *Shania Twain* sold around 100,000 copies. It did especially well in Seattle, Denver, Salt Lake City and Minneapolis, strong but not traditional country markets (perhaps they related to the snow better than the arid plains of Texas). Worryingly, it did nothing in Canada. Well enough for a debut – halve those sales and she would have been shopping for another deal – but disappointing.

In Nashville reality Mary Bailey's contacts, so impressive in northern Ontario, could not guarantee Shania overnight success. Her tough, no-compromise attitude had hit a brick wall of indifference. Nashville was a good ole boys' town; they ran it and it was their way or the highway. 'How far can you fight?' recalls Mary with a weary sigh. 'Realistically artists are a dime a dozen. A record executive has got 500 artists walking through his door. They misunderstand that there are artists who truly have something to say, who have a business sense as well, who say, "Look, if you allow me this opportunity, I think that I can . . ." They think you have developed an attitude. I didn't have the reputation of being the sweetest little girl on the block. But I had to, I'd rather them hate me and love her.'

Mary realized that for Shania to command the promotional back-up to take her to the next level she had to command some extra clout . . . and that she didn't have it. At times she thought, 'Am I the only one that believes? Can she be who I know she can be?' As it became apparent that the album was not going to catch, the doors slammed shut and Mary spent more and more of her family's money to keep the show going.

Not sharing her problems was a mistake that was eventually to cost her dear. However, it was Mary who took the first telephone call from the man who was to change Shania Twain's life way beyond the extent of her dreams.

CHAPTER THIRTEEN

The Svengali from South Africa

Although they grew up decades, hemispheres and continents
apart, there are many uncanny similarities between Mutt Lange
and Shania Twain's musical backgrounds. Both grew up in
places that were far beyond the known periphery of the music business,
both were marked out from their peers by an obsessive determination
to learn their craft and the type of music they heard as children was
straight-ahead commercial pop.

Robert John Lange was born in Mufulira, northern Rhodesia (now
Zambia) on 11 November 1948, the second of three boys. Mufulira is a
mining town on the Zaire border, right in the centre of the Copperbelt,
the richest seam of copper ore in the world. His South African-born
father, Ivan Gary Lange, was a mining engineer – not a suit-and-tie
office manager, more a pick-axe and shovel guy, a foreman in charge of
teams of native workers. In contrast, his mother, Elizabeth (_née_ von
Wartenburg), was a very cultured, sophisticated woman who came from
a landed family in Germany. He was always called John at school and
by his mother. But the Lange boys picked up nicknames young and got
stuck with them. The youngest, Bill, was always known as 'Slug',
because as a kid he was pudgy, slow and laid-back, while John started
off as 'Puppy', which soon changed to the less endearing 'Mutt'. It was a
comfortable colonial upbringing, but far from the verandahed luxury of
Happy Valley. There was domestic help but not hot and cold running
servants, as the Langes were at the lower end of the expat social scale.

While the white population was able to support a string of social and
sports clubs, it could not support a segregated high school in every
town. From the age of eleven the Lange boys were sent away to
boarding school, paid for by the government. John followed Peter to

Guinea Fowl, in Gwelo, Southern Rhodesia (now Gweru in Zimbabwe). The school was in a converted RAAF training barracks from the Second World War. Pupils' movements were controlled by blast of the air-raid siren.

Another student at Guinea Fowl was Johan du Plooy, now a doctor living in Canada, who played in the cricket team with John Lange. 'He was one of the opening bowlers,' he says, 'and I was the wicket keeper. He was a good all-round sportsman. He played rugby as well, but I don't recall him being into music at all back then. He was a quiet guy, always humble, friendly enough. He was never a big deal, never a bully. I got to know him better after I moved to Belfast High School in 1962.'

Belfast High was in South Africa, situated on the High Veldt of the Northern Transvaal, half-way between Pretoria and the Mozambique border. It took two days on the train from Salisbury (Harare), travelling down through Botswana, to reach the school. Du Plooy's parents had sent him there to learn Afrikaans and he never understood why John Lange ended up there. It was a state-funded co-educational boarding school which took in teenagers from all over Africa. The boys loathed it. 'It was extremely rigid, unbending, cold, isolated. It wasn't a pretty place, it felt to me like a prison.' At Guinea Fowl the educational system was English in origin and relatively liberal; at Belfast it was right-wing Dutch Calvinist, where discipline was all and fun – unless it involved maiming other boys on the rugby field – was unhealthy. 'Although we had girls at the school, we weren't even allowed to hold their hands,' says du Plooy. 'During school break the girls would go to one side, the boys to the other. We weren't allowed to mix except at specially organized social evenings where they kept us all indoors and watched us like hawks. Radios were not allowed in the school.'

'John hated Belfast High. If any of us could have got out of there we would. At one stage I wanted to run away and he did too. We discussed it but, of course, we never did.'

Lange was one of the youngest in his year, average academically and a reasonable sportsman. Even then he knew he wanted to be a musician. A pop musician. There he was at fifteen, blond hair cut so short it could only hint at curls, fair-skinned, freckled face, practising his guitar and telling his friends, 'I'm going to be involved in music,' to which they all went, 'Oh yeah, right.' That certainty did inspire Roland Deal to suggest starting a group. Deal, whom du Plooy remembers as a more naturally gifted musician, played piano and sang; Johan learnt to play the bass guitar 'very badly', James Borthwick was on drums and Lange on rhythm guitar and harmonies. They played British pop hits by the Beatles, Manfred Mann (an expat South African) and the Hollies. Despite their radio ban the school did allow the band to practise and even to play at school functions. Dancing, however, was not permitted.

'I don't think we had a name,' says Johan. 'John was never going to be the lead singer, he didn't have a good voice at all. Even back then he was more interested in making music itself than performing; he didn't want to be the star.'

Both boys graduated in December 1965. After Johan went to do his military service, they lost touch for several years. In 1969, while working as a medical rep, he attended a trade fair in Johannesburg. There, playing in a small tent off the main area, was a three-piece band, called Hocus. The bass player, who had sandy hair down to his shoulders, looked very familiar. It was John Lange, whom everyone now called Mutt. 'He always knew exactly what he wanted and he worked for it,' says Johan. 'It didn't happen by accident.'

During the early 1960s the political situation in Southeast Africa became increasingly unstable. The federation of Rhodesia and Nyasaland was always opposed by nationalists arguing that it existed only to serve the economic interests of the white population in Southern Rhodesia. Violent unrest led to its dissolution in 1963, with the two northern territories becoming independent as Zambia and Malawi. Zambia's leader, Kenneth Kaunda, had plans for the copper profits and the whites in Southern Rhodesia became increasingly militant in their refusal to accept black majority rule. By the time Ian Smith made his Unilateral Declaration of Independence in 1965 the mining industry was in turmoil. The Lange family returned to South

Africa, where, once he had completed his education, Mutt set about fulfilling his ambition.

Almost four decades later, it is hard to explain just how radical, nay inconceivable, an ambition this was. The local record business was no more than a cottage industry which grew more insular as the outside world slowly showed its disapproval of the apartheid regime. The only pop music Mutt heard in his youth was international, hits with strong hooks and melodies that stuck in the head. There wasn't much else out there. In the mining towns of Northern Rhodesia there were no radio stations, so music came from what records the expat community brought with them – and their tastes were often suspect. Long before he heard Elvis for the first time, little Mutt listened to Slim Whitman, and has loved him ever since. In the mid-1950s the Florida-born country singer, with extra added yodel, was hugely successful with hits including 'Rose Marie', 'Indian Love Call' and 'Serenade'. Somehow Slim touched a chord right across Africa. Nigerian superstar King Sunny Ade has described Whitman as one of his earliest influences and his band line-ups invariably include a pedal steel guitar.

While the guitar is ubiquitous across the continent, it is unlikely Mutt was exposed to much black African music as a child. A musician as accomplished as the Zimbabwean Thomas Mapfumo learnt his trade playing covers by the Beatles, Sinatra and Presley. The record bars were colourful places where the local artists were pressed by the dozen with covers made from wallpaper offcuts but not places where a young white boy would hang out.

In South Africa the music scene was even more segregated. 'The black music scene was traditional, not so vibrant as the unique sounds you hear coming out today,' says Geoff Williams. 'It hadn't evolved back then. There was interest in soul music, some great jazz and a lot of traditional township music. We weren't really exposed to each other's music. White audiences had vastly different tastes.' There was no television and the state-run radio stations played the international hits (alongside middle-of-the-road covers by bland white pop 'stars' like Gê Korsten, as tasteless as they were talentless). Anything more left-field could only be found in specialist import shops in big cities. Jimi Hendrix's *Electric Ladyland* was a proscribed text: a black guitarist with an album cover featuring topless women of all races it hit every puritan button available.

'The scene was so restrictive,' says Ralph Simon, 'with three million whites who didn't get involved in black music. As a white kid you didn't hear much black music unless you looked for it. The Beatles were allowed on the radio until John Lennon made the pronouncement that they were bigger than Jesus, then all their stuff was banned. When you took a record to radio you had to take the lyrics, and if they didn't pass muster with the censors at the SABC then you couldn't get the record played.'

South Africa's hippie revolution, such as it was, came late, but it did try to emulate its English and American predecessors. Acid trips, pot smoking, communes in the country and long, drug-fuelled and (sometimes) inspired jam sessions, often with black musicians like the legendary and exquisite sax player Kippie Moeketsi, were part of the scene. In its context it was wild, and by 1970 the government were stamping on long-haired deviants with boot, scissors and military call-up papers.

That was never Mutt's scene. He first played bass in a band called Sound Reason but quit for a day job as a sound engineer at Sonovision, a production house in downtown Johannesburg, working on radio soap operas and jingles for ad agencies. Jingles only lasted fifteen seconds and nobody cared much how they sounded. Except Mutt, who was obsessed with getting the right drum sounds. In the evenings he set about forming a rock band. To begin with he could not find a drummer, which is how Geoff Williams got a call. He was reluctant to go to an audition but when he did, he was knocked out.

'He was already Mutt when I met him,' says Williams, 'so there we were Mutt and Geoff. I thought, "Hell, these guys are really talented." I was asked to join and within a matter of months we were full-time. We weren't commercial, but to secure a gig and get some money we did a crash course learning hits. Mutt was always the driving force. When I first joined we had a lead singer, Colin, but Mutt was a far better vocalist than he was. From when we turned professional Mutt was more or less the lead singer. We cut back to a trio with Steve McNamara on guitar and had to keep it very tight.'

In 1970, Mutt quit Sonovision and the three rented a house on a fifty-acre plot near Mulders Drift, twenty kilometres from Johannesburg. Their gear was permanently set up in the lounge and each had their own bedroom. Getting it together in the country was not an excuse for Hocus to smoke bales of pot and drink themselves silly. They might have had long hair, but that was as far as the rebellion went. 'Hocus was an extremely clean band,' says Williams, 'Mutt and I used to have a few beers but he didn't smoke, and after he became a vegetarian, he didn't even have a beer.'

The band survived on a tight budget; their live work was supplemented by jingles for soap powder or soup cans. Mutt would write it, the band would rehearse and then drive into town to record it. Mutt was obsessed with getting their sound right and they rehearsed for hour after hour. 'He wasn't a raging dictator. Everyone did their own self-development on their instruments. Mutt more so than anyone. He was incredible; after a full day's rehearsal you could hear him doing scales in his room and he'd have the music out, getting into some new scale trying out a new finger grip, writing something.

'Some people get born with talent but he wasn't a born musician. He worked hell of a hard at crafting his profession, he listened and he learnt and he practised. His voice was so versatile. He had a kind of Van Morrison/John Fogerty voice, strong, forceful and quite distinctive. Mutt liked those big-voice people, but he also had a breathy voice full of little breathy bits and nasal intonations. If you listen to Bryan Adams, Def Leppard and Shania they all have very similar intonations in their voice, and I'm sure that Matt imparted it.'

Mutt was always trying to get the sound and balance right. Miking-up was primitive, if it happened at all, though they always tried to put a mike in the bass drum. Otherwise everything was balanced by ear. Mutt could never stand too much volume, so Hocus toned down.

They were fanatical about hearing what was going on. While their songs were tightly constructed and disciplined, with no freak-out guitar solos – Mutt hated showing off and would never hurtle around the stage – they still flowed. At the spine of every song were the bass and drums. Once organ player Alan Goldswain and singer Stevie van Kerken joined from the Music Corporation, Hocus could specialize in another of Mutt's great loves: vocal harmonies.

The Johannesburg music scene only consisted of a few small clubs, so Hocus lived vicariously through imported music magazines and albums. When *Melody Maker* arrived from England, they devoured every word. Reading the gigs pages was the equivalent of a refugee from behind the Iron Curtain staring in the window of a department store. 'Elton John had just started up and we'd see he was at the Roundhouse; Atomic Rooster was here, the Strawbs were there, the Moody Blues were doing a tour. We were astonished because there were huge-name bands just on a little strip ad in the corner.' While many of his contemporaries would have been using the gatefold sleeve of the first Crosby, Stills and Nash album for rolling joints Mutt digested every word on it. He knew which studio it was recorded at, where the mix was done, where it was mastered, who the backing singers were, what session musicians were hot. They talked about such minutiae all day – except when they were rehearsing.

Musically their major influence was American West Coast country rock, as pioneered by the Byrds, Poco, the Flying Burrito Brothers and the Eagles. British acts like Elton John, Emerson Lake and Palmer, Free, Rod Argent and King Crimson were also important. Although they never recorded an album, Hocus had a top ten hit in Rhodesia with 'Roll Me Over' while 'River Roll' picked up radio play in South Africa the next year.

Mutt spoke to record companies in the States who were impressed enough with the five songs that were completed to talk of a deal once their album was finished. It never was. By 1971, the band had grown to a six-piece, all pulling in different directions. Mutt had started to get some freelance production work. He and Stevie (whom he had known since they were four) had become an item and she was one of the country's most in-demand backing singers. He started to see a bigger picture than a run-down farm house on the outskirts of Johannesburg. Hocus split in November 1971. Their last gig was in Pretoria. Mutt and Stevie married the next day, Geoff was their best man.

More important was Mutt's burgeoning business relationship with Clive Calder (born 13 December 1946), who had coincidentally just formed two record and entertainment companies. With his partner, Ralph Simon (born 17 December 1946), he set up Sagittarius Promotions, involved in artist management and promoting shows at the Electric Circus in Johannesburg, while Clive Calder Productions was involved with production and song publishing. Clive was a live wire, a skinny blond guy, a fine cricketer who played the piano, and while he loved music, he was always more interested in the business side. He was *Billboard*'s South African correspondent, then hooked a job as an A&R manager at EMI Records. After an eye-opening trip overseas, he decided he knew how to make records and how to break them too. Like all great managers Clive could talk the talk; he told the Rhodesian Otis Waygood Blues Band, 'I'm going to turn you into the biggest thing South Africa has ever seen,' produced their first album in two days and then hyped the hell out of their first tour, reaching into small towns whose longest-haired inhabitants had previously always been goats. Clive also produced two albums (*Astra* and *Galactic Vibes*) with the acid-astral rockers Freedom's Children, sometimes described, by nostalgic South African rock critics, as 'the best band the world never heard' (Stevie van Kerken had sung on their first album).

In Mutt Lange Calder recognized he had stumbled upon a large uncut diamond. At a time when all around him were crumbling, Mutt held firm to his belief systems. He started to produce local artists – some of whom were also managed by Clive – and had instant success with Jessica Jones, whose 'Sunday, Monday, Tuesday' was a South African number one in 1972, while 'Waikiki Man' was a chart-topper in New Zealand and Rhodesia, and Richard Jon Smith, the first coloured singer to make an impact with all sections of the community. Mutt's other speciality was re-recording international hits for local compilation albums.

'Mutt was very well known as this budding engineer who could always come up with a snappy jingle,' says Ralph Simon. 'He always had that bent and flair for coming up with very good hooks and melodies. He studied the charts and those records that had commercial success. In a small market like South Africa you had to be very derivative. We put out an album called the *Greatest Hits of Johnny Nash*, and Mutt played and sang on every track, *The Greatest Hits of the Troggs*, and he'd sound like Reg Presley. He knew how to be a human jukebox.'

Even then, working with primitive equipment, Mutt knew what he wanted, and how to get it. The fundamentals of his technique and approach were the same back then. 'I was always amazed at his absolute focus and passion . . . he was like a single clear thought, but always relaxed,' recalls Paul Wright, who worked as an engineer at Sonovision with Mutt. 'This came out strong in those early days of multi-track recording. While most people were putting lots of layers down and then 'fixing it in the mix', Mutt would know *exactly* what picture he was creating right from the start. I also recall his comments making me aware of just how important the bass guitar is in the scheme of things . . . if you can sort of imagine all those harmonies building up out of the bass line . . . great things happen.'

In South Africa, Calder and Simon's interests stretched beyond pop and psychedelic rock bands. By February 1972, they had concluded recording, management and publishing deals with most of the top Black acts south of the equator. The idea, spearheaded by white Afro-rock group Hawk and black soul acts, the Miracle and the Triangle, was to look to the international market. Calder was ahead of his time, for the real interest in 'world music' did not take off for another decade. While local audiences enjoyed this multi-racial approach, the authorities did not. As government crackdowns effectively destroyed the local rock scene and sanctions made it very difficult to sell records abroad Calder and Simon made the decision to leave South Africa for London. From being sharks in a small pond they found themselves just another piece of bait, bluffing furiously to make their way.

Today Clive Calder runs the Zomba Group, the largest independent music firm in the world. Without Mutt Lange it might never have happened. Jive Records are home to Britney Spears, the Backstreet Boys, R. Kelly, *NSYNC, Billy Ocean, Steps, A Tribe Called Quest and Groove Armada, while Zomba is an interconnected web of fifty companies spanning six divisions: records, music publishing, production, music libraries, record/software distribution and export, film/TV music, and recording studios and instrument hire companies. Still privately owned, the company is estimated to have annual sales topping $1.2 billion. Everything Zomba does today they were doing in South Africa thirty years ago, albeit in microcosm.

'Mutt was very instrumental in the rise and rise of Zomba,' acknowledges Ralph Simon. 'He played a major role in the growth of it. Clive and I had both come from a music and music publishing/live entertainment background. We always felt we had the ability to develop a business that had the various legs of a publishing, record company, a music studio and a live business.'

In early 1974, Mutt left for London with Stevie. They were signed to a singles deal by Phil Carson at Atlantic Records, and while he cut a couple of sides, nothing seemed to happen. To make ends meet the couple sang backing vocals for The Crazy World of Arthur Brown. Clive and Ralph arrived the next year, having landed Richard Jon Smith a deal with Polydor. After they had Mutt produce Smith, they started pushing him hard. 'It was largely an attempt to get Mutt some work when the Atlantic deal didn't come together,' says Simon, 'which led to the whole notion of managing producers – which we were the first to do.'

In the days of punk and Rock against Racism benefits, being a white South African required a lot of explaining in the English music scene. Nobody knew that in the early years Zomba's cash-flow was helped by the ANC (African National Congress). Funds were invested in the company in England, who in turn arranged for envelopes stuffed with cash to be tossed over the fence of a convent in a Johannesburg suburb to help pay the legal costs of defending anti-apartheid cases.

'Mutt was the only thing Clive had; he managed him as an artist as well,' says Nigel Grainge, the head of A&R at Phonogram who, in 1975, gave him the first City Boy album to produce. Over the next two years he also did albums for Graham Parker and the Rumour and displaced country rockers Clover (whose lead singer was Huey Lewis), while at the fledgling Virgin Records Simon Draper had Mutt produce the Motors, whose 'Airport' was a big hit single. His big breakthrough came from Grainge, who had signed the Boomtown Rats to his new Ensign label in late 1976.

Grainge liked Mutt because he too was a record nut, a compulsive collector, a real fan. When he was in South Africa, he had devoured every scrap of information available on album sleeves and that desire to know everything has never left him. 'Most record producers are closeted in a studio and not aware of what is going on outside; very few of them take the time to discover what they are competing with,' says Grainge. 'They are usually a year behind everybody else. Mutt always wanted to know what was happening. He'd make lists and say, "Come on, Nige what shall I get?" One of the reasons we got on so well was that he reacted so well to all the obscure stuff I was into. He loved bands like Spirit and Quicksilver Messenger Service, all those classic American acts of the late 1960s, and would always look for that kind of vibe. Even in 1975, there would still be a huge slew of obscure stuff that would come through Warners and Columbia that would be exciting. Steely Dan were just being launched.'

That is one of the secrets of Lange's success. He listens to music all the time, to all music, to pop, rock, country, heavy metal, AOR, reggae, soul, folk, teeny bop, rap and punk, judging it on musical merits overlaid by a sound commercial ear. Because he is not bound by genre, he is able to cross over, taking bits with him to sprinkle into the mix like fairy dust. Mutt's early successes came with bands where he harnessed the collective energy and created a distinctive sound – but always with a commercial edge and melodic heart. With his help the Rats, a ragged bunch of Dublin proto-punks, became regular chart-toppers. Their first meeting was not a success, as Bob Geldof recalls in his autobiography *Is That It?*:

'Chris [Hill] and Nigel introduced us to Mutt Lange, a brilliant record producer who was then relatively unknown, but who has gone on to become one of the most successful in the world. We played for him at Chessington. "What do you think?" the Ensign man asked him hopefully. "I think they're terrible," he replied, in his clipped South African accent. "What on earth do you expect me to do with this lot? I really would rather not get involved."

'They took him to see us perform and he changed his mind. One week into recording at Dieter Dirk's studio in Stommeln, just outside Cologne, we began to wish that Mutt had stuck to his first instinct. Robert John Lange was a martinet. He was a perfectionist who drove others as hard as he drove himself. We had made our demo tapes in a little studio owned by Eamonn Andrews in Dublin. The whole thing had taken a couple of hours. We just ran through the songs a few times and picked the best version. With Mutt the recording lasted eight weeks. We did seventy-eight takes alone for "Lookin' After Number One".

'We had in our brief two-hour experience in the studio played together as if it were a live performance. Now we were required to create a layered production with each instrument playing on its own away from the others. The sound had to be broken into its component parts in order to give the producer greater control in the final stages of mixing the instruments together. It caused us enormous initial difficulties. For the first time we actually heard ourselves individually, and we were embarrassed because some of us were playing completely different chords to the others. We had been playing these mistakes live for months. We lived in an apartment connected to the studio and often worked from 10 a.m. through to 2 a.m. Mutt was obsessive about detail and would spend hours going over and over the same thing until in the end we lost the feel of it. We felt inadequate, the more so because Mutt himself was a brilliant musician and was impatient with our fumbling.

' "Hit it harder, hit it harder, Johnny," he would call through at

Fingers pounding the keyboard. "Harder, Pete, it's not coming through." In the end Pete's fingers were raw with playing. Mutt was a bass player himself and, unintentionally, he kept belittling Pete's ability. "That's no good. You're not playing it properly. It goes like this." Then he would play it and completely outclass Pete.'

The Boomtown Rats were also a big break for Calder and Simon, as Grainge recalls: 'I knew nothing about publishing when the Rats deal had been done, and when we were talking to Mutt, Clive then asked Fachtna O'Kelly, the Rats manager, what they were going to do with their publishing. They didn't really know, so Clive offered to set up their own publishing company through Zomba, which he did for a handling percentage. Smart. We never made a penny out of the Rats because of the structure of our deal and he built his empire on them without the outlay of a penny.'

Steve Brown, now a successful record producer, worked as a tape operator and engineer for Phonogram in the late 1970s. He worked with Mutt on recordings with City Boy, the Rats and Graham Parker. Frequently Steve was close to tears from sheer exhaustion. 'If I hadn't have worked with him,' says Brown, 'I'd have doubted myself when I got into sessions where things aren't going well and you, the producer, have to pull them together. He was a big disciplinarian, which I liked. If you are going to call a recording session you are there before it starts to get your bits and pieces together. It's a business, not a coke-snorting, booze-drinking madness.'

Mutt developed his own idiosyncratic routine. During the recording sessions for the second Rats' album, *Tonic for the Troops*, Brown recalls Mutt insisted on a minimum six hours' sleep a night but 'he'd still be awake two hours before anyone else. Then he would put on his track suit, eat some breakfast or energy food and go out running for at least five miles, come back, eat some more food, shower and go to the control room half an hour before anybody else. He was a vegetarian. In terms of discipline he was way out of his time. We never talked religion, but I would imagine there is some force that drives him on; he had a very disciplined lifestyle.'

He drove musicians hard. Says Brown, 'City Boy were post-punk, good players, they wrote pretty good songs and he stretched them as far as they could go. We'd do sixteen hours a day, six days a week. It wasn't clinical – we were going for performance but performance goes with feel. Mutt is into feel. It's not just getting the notes right, it's getting the feel too. Mutt is totally soulful. As an engineer I was waiting for the performance so we could move on to the next thing. Steve Broughton was doing a guitar part. He did it for about three hours and I saw him performing his heart out doing what I thought he would never achieve. He looked up at Mutt and Mutt wasn't looking at him, so he looked over at me and I went, "Yes," gave him the thumbs up. Mutt gave me such a look and said "No." It took another four hours to get the thing right.'

Yet however hard he pushed the artist, Lange pushed himself harder. Many nights he sent the bands home, and while the engineer hit the buttons, he went out into the studio and replaced some instrumental breaks and added extra backing vocals himself. He stood behind the mike, cupped his hand behind his ear, like some ageing folk singer, to get the tuning just right and when he sang, he literally threw his body at the microphone, giving a virtuoso performance nobody ever saw. 'He is not a great musician,' says Brown, 'but he is very competent and he has a great deal of feel. What he loses on the technical side he gains on the feel and soulfulness. His feel for backing vocals was totally amazing, which manifested itself on all the Def Leppard records.'

If genius always requires 99 per cent perspiration Mutt insists on delivering 99.9 per cent. For all his success he is aware of his limitations. As he once explained to Helene Bolduc, it does not come naturally to him, and it never has. While David Foster can go and work on a project for a month and he's done, to achieve the same result Mutt knows it will take four months and that he will have to work harder. But because he's a perfectionist he will stick to it until he gets there. All it takes is time and focus.

Before the advent of computerized mixing desks in the late 1970s, the producer's job was still considered by many to be to transfer a live performance on to vinyl. Lange had always looked beyond that and technology caught up with his vision. He and Geldof argued a great deal as Mutt started dissecting songs, taking the melody and saying, 'We must change those two notes because it is derogatory to the scan of the song.' If he lost the argument with Geldof, which did happen, Mutt employed his final weapon. He sulked.

'If a producer is sulking you are not going to get much work done, so you might as well try and get where he's coming from,' says Brown. 'Bob used to say, "The guy sulks and I can't stand it." And Bob was a champion sulker of his own.'

Lange was not available to produce the Boomtown Rats' biggest hit, 'I Don't Like Mondays', although he did the rest of the recording for their third album, *The Fine Art of Surfacing*. Then he switched musical genres to Aussie hard rockers AC/DC. For their second outing together, Lange had to help them overcome the seemingly insurmountable loss of original singer Bon Scott. *Back in Black* went to number one in the USA and Australia, eventually selling 19 million copies. 'He really can hear it,' says Ralph Simon. 'He evolved the way Brian Johnson sang after Bon Scott died. They made four albums together and he brought a tacit commercial edge to them, added backing vocals which really lifted the broader acceptability of the new heavy metal.' Mutt was a hard taskmaster but an adept at creating diamonds from chaos. Few men could have salvaged Def Leppard not once but twice.

Lange's production on *High 'N' Dry* in 1981 set up Def Leppard in America, but during the recording of their follow up *Pyromania*, guitarist Pete Willis was grappling with a drink problem. He kept appearing at the studio either drunk or not at all. 'On the road there is a semi-excuse for getting kinda crazy, because it is not a natural way to live,' said singer Joe Elliot. 'Then Pete started acting like that in a fixed place – in the recording studio. He pitched up to play a guitar solo drunk; if he'd had the guitar on backwards it would have sounded as good. Mutt just bawled him out told him not to come back to the studio until he got his act together. Basically he never came back.'

The huge momentum that *Pyromania* created appeared lost on New

Year's Eve 1984, when drummer Rick Allan lost his left arm in a car crash. In December 1986, on the way to the *Hysteria* recording sessions in Wisseloord, Holland, Mutt too crashed his car and spent three weeks in hospital with leg injuries. During those same sessions, Mutt left the control room to relieve himself. Elliot, scarcely the most accomplished musician, picked up a guitar and began to fool around. Mutt came back in and announced, 'That's the best hook I've heard in five years.' The hook became the chorus for 'Pour Some Sugar on Me', the album's anthem. *Hysteria* sold over 15 million copies. 'It became the most important song on the record,' says Elliot. 'And it was done almost by accident. Had he not gone for a piss . . .'

Ralph Simon believes Mutt's influence on Def Leppard was greater than its members ever realized. 'Having come from the background of being a sonic constructor and knowing how he heard the end sonic architecture, Mutt knew exactly what he had to do. He would either sing the parts or the backing vocals, and if you listen to Joe Elliot – who could never really sing properly – and then early Mutt work, Mutt's phrasing punctuated everything he did.'

Lange had a fanatical attention to details. In the days before CDs, the final step in making an album was the cutting. As you cut towards the centre and the grooves got closer together the sound quality decreased, so it was important to push the levels back up. 'When I was cutting *Hysteria* to vinyl, Mutt would send the album up one track at a time and get that absolutely right,' says Steve Brown. 'Mutt notices everything and he wants it spot-on side one, track one and then he would send up track two. That had to run right, with the right space in between tracks and the right EQ. That happened twice a day. The album was done after six days, most took one or two at the outside. It made a bit of vinyl perfect.'

The success of Def Leppard and AC/DC showed that Lange had the right ears for the lucrative American market. His work with Foreigner on *4*, helped turn them into an FM radio staple, and the Cars wanted the same gloss. Like Mutt, their leader, Ric Ocasek, was a stickler for getting it just so, and hang the time and the expense. Mutt, despite his painstaking approach, did bring his projects in on budget, whereas the Americans were profligate with studio time. The recording process was so intense Mutt almost had a breakdown – and he never worked with the band again. 'Mutt's a definite stickler for feel,' said keyboard player Greg Hawkes. 'He'd sit there with somebody for hours working on a part, and only looking for the feel. If he didn't hear the feel, it wasn't down on tape. Mutt would always refer to the demos and say, "You've got to have the feel of this," or, "This doesn't have the feel of the demo – do it again." That's the point of creativity, it's always trying to get that feel.'

It was Mutt who insisted that 'Drive' was a hit. 'It was a simple song, direct. I thought it was kinda weird for a single,' admitted Ocasek. 'It was all two, three chords and droning; the subject matter was kind of depressing. But Mutt always said, "It's a big single." And I always went, "Sure." ' 'Drive' was a worldwide smash in 1984, and the following year was used so effectively during the Live Aid concert that it still tugs at people's consciences today.

Mutt had strong views on lyrics. 'Lyrically, negativity wasn't in Mutt's vocabulary,' recalls Joe Elliot, whose songs took on a darker tone when they stopped working with him. Ric Ocasek also disagreed with Mutt's views on words. 'I think it's still a kind of poetry, or some sort of poetic form with music,' says Ocasek. 'Mutt Lange used to say, "Nobody ever listens to the lyrics anyway, so who gives a shit?" I like Mutt, but he just has firm beliefs about things like that.'

In his songwriting Mutt returns time and again to the same sources for inspiration. One particular favourite is B.W. 'Buckwheat' Stevenson's 'My Maria', a US top ten hit in 1973. (Stevenson, a Texan equally at home singing country, blues and rock died in 1988 following heart surgery. He was thirty-nine). 'Mutt always goes back to B.W. Stevenson, because he feels that the melodic integrity of the pop hook was what fed his muse,' says Ralph. 'He uses a lot of hits from the late 60s and early 70s as a touchstone and reference point, as guidelines for how he should meld someone. He knows how to construct a song that has the common touch.'

Working with Mutt was an exhausting, long-winded process. The perfection he sought was time-consuming and could be bad for band morale. Stars used to being cheered every time they stumble up the fretboard do not like being told to do it again and again. And again. Few acts could face a third album with Mutt unless commercial sense triumphed over ego (AC/DC managed four albums). The Rats constantly tried to escape, while *Hysteria* was started with Jim Steinman, and continued with Nigel Green before Def Leppard realized how much they needed Mutt.

In 1989, Bryan Adams was going nowhere. The Vancouver-born rocker had spent two fruitless years trying to follow up the disappointing *Into the Fire* and sessions with Steve Lillywhite and Bob Clearmountain had to be scrapped. He started working with Lange. 'Mutt's a lovely guy,' said Adams. 'I've got nothing but fantastic things to say about him. He really pulled me out of a rut. I'll be forever indebted to him.'

'Let's be honest, Mutt could work with my mom and have a hit record. We come from similar backgrounds and with similar musical interests. When we first started writing together, it was obvious that we were going to make a good record together . . . the fact that we've carried on since that is due to the fact that we've had some great moments making music, not to mention a few dodgy Indian curries!'

The two of them hit it off, established a method of working together that neither had ever had before and which Lange was later to refine to perfection with Shania. Lange forced Adams to rethink his whole modus operandi. 'He made me realize there really were no rules, and that a song just has to have something special, no matter what it is – that you have to come up with it, make it work, stretch it, rip it apart, strip it down, take its clothes off and see how it looks. One of us would come in with an idea for a song, and we'd try and set up some sort of structure for it, then puzzle over it for a while, try and come up with a middle eight; then he'd come up with some genius rhythm thing for it, and we'd go back and listen to that, then realize the verse wasn't very good; so we'd erase that, rewrite the verse – it was unbelievable!

'He'd take old songs that Jim Vallance and I had written, which I thought were quite cohesive, and he'd listen to the chorus and say, "That chorus is quite a good verse." I've never met anyone like it in my life. He really is an all-encompassing producer: he writes, arranges, sings, plays. There were times when we were working around three in the morning, and I'd go, "Look, I can't sit here any longer," and he'd say, "OK, man, see ya later." So I'd go off to bed, wake up around ten or eleven, go back to the studio and he'd still be there – and not only had he not gone to sleep, he'd also sussed out the problem we'd had the night before!'

That cut both ways. After their first collaboration, Mutt swore he would never work with Bryan again. At times, Bryan's attention to detail was so intense, that Mutt had to go out in the woods and take a walk around the house. If Mutt, with his obsessive approach, couldn't take it, it must have been bad. However, they did end up doing songs on two more albums.

Their major songwriting collaboration was '(Everything I Do) I Do It for You', used as the soundtrack for the movie *Robin Hood: Prince of Thieves*. It topped the UK singles charts for sixteen seemingly interminable weeks in 1991 and sold millions. *Waking Up the Neighbours* was a massive hit, another 10 million-seller. There were criticisms – Adams was not a big fan of Mutt's trademark layered backing vocals and Joe Elliot dared to suggest it was just a Def Leppard album with a different vocalist (he later apologized). In the early 1990s Lange also collaborated with power balladeer Michael Bolton, co-writing the hits 'Said I Loved You . . . But I Lied' and 'Can I Touch You . . . There?' and producing the album *One Thing*. In December 1993, the month he married Eileen Twain, Lange had three songs simultaneously in the top ten of the US top 100 singles chart: 'Please Forgive Me' (Bryan Adams), 'All For Love' (Bryan Adams, Rod Stewart and Sting), from *The Three Musketeers* soundtrack, and 'Said I Loved You . . . But I Lied'.

He appeared to be at the height of his profession. In fact, his greatest triumph was still to come and from a most unlikely source. Country music. During his career Lange had dabbled in country – recording albums with Clover (who later metamorphosed into Huey Lewis and the News) and the Outlaws – without much success. By 1993, he was ready for another challenge. The Garth Brooks explosion had shown that Nashville had the power to shift millions of units but their sound was still outdated and thin compared to what he could deliver.

CHAPTER FOURTEEN

A Spiritual Man

Mutt Lange's love life was nowhere near as successful as his recording career. It was remarkable only because all the women he married or became seriously involved with continued to adore him long after they broke up. They also ended up as friends with each other, perhaps because they realized that any long-term relationship with him was doomed. Mutt was a serial monogamist, yet his one true love, the only mistress who could always captivate him and take him away, was his Muse.

He was a difficult man to be married to, charming and attentive when his attention was focused on the girl but impossible to distract once he entered the recording studio. In there, time, life and love receded into mist. In *Is That It?* Bob Geldof suggests that Mutt's demanding producing on their first album was partly due to the strain of the break-up of his marriage to Stevie. During the recording of the Rats' third album, 'a Swedish girl was always in the studio with him,' says Nigel Grainge, 'probably because he spent so much time in the studio it was the only time to keep up with him. He pretty much ignored her.'

In the only extant picture of Hocus one can see Stevie resting her hand on his knee, staring straight at the camera, while Mutt has just the tips of his fingers on her wrist and the skewed look of a man who would rather be somewhere else. Mutt's second wife, Olga, was quite different to Stevie. Despite her name and Scandinavian ancestry, her upbringing and accent were cut-glass, upper-class English. Olga was a stunningly pretty blonde, a former model always surrounded by a cloud of gorgeous women. 'She was a party girl, into the club scene, very high-spirited and shared his passion for all things Indian,' says Alison

Green, an American music business lawyer, who met them both at a party in their house at 4 Fernshaw Close in Chelsea. 'She loved to throw dinner parties, she had like a salon, the Gertrude Stein of rock and roll. She bonded with all the bands he produced, she was a people magnet, the most outgoing girl you could ever meet. She and Mutt were complete polar opposites.'

When he was present at his wife's party, Mutt was excellent company. Conversationally he had a wide range of interests – everything from gardening, high culture, ballet and painting to sport, especially rugby and football, and geopolitics – and was a polite listener. 'He was a really nice guy, very quiet, very mellow,' says Alison. 'I don't think he had an evil bone in his body. His biggest single vice was being a workaholic, so focused that the world ceased to exist. His work habits were legendary. He'd disappear for days on end, lock himself in the studio, sleep on the floor until he was physically ready to drop.

In 1980, when Mutt was working on Foreigner's 4, he was poised to become one of the biggest producers in the world. While he was raking in the money, there was such demand for his services that he would go sequentially from album to album. When he eventually finished a project and had driven himself to the point of exhaustion, he and Olga headed off on holiday, where he recharged his batteries before throwing himself into the next one. By the mid-1980s rock and roll widowhood had palled with Olga, who reluctantly called time on a marriage that was no longer a marriage. 'Olga was devastated by the break-up,' says Alison. 'She was crazy about Mutt, she adored him, she really, really, loved this guy. But as time wore on, she recognized this wasn't a phase, it was a lifestyle, ingrained in his personality and it just wasn't going to change. She wanted kids, somebody to share her life with.'

Money was never an issue to Mutt. After he and Olga split he bought a mansion in Surrey. He decided to build a shrine outside his bedroom window. Unfortunately there was a 300-year-old oak in the way. He paid thousands of pounds to have the oak moved and replanted. He gave Olga the house in Chelsea, never abandoned her and supported her financially without a quibble. Clichéd as it sounds, he has remained friends with all his exes, helping Stevie emotionally when she went through problems, giving her a song to record on her solo album, which was released by Silvertone (part of Zomba). After their divorce, Olga discovered a rock band, Romeo's Daughter. They were signed to Jive, their publishing went to Zomba and Mutt produced their first album, keeping it all in the family (and the family bank account, if it had proved to be successful).

Although he has worked for years with bands who were devotees of sex, drugs and rock and roll, Lange was never interested. After 'workaholic' the word that describes him best is 'spiritual'. It comes up again and again. 'He was very spiritual and for all his fame and fortune very humble,' says Alison Green. 'They had a meditation room in their house, but what was so cool about Mutt and Olga's marriage was that he never expected her to follow his beliefs. They shared this bond, but while Olga found her own way to follow, with Mutt it was the core of his being.'

Recording studios are inherently stressful places, cocoons fuelled by artificial light and air where the body's natural rhythms soon become reversed and daylight, unless it is dawn, becomes an enemy. Mutt Lange has a unique reputation in the business for remaining calm and composed. He is an ascetic amidst excess, a monk amongst the mayhem. Those who have worked with him knew he was a vegetarian, an exercise fiend, who did not drink alcohol, smoke or take drugs. Most did not inquire further, and Mutt never volunteered much. Steve Brown assumed that because he didn't eat eggs he must have an allergy to them; Mutt chose never to correct him. However, for those who are interested, Mutt Lange has a great impact on their lives . . . and not because of his musical abilities.

'Mutt has had a guru in India for thirty years to whom he has always been very spiritually devoted,' says Ralph Simon. 'He never did want to be in the limelight. Sometimes it's almost as if he is using his spiritual path to take him through to the end result. For him the path he follows is in trying to construct some kind of 'happiness shrapnel', musical pieces that have an enormous impact globally. The impact of his songs is far greater than [that of] many political leaders.'

He does not preach or proselytize but leads by example. It is hard to find anybody who will say a bad, or indeed, any, word about him. The word friends, and ex-wives, use to describe their feelings for him is inevitably the same: 'love'. He is, and wishes to remain, an intensely private person.

Bryan Adams has said a little. For years Bryan suffered with facial skin problems and he had given up eating red meat. Following Mutt's example, he stopped eating anything with a face: no chicken (or eggs), no fish . . . He also started to explore Lange's spiritual path. 'He improved my spiritual life. I'm not incredibly religious or spiritual, but I learnt a lot of ways from him, the laws of karma. I read books on his path and it's very interesting.'

It would be easy to dismiss this as another musician's fad, a twelve-step programme for the spiritually disenfranchised, except Mutt Lange has been following the same path since 1970. Even as a teenager at Belfast High he was interested in metaphysical matters. 'John had none of that anger you often get with teens,' says Johan du Plooy. 'He was so busy with sport and music that he didn't have time to be idle and angry. There were people who had that anger, but he was a gentle young guy, well liked and respectable.'

The catalyst was the arrival of a charismatic boy who lived in the Sudan, nicknamed 'the Camel'. 'The extent of my faith at the time was, if you were nice to Granny, kind to the cat then you'd go to heaven and here was this young guy who actually believed, really believed. It was the first time we'd ever really been exposed to Christianity. We got a group together, John, me and a guy named Spooky – David Sphour. We'd spend weekends at Spooky's farm outside of Belfast, have these heavy discussions about religion and play with his monkey, which would run up if you put sugar in the tea cup. John was a very strong Christian at the time when we were being exposed to different philosophies. There weren't many of us and the rest of the school ignored it completely. How much it influenced his later life I don't know, but it certainly did mine.'

The second and most radical stage of Mutt's spiritual development happened in 1970, when he was living in the farmhouse with Geoff Williams and Steve McNamara. 'Hocus had a recess over a long weekend and the three of us went our separate ways to catch up on personal things,' says Geoff. 'It was over that weekend that Steve was exposed to the path. On his return, he told us all about this Eastern philosophy. It was very strict: no stimulant substances, no alcohol, not eating anything living at all. Fish, eggs, both would be the taking of a life. Mutt and I were a bit sceptical, but we all had a live-and-let-live attitude.'

Mutt didn't follow McNamara immediately, for he is a man who takes his time before committing himself to a cause. When he did at the end of the year, he did so absolutely. 'Mutt is an all-or-nothing guy,' says Williams. 'He does not profess to be something and then have a T-bone steak for his birthday. I would put money on it that Mutt has not had a drop of alcohol in the last thirty years. It didn't cause any open friction or animosity, everybody was most tolerant. Mutt is very private and once he decided it was right for him, he never tried to convert other people. He did pass the odd comment sometimes. If I was cooking a piece of steak in the pan he might walk past and go "moo".'

The path that Mutt follows is called Radhasoami Satsang. It was founded by Shiv Dayal Singh in the Punjab in 1861, a breakaway from Sikhism, which was in a state of turmoil after the Sikh kingdom had been defeated by the British. Sikhism, too, had been born during a time of chaos. In the early sixteenth century, as the Muslims were establishing military supremacy in northern India, Nanak, the son of a Hindu merchant in Lahore had a vision of God's presence while bathing in a river. According to legend, after a full day of silence, he pronounced, 'There is no Hindu and no Musselman (Muslim).' Shrewdly he adopted a unique garb which combined both Hindu and Muslim features, notably the turban. The faith he developed was eclectic, stressing the unity of God and the brotherhood of man. From Islam came the concept of a single Creator, called the True Name, and the futility of idol worship. From Hinduism he took the ideas of karma, reincarnation and the ultimate unreality of the world, while utterly rejecting the caste system. Sikhs believe spiritual release can only be obtained by taming the ego through devotional singing, constant recitation of the divine name, meditation and service. Nanak also emphasized the unique role of the guru (teacher) as essential in leading people to find God.

Nanak was succeeded by nine further gurus, the tenth of whom, Gobind Singh, turned his teachings on their head. In 1699, he founded the Khalsa, the Community of the Pure, and turned the Sikhs into warrior priests. After Gobind Singh's assassination, the *Adi Granth* (the collected writings of Nanak) was declared to be the guru. No further human gurus were allowed. As warriors the Sikhs fought the Muslims, eventually ruling most of the Punjab before losing two wars to the British.

Radhasoami Satsang went back to the earliest tenets of Sikhism – vegetarianism, abstinence from stimulants and repeating the name of God – and the teachings of medieval, often rebel and unorthodox, Indian 'saints'. Primarily it was a modern manifestation of Sant Mat (Path of the Masters), a philosophical school which some claim dates back to the dawn of recorded history and which stresses the importance of listening to inner sound. Most radically it was led by a 'living' guru, as practitioners are initiated by a master who has reputedly already made the inner journey.

The idea of the path of sound and light is universal. Versions can be found in many of the world's major religions, including Christianity – it is referred to in St John's Gospel. Sant Mat practitioners try to merge their soul with a 'true' and 'pure' God, minus the beliefs, practices and rules that make up most organized religions. They believe it to be a scientific method of entering the kingdom of heaven while living in the here and now. They hate being described as a 'religion' or even worse a 'cult'.

The meditation technique requires acute concentration on a point behind and between the eyebrows, called the ajna chakra ('seat of the soul'), which acts as a gateway into the human soul. The senses are withdrawn and 'collected' at this point. At worst, practitioners claim that this meditation clears up the clutter of everyday life; at best, it leads to contact with the true God and a finding of the true self, which in turn leads to wisdom, unconditional love, fearlessness, connectedness, bliss and spiritual immortality. (And in Mutt Lange's case marriage to one of the most desired women on the planet and a fortune running into hundreds of millions).

Radhasoami Satsang came to the West in the early twentieth century. Kirpal Singh was the first Sant (Perfect Living Master) to visit the United States in 1955 and later founded his own independent organization, Ruhani Satsang. It is now known as the Science of Spirituality/Sawan Kirpal Ruhani Mission, whose current head is Rajinder Singh, who was an electronic engineer and researcher at AT&T until he was selected as the organization's new leader by his own spiritual teacher, Darshan Singh. Unlike many similar sects it does not encourage active recruitment and proselytization. As Mutt did, people discover it through word of mouth or educational seminars publicized on the alternative spirituality circuit.

While a person's religion should be allowed to remain a private matter, the problem is that, when Shiv Dayal Singh announced that there were once more living gurus, he declared open season. Anybody with a few acolytes could be anointed a guru and command absolute obedience from their followers. Scattered around the world there are currently over one hundred different groups that follow parts of the Radhasoami tradition.

In 2000, tabloid newspapers in America and Britain attempted to link Mutt and Shania with a controversial Sant Mat offshoot led by Thakar Singh, which has many followers in Germany and Switzerland. While Thakar claims to follow the path of Kirpal Singh, he split from Kirpal's designated successor, Darshan Singh (whom Mutt continued to follow), in the late 70s and set up his own sect.

Mutt Lange is not a follower of Thakar Singh. He meditates and exercises regularly, sticks to his vegetarian diet, eschews alcohol and drugs. He may have practised sexual abstinence in the past but he has also been married three times with various girlfriends in between. 'I never heard Olga complain about that,' laughs Alison Green. 'If they had no sex, it was because Mutt was never home.' While there is a delicious irony in the idea of the man married to an international sex symbol refraining from sex with her, both his and Shania's friends always laughed at the idea that their relationship was platonic long before they learnt she was pregnant.

There must also be a shadow cast by Mutt's beliefs. He may be gentle and charming but by his very nature he is a controller. People who are drawn to him are then attracted by his beliefs. Both Mary Bailey and Shania now follow the same path.

Just because he does not appear to have any enemies in a business that enjoys enmity does not mean Lange is a pushover. 'Mutt was never a guy to suffer fools, he wasn't a guy to suck up,' says Alison Green. 'He picked business managers who were really tough and totally insulated him from anything he didn't want to deal with. One way he could stay really nice was by putting up this protective zone. Clive Calder was tough . . . like steel would break on that guy. Mutt was his cash cow and Clive wasn't letting anyone interfere with that relationship. Clive took care of business beautifully and Mutt did what Mutt wanted, which was to create with absolutely no interference . . . and they all got exceedingly rich.'

It is much easier to be a nice guy if you have one of the record industry's hard men in your corner. Mutt continues to be represented by Zomba, headed by Clive Calder, a notoriously tough negotiator who gives no quarter in his deals. 'He's legendary for being hard,' British record company executive Dave Bates, who has known Calder for over twenty-five years, told *Billboard*. 'Some people might say he's too hard, but it's his money, his expertise and their choice. If you get involved with Clive and he really believes in you, you've got every chance of success. He's not a charity; he's a business that happens to work in music.'

Mutt's exact relationship with the Zomba group is a source of much speculation. Because it is a private company, nobody knows who has a piece of it. Industry observers are convinced that Mutt must own a percentage of a corporation he has done so much to build. Ralph Simon, who surely knew when he split with Calder in 1990, is non-committal, saying, 'I think it extremely unlikely that Calder would give Mutt any interest in the Zomba structure.'

In 1993, Mutt Lange was one of the most private, but most powerful, men in the music business, with fast-track access to all the movers and shakers who mattered and quite capable of using his clout to get his own way. He was quite prepared to give Shania Twain what she had always wanted, but much of it, initially, would have to be on his terms.

CHAPTER FIFTEEN

Enter Prince Charming

The legend is simple. It was a *coup de foudre*, love at first digital glimpse. Mutt saw Shania's video and fell in love with her. He knew he had to have her, so he pursued her until he did. In riding to the rescue, Prince Charming turned her career from squatting in the basement to owning the castle.

When he was working in his studio, Mutt liked to watch Country Music Television and saw Shania's video. Shania says they met because, 'David Rose who worked at A&M in London would give Mutt new stuff coming in and my CD and video package was one of them. Mutt was very intrigued. He loved my voice, loved my story, he liked my video too, but more than anything my story drew him to me.' Everything about the clip that had upset the programmers in the States had the opposite effect on Lange. He fell for Shania big-time and when he subsequently listened to the album, he felt she was a major talent.

He was certainly struck enough to set about breaking his cardinal patterns. Mutt, who had not worked with a woman singer successfully since Jessica Jones, actively set out to pursue an unknown artist. He hadn't done that for years. He hadn't broken a new act since Def Leppard. As one of the top producers on the planet, with combined album sales well over the 100 million mark, he commanded a royalty of five per cent and an advance running into six figures. Only established acts could afford him. Nashville was probably the only recording centre in the world where his name meant next to nothing. The first time he called and spoke to Mary Bailey, she thought he was an over-enthusiastic fan.

'It came through a business source that there was a fellow who wanted an autograph, and so we signed a picture,' chuckles Mary.

Shania signed it but left the 'e' off Lange. Over in England Mutt called the office and went into charm offensive. 'I got a phone call from Mutt. I knew he had something to do with the music business but I had no idea he was a producer, I just thought he was a guy with a strange name. Anyway, I had a conversation and he was just so wonderful to talk to. We started conversing back and forth and it was quite a while before I got Eilleen and Mutt to actually have a conversation. I kept saying to Eilleen, "You have to phone this guy," and she was saying, "Later, I'll get around to it." '

The clincher came when Mary mentioned to Luke Lewis that this English man was calling up and seemed interested in Shania. Lewis, one of the few people in town who knew just how important Lange was, was gobsmacked. When Shania eventually phoned him from her apartment, she had no idea who he was, just this Brit Mary was insisting she talk to. His first question to her was: 'Do you write?' This sounded great, because she was fed up with fighting the Nashville system of getting as many different songwriters on an album as possible – lots of pie for everyone.

'Yes,' she replied hesitantly.

'Can I hear something?'

'OK,' she said, 'I'll send you a tape.'

'No,' came the firm reply, 'I want to hear something right now, sing some stuff for me.'

Bizarre though the request sounded, it was music to her ears. None of this 'Let's schedule a songwriting session a week on Tuesday.' This was organic, a creative spark from a guy 6,500 kilometres away. Shania propped the phone receiver on the cushion of her couch, pulled out her guitar and started playing songs, her songs. She played 'Raining on Our Love' and 'Whose Bed Have Your Boots Been Under?', 'That Man of Mine' and 'Home Ain't Where His Heart Is (Anymore)'. Each time she finished, she waited for his response; each time he said he loved it and asked why it had not been recorded. Playfully she asked what he was working on, and so he sang her what was to become Michael Bolton's 'Said I Loved You . . . But I Lied'.

Everything Mutt said was what she wanted to hear. He praised her voice but obliquely criticized her first album. 'The way you're singing right now,' he said, 'even though it's over the phone, that's the voice I've heard bits and pieces of. That's how you should be sounding all the time. If you're doing your own stuff, you'll be able to get that.'

By the end of that first conversation they agreed to start writing songs together, sending packages back and forth by Federal Express, singing and chatting over the phone. 'I didn't know who he was,' insisted Shania, 'just this guy with a weird name. I trusted him because he played me some music of his on the phone: there was a musical trust and a bond there before anything else. I love our relationship and the way it all started, it was so real, based on no inhibitions. I was not intimidated by who he was.'

At the time Lange was recording with Michael Bolton and writing with Bryan Adams. Bolton recalls, 'I had never seen Mutt like that before. He was as focused on Shania as he was on his work. He just had an instinct that she was it for him.' When Mutt learnt that Shania would be appearing at Fan Fair in June, he convinced Adams, who loathes country music, to make the trip to Nashville with him. He told Shania he was thinking of coming down 'with Bryan' and asked, 'Why don't you come and meet me?'

'He figures I know who he's talking about,' said Shania, 'then he starts talking about things, referring to Bryan Adams' music, and I said "Can you hold on a second?", went over to the record collection and I had bought *Waking Up the Neighbours*. I pulled it out and there is his name on the back. I didn't say anything, acted like I'd known all the time, but I was so embarrassed.'

The International Country Music Fan Fair convention takes place every June in the Tennessee State Fairgrounds. It is unique in the music industry in that it allows 25,000 fans an opportunity to actually meet, chat, collect autographs and maybe even have photos taken with their favourite stars. There are parties galore and concerts in which even the biggest names perform a few numbers. The price the fans have to pay is hours queuing for everything from autographs to food and toilets as well as sky-high souvenir prices. For record companies it is a cost-efficient way of introducing new acts to a committed audience.

Nobody paid much attention to Shania Twain at Fan Fair '93. Her record company were far more interested in Billy Ray Cyrus, whose cloying, irritating but infectious 'Achy Breaky Heart' had become an international hit. Until Mutt Lange turned up backstage with Bryan Adams. As Adams was pumping the flesh, Mutt, who is uncomfortable with such things, shrank into the canvas. His eyes kept searching the crowd looking for one person. Shania came in and had Mutt pointed out to her. He was not what she expected: 'Tall, thin, blue eyes, blond with long curly hair, so neat looking.'

Shania is not physically spontaneous – 'I'm not a huggy-touchy person, which in America can be seen as quite odd' – but the moment she saw him, she ran straight over and hugged him, enveloping him in a cloak of her arms as if she had recognized the missing part of her soul and was not prepared to let it go again ever. Giddy, she rushed over to Mary saying, 'Come here, come here, this is Mutt.' Mary, too, was captivated. So were Mercury, once they realized that Mutt was serious about working with Shania and indeed that he was going to stay in Nashville and write with her for the next two weeks.

By that point Mutt's interest in Shania was more than just a professional crush. He was seriously smitten. Sitting in the back of the limo taking Bryan and him back from Fan Fair, he raved about her. The problem, he told Bryan again and again, was that she had a fiancé.

'I can see that might be a problem,' said Adams drily. 'Let's see. On the one hand . . . carpenter. On the other hand . . . world-famous record producer. World-famous record producer. Carpenter. Yes . . . tough call.'

Shania was smitten in a different way. She maintains that she had no romantic interest in Mutt before they met – 'I didn't expect him to look the way he does,' she admits. 'I thought he was fat, I pictured him as this workaholic, I figured he probably sat down all the time, an overweight guy with long greying black hair in a ponytail.' But he had already reached her in a way Paul never could. Music had always been, will always be, more important to her than sex. 'I didn't fall in love right off the bat, it took about . . . a month,' she laughs. Those first weeks in Nashville, they didn't do much writing, just swapped stories and laughed a lot. For Shania it was a revelation. She had never met a man like him before. Here was this guy, OK, so he was older and he was rich and powerful, but she already knew people like that and how to play them. But she couldn't play Mutt, because he wouldn't respond. Instead, he teased her just like Jerry used to, christened her 'Woody' because 'I had short bangs when I met him and he thought I looked like Woody Woodpecker.'

Just as he had with Bryan Adams, Mutt turned the way Shania thought about her songs upside-down and round about, made her look at them in a brand new way. First he told her, 'We need to go into your catalogue. I want to know what you've been writing, then we'll go from there.' He showed her how verses could become choruses, choruses become hooks. He told her, 'No that lyric's not quite there yet.' Her lyrics moved from the generic to the personal. Instead of resorting to cliché, she came over sassy, teasing but self-contained and strong – the antithesis of the Nashville woman in song but spot-on in terms of 90s reality. Mutt believed that titles were essential; they could colour the flavour of the song, that one word can make a difference. Changing 'That Man of Mine' to 'Any Man of Mine' altered the entire sexual dynamic. The singer was now in control, no longer passive. So simple to see. So difficult to do.

Mary Bailey describes Mutt as 'a gentle soul' and you don't get many of them in the music business. He was so calm, so comfortable, at ease with himself, but there was nothing weak about him, nothing that could be pushed aside like yesterday's man. The absolute calm he radiated came from power. Shania knew, as women always do, that he was attracted to her, but he didn't make any sudden lunges, or indeed any sexual moves at all. Men had never done that to Shania, so it intrigued her all the more. She connected with Mutt on non-physical planes, musical and spiritual. It sounds trite, but sex was irrelevant.

'No, I wasn't surprised when they became romantically involved,' says

Mary. 'Because they were so compatible artistically. With Mutt, his personality, his kindness and his warmth, it was probably a very natural progression. So it didn't surprise me and I don't think it did change the basis of our relationship.'

Others might disagree. Along with an intense love, Mutt brought the ability to make things happen. Not just total financial security for several lifetimes but serious business connections. Access to the best studios, to the best musicians, the best lawyers. Fine, Jive were not going to take over her contract as their expertise was in teen pop and rap/R&B, but they knew all the people who could make things happen outside of the country market.

What moved Mutt and Shania from the professional to the personal was a writing trip they took to Europe. He suggested she come over on Concorde, but Shania had never heard of it, did not know there was such a thing as a supersonic airliner. They disappeared inside his home to write and then travelled on to Spain, Italy and Paris. 'We pretty much wrote almost all of the album before we even revealed our feelings to each other at all. Which wasn't long,' said Shania, 'I've always been that way. I've never, ever, ever let a guy know the way I felt about him until I know. Because I'm just never a fool for that. I don't know whether I'm just really old-fashioned that way or what. But I just always felt there's no point making a fool of yourself.'

Shania has said repeatedly, 'We were meant to be together,' but the actual moment of revelation came one day in Spain. 'We just hugged. We'd hugged before. I mean, goodbye, at the airport. But that time we didn't let go for the longest time. It was so intensive I thought: "I really don't want to let go of this person." At that moment we knew we had a lot to talk about.'

'It wasn't a kiss. It wasn't like a very sexual moment or a passionate moment, it wasn't. It was a very sweet, honest moment.' For Shania that was it. From that moment on it was all cut and dried. 'Looking at him the day I fell in love and looking at him the day before? Two different things.'

Before she could commit to Mutt, she had to tidy up a few loose ends. One of whom was her fiancé. Unable to find regular work in Nashville, Paul Bolduc had returned to Timmins. In August, Shania went up for a visit and broke it off. Paul was very upset but he knew that to Shania the music had always and would always come first. He could not compete. 'They split up, stayed friends, and he understood,' says Helene Bolduc. 'Not because he wanted it, of course, it's always hard to go through leaving somebody you've been with, but he totally understood the love she had for the music and he had a lot to learn about it. He couldn't do what this guy [Mutt] could, and she loved to be with the person that just heard and saw her for what she was.'

After Paul and Eileen split, Dean Malton used to see him at the Cottage, a bar in Huntsville. 'He didn't show if he was upset. He didn't run away from Huntsville, go hide anywhere. He was back in town doing his thing, and hanging out on weekends in the bar. Paul had a good circle of friends, and being a very good-looking guy, he moved on relatively quickly.'

For Paul the wounds were still raw on 21 September when Shania came back to Timmins to play a gig in a gymnasium of Ecole Secondaire Theriault (the French High right next door to her Alma Mater). Mutt came along to mix the sound. For Timmins the show was a major deal. 'We were so proud that someone actually had an album out on a major label and they would come back and play,' says John Emms, who reviewed the show for the Timmins *Daily Press*. To Emms' ears the band were not up to scratch, better than Longshot but nowhere near the standard of platinum Canadian artists like Tom Cochrane or Bruce Cockburn. (Mysteriously the first four paragraphs of his review were never published.) It must have felt the same to both Shania and Mutt. Aside from TV appearances and a handful of showcases, she did not give another live concert for almost five years.

'We were all hoping for the best, but for the first few songs Shania was beside herself with nerves,' says Emms. 'I could hear the mistakes, I could hear the fluffs. But once the nerves went, she was out front and she was shaking it. In the end it was triumphant and everyone was ecstatic. Even though the band didn't play that well, it was a wonderful evening, everyone was happy.'

Once she had relaxed, Shania remembered where she was. In Timmins she was still Eilleen, who had nothing to prove. Graciously she announced, 'I'm always going to be grateful to J. P. Aube for giving me the opportunity to have my first professional job at the Escapade Hotel.' The crowd cheered, J. P. squirmed in his seat with pleasure.

After the show J. P. and his wife hosted a party for the band at their house. When Mutt arrived, he promptly took his shoes off at the door, very much the custom in northern Ontario. He charmed Charmaine by immediately noticing and then asking informed questions about her collection of abstract paintings. 'Mutt is a very interesting guy, very calm, a person with no airs and no pretensions, very sincere, attentive and considerate,' says J. P. 'It was just before they got married and they were very comfortable with each other.'

Six weeks later, soon after they arrived in Paris, Mutt proposed to Shania on bended knee, presenting her with a 2.5 carat ring. 'I knew it was coming,' said Shania later, 'because he had invited my sisters along.' Jill and Carrie Ann were worried, telling her, 'You just met this guy, you can't get married.' It was so out of character for their cool, calculating sister. She was the one who always looked but never leapt, the one who kept her head when all around were swooning. Mutt was the only man she'd ever been with who was more centred than she was. Although he only influenced by example, they could see subtle changes in her. Doubtless, as family members always are when confronted with the whiff of cult, they were concerned about his allegiance to Sant Mat. However, they soon realised it was no danger and on the plus side he was good-looking, charming and fabulously wealthy, so maybe Leeni had finally met her true match . . . and anyway it would take a meteorite strike to change her focus.

Shania and Mutt were married at Deerhurst on 28 December 1993. It was a small ceremony, family and close friends only. Helene and Larry Bolduc were invited, but chose not to attend. 'I did it for Paul, I didn't want to hurt his feelings, I knew he still cared more than just being friends with her,' says Helene. 'Everything was really fresh, and still a little bit raw. Eilleen understood my position very well. She said, "I would love to have you there, I will miss you if you're not there, but it's up to you." I thought of her all day.'

It was a formal affair. The bride wore white, a low-cut dress with a halter top, long white gloves stretching above the elbow and a floor-length train from the floral band in her hair. Mutt, a good head taller than his new bride, wore a tuxedo with a traditional pleated shirt complete with wing collar and studs; his hair was on his shoulders and he had a pair of white roses in his buttonhole. Jill's daughter Mandy was the maid of honour and her little brother Jarret the ring bearer. The wedding cake was a classic three-tier affair, and the picture of them cutting it shows Mutt beaming out to the world while his new bride looks up at her Prince Charming in absolute adoration. Those watching remarked that they had never seen Eilleen look so happy.

For the first time in her life Eilleen Twain understood what it meant to be free of financial worries. She could, perhaps, have let her dreams pass on down the river, but she still believed, as she always has, in her destiny. She had always accepted without qualm if people wished to invest their money in her talent, for that was her due, but the idea of being a kept woman filled her with horror. More than ever she was determined to play the new hand she had been dealt, to break the bank and to prove the doubters wrong.

For their honeymoon the Langes set about recording the most expensive album in the history of Nashville.

CHAPTER SIXTEEN

The Great Nashville Bank Robbery

Although other Nashville folk have their doubts, Mary Bailey insists that Mercury would have made a second album with Shania whatever. She does admit: 'Having a proven producer with an unbelievable track record, who's expressed interest in a new talent, absolutely brought credibility to the team. I was very comfortable with Eilleen being with him, knowing that they started writing with a purpose, a purpose of an album. As a manager I'm totally going to support that. Number two, it allowed her the opportunity of being relaxed and finally having someone who was on the same wavelength. For me it was finding someone who believed in her as much as I did.'

Luke Lewis was ecstatic at the idea of a Lange/Twain collaboration from the get go. 'I was completely out of my mind excited about it,' he says. 'The guy had written a zillion killer songs. I came from a rock and roll space and it didn't scare me. Our initial conversations were about the budget, because he was wanting to spend – for what was going on here at the time – an extraordinary amount of money on the record.'

The average budget for a Nashville album was $125–150,000 and Mutt hadn't done anything that cheap since 1976. Despite his track record, he had never made a country hit. The simmering differences between Shedd and Lewis boiled over into war. Shedd liked to point out that Billy Ray Cyrus' debut (admittedly recorded with his backing band) had only cost $65,000, and the figures that were being batted about for Shania were closer to $400,000.

'Harold didn't want to do the album, I mean at all,' says Luke, 'didn't want to sign off on the budget. I was working in this precarious position with him with my bosses trying to keep us at peace with each other. We were at each other's throats, we had completely different philosophies. Not to slight Harold, but he didn't get Shania. To my mind Norro Wilson and Buddy Cannon – who doesn't get enough credit around here at all – those were the guys who heard something special in her voice and personality.'

Mutt, doubtless after much consultation with Clive Calder and Steven Howard at Zomba, solved the problem by making Lewis an offer he would be daft to refuse. 'Mutt said he would cover everything over 200 grand,' says Lewis. Him and her – she was definitely involved – made a really righteous move which took me out of the line of fire politically, allowed them to do it, and spoke to their own belief in what they were doing.' Those who know Zomba's deals doubt that Mutt would have financed the recording out of his own pocket unless he got a higher royalty than his usual five per cent. He probably ended up with six to seven per cent rising with increased sales. The cost of *The Woman in Me* has been variously estimated as anywhere up to a million dollars, though it's eventual cost was closer to $750,000. If Mutt had been charging his full commercial rate, it would have been far higher.

It was a masterstroke, in one move sidelining old Nashville, while ensuring that the new guy, Lewis, was utterly committed to the project. He had to make it happen. Provided, of course, that Mutt and Shania came up with a half-way decent record. *The Woman in Me* was much, much better than that.

'Mutt Lange studies whatever he's going to go after,' grins session drummer Paul Leim. 'He was coming into town for the first time, and he knew every musician he wanted, just like the notes he wanted and the licks he heard. This was like a bank robbery, planned from the very beginning. He came to Nashville, robbed the bank and took all the money. It was great.'

Paul Leim is the only musician to have played on the first three Shania Twain albums. He played on about half of the first album, all of *The Woman in Me* and for *Come On Over* was promoted to be session leader. 'On the first record she was another hopeful. She's a beautiful young woman, but it wasn't quite different enough to me,' recalls Leim, who had relocated from LA in 1989. 'The tunes that they had were good songs, and they could or could not have been a hit on anybody, and they just happened to not be on her. The most successful artists I've worked with,' like Lionel Richie and Amy Grant, who have been the most focused on what it is they're doing, are the ones that write their own material. When it starts coming from the heart, that's when it really starts making a difference.'

In LA Leim was used to working with producers who thought nothing of spending three days to get a single part sounding right. In Nashville, due to a combination of budget and tradition, the emphasis was on speed and feel. Top session musicians were given their head. 'Normally we make up our own parts,' says Joe Chemay, who played bass on *Come On Over*. 'We make a living being spontaneous, throwing ideas out constantly. We listen to something, everybody just goes on and plays it, everybody listens to each other and you just go on until the producer is satisfied. Then in the mix the producer would discard what he did not want.'

What Mutt required was the opposite. As a sonic architect he carried the complete picture for every song in his head but required the players to listen to everybody else, so that the songs are interwoven from the roots up. 'If this was 100 years ago, Mutt Lange would be Beethoven,' says Leim shaking his head with admiration. 'He hears it all in his head, he hears every guitar, he hears every bass note, every vocal. He is the one responsible for making hit songs, regardless of what it takes. It doesn't matter if it takes a day, an hour or a week.'

For the *Woman in Me* sessions at Sound Stage Studios Mutt set aside one full day for each backing track – a long time by Nashville standards, where session musicians expect to lay down three tracks a day. After he had finished his eleven days with Shania, Leim went back to Sound Stage to record with Linda Davis. During a break he popped in to see how Mutt was getting on. Mutt asked him, 'So what have you got done?'

'Oh, we got one,' replied the drummer.

'You've got one what?'

'We've got a track'.

'It's only 11.30 in the morning,' exclaimed Lange. 'How do you do that? How can you get what you want in that amount of time?'

(The answer is that John Guess, the highly successful producer of Davis' album *Shoot for the Moon*, had a different approach. The album came out in 1994, a year ahead of Shania's. It was a good record, full of sharp, questioning songs, but it did not even go gold. *The Woman in Me* sold 12 million.)

Mutt had already done his research. When the session leader, guitarist Larry Byrom (once of Steppenwolf), recommended the best players in town, Mutt knew the names and work of everyone suggested and many of those he finally chose – like Leim – had experience playing pop. Bassist Dave Hungate was a founder member of the million-selling corporate rockers Toto, pianist Matt Rollings had played with Lyle Lovett, and guitarist Dann Huff had almost cracked it with country rock band Giant. On top of that pop-flavoured rhythm section Mutt added the solid country roots of guitarists Brent Rowan and Brent Mason, fiddlers Joe Spivey and Rob Hajacos, while much of the pedal steel work came from John Hughey. Hughey is a legend in his own right, having given Conway Twitty's songs their distinctive sound and toured with Loretta Lynn and Vince Gill.

Sessions began every day at 10 a.m. Mutt assembled his core musicians, played them his demo and discussed what he wanted. Sometimes, if he needed early input, he telephoned and played ideas over the phone. (Leim recalls: 'The first time I ever heard the line "when I have a bad hair day" [from "Any Man of Mine"] was Mutt singing to me over the telephone from England. He was concerned, asking me, "What do you think of that line?" ') In the studio those musicians who used charts made notes. During the first run-throughs, he might ask the electric and acoustic guitars to play specific figures, get the bass and drums to play exactly the way he wanted. Moving on to the verse, he would stop and start, then explain in specific terms the way he wanted it. Once the basic track was down the real work began. Replacing everything.'

For Mutt everything starts from drums and bass. So Leim went back into the studio until the drum track was spot-on, while the other musicians rehearsed their parts. That might take until 8 p.m. When the bass part was being replaced, the bass player listened only to the drum track. 'Mutt's specific all the way down to when the bass cuts off. The bass should not be playing when the snare drum is hitting. We are talking in terms of milliseconds but it cleans up the track.' That attention to detail was carried on to every aspect of the recording process.

In the studio Mutt has no sense of time passing; he is so focused he doesn't know if it's ten in the morning or ten at night. It nearly finished off fiddle player Rob Hajacos during 'If It Don't Take Two'. Mutt had him in the studio for two hours, correcting everything. The third F beat of the second bar on the first verse, the second upbeat of the eighth bar, he knew each one, had it marked in his mind, and knew when it was right. During one break, Mutt heard a groan from the studio and asked offhandedly, 'Is there anything else?' Rob replied, 'Have you ever stood for two and half hours and held a fiddle under your neck? I can't move my head.' Mutt was horrified and immediately called a break, asking Rob, 'Can we get you something to eat, can we get you a drink . . .?'

Like film directors, record producers can all too easily become tyrants. Not all the musicians, used to the easy-going approach of Nashville producers, could cope with Mutt's demands. In Music City they call it 'burning the bees'. Says Leim, who was used to such demands in LA, 'With Lionel Richie we cut "Truly" for three days, and "Stuck on You" for three days. And to me "Stuck on You" sounded the same three days later as it did the first time we ran it down. But they'd heard something else and it was my job to get whatever it is they wanted. Some of the guys from here said, "I just can't take that pace, I can't do it over and over and over again, it's done." I'm sorry but if the guys were getting frustrated because he sees the vision and they're not able to capture that, then they are in the wrong.'

Mutt never raised his voice, he was always reasonable, polite and nice with it. He could always coax one more performance out of his musicians, saying to Leim, 'That was a wonderful performance, that was great, but can we do it one more time and just keep the hi-hat closed just a little bit?'

'That's why I'm saying he heard everything in his head,' says the drummer, 'and if anything distracted him away from what he wanted to hear at that time, he noticed. If you listen to his records, if you listen very specifically, you will hear a fiddle for a second, then it will go away, and then all of a sudden there's a line on an acoustic guitar, and then that would go away, and it will be this Duane Eddy electric guitar part. And then that will go away and go back to the fiddle.'

'(If You're Not in It for Love) I'm Outta Here!' begins with a scream of sheer frustration. Legend has it that it was Leim brought to the end of his tether by Mutt's demands. Not so, he laughs, 'Larry Byrom was supposed to start the song with the guitar riff and kept trying to get it right. He would stop, and say, "Wait a second, here we go." I'm trying to keep the energy going and when you concentrate that hard you're totally focused and he stops again . . . and again. I was like, "We've got to do this, we've got to do this now!" I just lost it, I screamed "aaargh." So then I went "three, four, five," I don't even know why I started on three . . . so Larry started at that count of five when there's not five beats in a bar anyway. And Mutt left that on the record!' At the end of 'No One Needs to Know' Leim quipped 'Here's your record, boss.' Mutt left that on too.

'My family is Leim, it's German, right?' says Leim. 'Mutt paid me the biggest compliment I've ever had. I'm not patting myself on the back. We cut this track and he said, "Bloody amazing," and I went, "What?" and he was just listening down the drums, he said, "German precision and American feel." He couldn't have said anything that made me feel any better than that, it was awesome. He made me feel like a million bucks, he's a wonderful guy. And a lot of rock producers, and pop artists I worked with in the 80s – whose names will remain unmentioned – are not nice at all.'

✶ Shania has always been at her most comfortable when dressed in jeans and cowboy boots. Also taken from the photo session to accompany the Harry Hinde album. (*Denise Grant*)

✶ The original cover for Shania's first album was shot outside Timmins in the winter of 1993 with Cane the timber wolf. Her buckskin jacket is now on permanent display at the Shania Twain Center in Timmins. (*Mercury Records*)

✶ Frolicking in the snow in 1993. (*CMT Europe*)

✳ Mutt Lange in his band Hocus in South Africa in 1971. Clockwise from top left: Alan Goldswain, Geoff Williams, Mutt Lange, Stevie van Kerken, Steve McNamara. (*Geoff Williams*)

✳ Shania and Mutt cut the cake at their wedding. (*American Media Inc.*)

✳ The Queen of Country meets the Prince of Wales at Party in the Park, 5 July 1998. Shania's stage clothes were still being fitted in the car. (*The Press Association Ltd*)

✷ A star performance at Party in the Park, 1998. Shania always insists on playing guitar on at least one number. (*Tim Auger/Retna*)

✳ Shania with braids performing at Reunion Arena, Dallas, on 12 September 1998. (*Neal Preston/Retna*)

✳ Shania in her trademark leopardskin at the CMA Awards 1999. (*John Kelly/Retna*)

✱ In order to help break *Come On Over* in Europe, Shania's image changed radically. The denim country girl became an international sophisticate. (*Willy Camden/Mercury Records*)

✴ Reflecting on fame and showing a little leg. (*Willy Camden/Mercury Records*)

✱ Showing off her awards for Best Country Song ('You're Still the One') and Best Female Country Vocal Performance at the 41st Grammy Awards on 24 February 1999. (*Steve Granitz/Retna*)

✱ Shania the rock goddess performing in New York. (*Ebet Roberts/Redferns*)

✴ Mutt Lange hates having his photo taken. He and Shania were snapped leaving a performance of *Swan Lake* in London in 2000. (*Big Pictures*)

✴ The 'Man! I Feel Like a Woman' video shoot and Revlon ad campaign, 1999. (*CMT*)

While it was the Mutt Lange Show, Shania had a tremendous amount of input, she was in the studio all day, every day, six days a week. There was no antsy behaviour, no disappearing off shopping or hanging around doing her make-up. She sang every pass every time, giving full-on guide vocals to every backing track. He treated her the same as every other musician, except occasionally when they got into arguments over vocal parts.

'I think you ought to sing it like this,' said Mutt, to which she might reply, 'Yes, but I feel that if the words are more intimate I ought to be more like this.' Then they would start what Leim calls this 'Oh honey thing . . . with Mutt saying, "Well, honey, I think it ought to be," or "Sweetkins, I think it ought to be" and "Sugar baby, why don't you try it like . . ." Mutt is very demanding at what he wants, but in such a gentlemanly fashion, you can't get mad at him.'

The final vocals were all recorded up at ARP Track Productions in St Anne des Lacs, near Montreal, Quebec. If Shania paints with words and melodies, Mutt paints with sound. He got to work, deconstructing every instrument on every track bar by bar and putting it back again triple-tracked, sonically enhanced. At one level it is a purely artificial construct but stitched back together and placed in its correct position in that extraordinary *mélange* that he calls a song it sounds anything but, Shania's albums crackle with an almost metaphysical energy, just as Michael Jackson's did when Quincy Jones was behind the control panel.

Each melodic hook was accentuated by leaving an infinitesimal space around it and every bass drum beat punched like Mike Tyson. All the vocals, but especially the harmonies, are classic Mutt, multi-layered so that it appears one voice is singing with the force of a choir of angels. He employed the same technique on the strings, stacking fiddles so they sounded both like a fuller, richer solo instrument and a full orchestra. Second-guessing the arrangement is as effective as bottling clouds – one moment there is a soaring pedal steel riff, and when you expect it to come again, he unleashes a guitar solo that would have a Def Leppard fan shaking his mane in approval.

The album was mixed at Le Studio in Morin Heights, Quebec. Tragically Le Studio's engineer Lynn Peterzell died of a heart attack soon after the record was finished in October 1994. When Mutt finally pronounced the record finished the Mercury Nashville execs flew in to listen to a playback. As dusk approached Shania covered up her nervousness in her usual way, she fired up a chainsaw, gathered enough logs and lit a roaring fire.

The Woman in Me was, still is, a ground-breaking album. That in itself was not enough. Every musical genre is full of great records that millions do not know exist. Some, like the extraordinary *The Velvet Underground and Nico*, initially reviled and a commercial disaster, hang around long enough to be regarded as among the most influential albums of all time. Country music has long had a habit of ignoring exquisite gems – Guy Clark's almost perfect *Old No. 1* and anything Gram Parsons ever recorded – because they were too different. In 1994, *The Woman in Me* sounded unlike anything else. And Mercury had to sell it. It was scary.

Internal reaction was not universally euphoric. 'I was taken aback,' admits John Grady. 'I knew it was tremendous music, I didn't know if it would fit. Fortunately I've had a history in the more successful companies I've worked for of having to deal with records that didn't fit.' The then head of promotion didn't hear it at all, and suggested to Lewis it needed to be sent back and remixed. Many of his staff were scared to death by it. 'We can't understand the record,' they whined, 'it's too pop, it's so obvious.' (In a sense they were right, because when Shania's songs were played on the radio they stood out a mile, popping, fizzing making other productions sound flat in comparison.) Lewis countered by hiring promo men who had worked pop radio.

Luke was convinced. When he called Alain Levy, the big boss at Polygram, and told him, 'I'm going to spend an out of the ordinary amount of money chasing this thing because I believe,' Levy, who had liked seeing 10 million Billy Ray Cyrus records come out of nowhere and who knew just what Mutt Lange could do, turned him loose. With a release date of 7 February 1995 there wasn't a lot of time to spare.

Most of the money went on radio promotion, with a disproportionate (for Nashville) amount on videos and photo sessions. Initially the marketing plan went badly awry.

The first hiccup occurred in Cowboys, a Nashville line-dancing club. At the time country dance clubs were really happening and the idea was to launch 'Any Man of Mine' through the clubs. Luke took a rough mix to the DJ at Cowboys and asked him to play it so he could gauge the reaction. It was a fiasco. 'I don't dance – not country dance – so I walked into it cold,' he laughs. 'The problem is in the way the song is structured. It starts out as a line-dance riff and then it turns into a two-step riff. People started the song doing a line-dance and then it runs into this two-step when you don't have a partner. What a dumb-ass thing. It wouldn't have occurred to me in a hundred years.'

It was decided to hold 'Any Man' and go with 'Whose Bed Have Your Boots Been Under?' ' "Boots" was a little more formatic and it didn't have that – "Pour Some Sugar on Me" guitar riff that made radio programmers crazy.' The first video, made in England, featuring a pair of animated boots, was too clever by half. The decision was made to junk it, and instead, Mary convinced Mercury to employ the services of a man who knew how to bring out the best in beautiful women.

As an actor, John Derek had enjoyed only fleeting success; as a lover, he had a far better track record, numbering Jane Fonda and Brigitte Bardot among his conquests and Linda Evans and Bo '10' Derek among his wives. Derek was an autocrat who knew what image he wanted to achieve and, like Mutt, he was married to a much younger woman. At their first meeting Derek took one look at Shania and announced, 'Somebody get me a knife. I've got to cut that nose off!' and wanted to back out of the project. Bo, who had bonded with Shania immediately, convinced him to come back on board.'

Derek took control, spiriting Shania to California to shoot on his property, where she did some very sexy photo sessions which were used to good effect. He stamped a specific image on the album cover artwork, and the Christmas promotional calendar that was sent out to radio stations, retailers and media. Mercury also used the shots in an advertisement in *Sports Illustrated's* college basketball preview issue, which, while it might not have been traditional country market, certainly raised more than flickers of interest.

John also shot the videos for both 'Boots' and 'Any Man of Mine'. Looking at them, it's hard to know what the fuss was about. Boots is set in a diner where Shania sashays around in a backless, clinging burgundy dress, flirting with a bunch of central casting rednecks, who ignore her. These scenes are cut with sequences of her playing a guitar and singing, wearing a sleeveless waistcoat that ends above her midriff. At no point can you see the tummy button that was about to become so famous a comic later quipped it should have its own agent.

'Any Man of Mine' really caught the imagination. The scenes of Shania in a field wearing tight jeans and a blatantly bare midriff were shot separately by director Charley Rendazzo and spliced together with Derek's sequences that showed Shania metamorphosing from cowgirl to society sophisticate. Again scarcely taboo-shattering . . . but very sexy.

Shania called the shots in terms of what she wanted to wear and how she wanted to be presented physically. 'For the country music image, it was definitely different and sexier. I came to Nashville with a certain amount of naivety,' said Shania. Being Canadian, she was more aware that there was life outside country. Back home she had watched *Much Music*, listened to other musical genres and took all that into account. 'I wasn't really aware that I was being that controversial, until people started to say "Your image is too sexy," and that I was going to be intimidating to women. I said, "Are you crazy! Everybody shows their midriff, just relax." I'm young I want to enjoy that, I'm a woman and I want to enjoy it now while I can. I was just lucky that somehow it clicked and it worked.'

If Shania knew exactly what she was doing, there was still that risk that CMT might simply ignore her. They tried. Says Lewis, 'I never had a moment when I choked and thought, put on some clothes, girl. It did occur to CMT, I hate to bash them but the truth is they had a committee out there that decided that her videos were . . . not suitable.

They can absolutely take no credit for breaking Shania Twain, they were not supportive. OK, they have been since – but at the beginning it was pulling teeth, one of the biggest pockets of resistance we ever met. It was frustrating they were playing everything and suddenly went shy on us.'

While MTV and VH-1 had a radical effect on rock and pop music, CMT and TNN have been much less influential on country music sales. 'There's a lot of people in this community,' agrees Retta Harvey, 'who still don't feel that video is a viable form of exposing an artist and getting an artist to sell. I don't think CMT on its own has definitely broken an act. Shania has helped them more than they've helped Shania. She's certainly brought in a hell of a lot more viewers than they had.' Videos helped cement Shania's image as somebody new and exciting, but first Mercury had to generate interest.

The key to turning 'Boots' into a hit was radio play. Lewis knew that if he didn't get the first record away the whole album could be lost – and maybe his career with it. The six markets that had gone with the first album all played it. It wasn't the first Shania Twain record for those markets, it was the next one. That was enough to get a low chart placing on 14 January 1995, but the twitchy promo men were being proved right, as other major stations were reluctant to follow suit. The record began to lose momentum, the chart position slipped. As it was on the verge of being lost for good, Luke 'went to the wall': he pounded on the amenable stations to keep with it. 'Go with me on this,' he implored them, 'long enough to see what reaction we get from the public.' They did, and suddenly the public got it, calling in, wanting to hear it . . . and buy it, too. The record climbed to eleven, although there were still radio stations that never played it at all.

'I'm not sure without those six markets it would have made it,' admits Lewis. 'It is a very unusual thing in country music, as the programmers are in lock step and they all play the same records every week or they don't play them and there are very few regional break-outs – in fact, I can't think of one since. "Boots" was a much bigger hit than anybody remembers. It sold a half million records very quickly on its own. By then we all knew "Any Man of Mine" was the one that was going to blow it wide-open.'

At CBS Luke had seen the way. Frank Dileo, the Head of Promotion, had stacked the singles off *Thriller* (later, he went on to manage Michael Jackson). Before one had reached the top of the charts he started the next one off by releasing it to radio. 'Any Man of Mine' debuted on 13 May, and after some stress-inducing staggers of its own, climbed all the way to the top, spending twenty weeks in the charts. Long before it was cold, 'The Woman in Me' was out, soon followed by '(If You're Not in It for Love) I'm Outta Here!', which also made it to number one. In 1996 'You Win My Love' and then 'No One Needs to Know' both went to the very top. Eight singles were released from the album, unheard of in Nashville. This tactic might have pissed off country radio program-mers, who liked having to play the same records for months, but it helped to build, then maintain momentum. 'For me that wasn't out of the ordinary at all,' says Lewis. 'It was pop rules. There are differences in marketing country, but not really; you get records in the stores, get them on the radio, get them exposed in the press and you put them on the road – which was the one thing we didn't do.'

With radio firmly onside, the visual impact of Shania's videos kicked in and the album started to sell by the truckload. Whenever the mould is broken, rumours of skulduggery follow as close behind as shadows. On Music Row stories circulated that the sales had been boosted by the carpetbaggers (Lange and Lewis) using dirty pop tricks, buying thou-sands of records and then storing them in a warehouse while the album shot up the charts. 'They said Mutt and I went out and bought the first 250,000 records. I wish I knew how to be that manipulative,' Lewis grins. 'Actually I do know how . . . but not to that scale.'

Such sales manipulation is much harder to achieve in America than in Britain and much less common. In the UK it has generally been confined to hyping the sales of singles. Prior to 1991, the US album charts were notoriously easy to rig but the arrival of SoundScan had made it far tougher. To make enough of a chart impact needed 50,000 added sales (half the original pressing of 100,000), which would have been prohibitively expensive. 'The story is unbelievable,' says Larry le Blanc, *Billboard*'s Canadian correspondent. 'Most record stores in the States don't carry a lot of country music product, most country records are sold through chains like Wal-Mart, which only stock a few copies. If you had one or two chains reporting that they had sold thousands, SoundScan would ask how come it is not selling through Wal-Mart. They would have noticed really quickly and they were looking for that stuff. Secondly, there wouldn't have been enough of a shipment out there for him to buy out.'

The sales of hit records generally resemble the screen of an EKG machine, or the stock market on a volatile day, up and down all the time. Blips occur between singles releases or TV appearances. What still stuns John Grady was the way *The Woman in Me* displayed a steady rise. The record never went back, it just kept going up all the way until Christmas when the market got so inflated it had to go down a bit.

'I was asked, "What was the most single important thing you did in this?"' says Grady. 'The answer was: I never ran out of the record. I didn't get in its way. It was its own vehicle, a living being. It didn't sell because of a marketing plan, or anybody's tremendous idea out of here.' Lewis, aware that he is being watched over his shoulder by Clive Calder, who knew all about making hit records happen, says succinctly, 'If I can take credit for anything in this whole process it's that I didn't fuck it up.'

The next step was to hire a band and go on the road. This threatened some logistical problems. Mary Bailey had her Nashville office in a converted apartment on 20th and Grand, and as the record picked up momentum so her staff increased, and became stretched and stressed. Mutt and Shania were living 2,400 kilometres away on his 3,000-acre estate on Blue Mountain Road outside St Regis Falls in upper New York state, part recording studio, part guesthouse. To play the songs to Mutt's exacting standards required more than turning up and plugging in. Hiring musicians who lived in New York made it easier for him to supervise rehearsals.

The first musician to answer the small classified ad in Albany's *Metroland* was guitarist David Malachowski, a graduate of Boston's Berklee College of Music who had toured with Janie Fricke and John Michael Montgomery. Mutt and Shania checked him out at a small club gig in Burlington, Vermont, and a few days later he found a message on his answer phone: 'Hello, David, this is Mutt Lange calling. I'd like to talk to you about putting a band together . . .'

Malachowski reeled off an impressive list of names: bassist Graham Maby had been at the nucleus of Joe Jackson's band for years, while drummer Gary Burke and Allison Cornell (fiddle, keyboards,) were also Jackson veterans; guitarist Shane Fontayne had toured with Lone Justice, Peter Gabriel and Bruce Springsteen. They passed the first test. 'I know Shane, he worked with me on a Bryan Adams album,' said Mutt, then he paused. 'Why don't you put the band together?'

On 14 June Mutt, who drove up from Michael Bolton's house in Connecticut, and Shania, who flew in from England, arrived at Sweet-fish recording studios in Argyle, New York. The band, augmented by Marc Muller (pedal steel) and Phil Skyler (Keyboards), began to play. 'Mutt sits near the far wall and leans forward, putting his head close to his knees, to listen,' writes Malachowski in his Internet diary. 'Shania sits facing us, on a stool. We perform 'Any Man of Mine' first and really hammer it. When we finish, Shania gets near hysterical, laughing with delight. "That was great! Those guys in Nashville, they can't rock out," at that moment, I knew we had the gig.'

Next up was 'Boots', which had Shania giggling at the nifty ending, and then 'The Woman in Me', where she got serious, and delivered 'a devastating, emotional take of the song'. At the end she said, 'Terrific, great, you play very well together.' They chatted for a while, discussed plans to open a tour, when Shania prophesied, 'I'm never gonna win any awards.'

With Shania's old Kirkland Lake colleague Eric Lambier replacing Skyler, and the addition of a couple of Nashville musicians, Randy Thomas and Dan Shaefer, that was to be the core of her live musicians for the next eighteen months. Within a fortnight, Shania was in the UK, playing a series of small promotional gigs in London, Manchester and Glasgow. At the time they raised polite flickers of interest, but have now reached legendary status with the media, who claim to have been there in sufficient numbers to fill an arena. It is indicative of Shania's international ambitions that, at a time when she was on the cusp of her American breakthrough, she was prepared to go abroad.

Once back in the States, Shania shuttled between major TV shows, *The Tonight Show* with Jay Leno and *Live! with Regis and Kathy Lee*. Plans were discussed for the band to rehearse up at the studio during the autumn prior to going on tour the following January. On 30 August, she and the band performed at a Mercury showcase for radio pro-gramme directors at the Ritz Carlton in Laguna Beach, California. Luke Lewis got up to introduce the act and announced, 'Shania has just turned down a lucrative tour with Wynona, to concentrate on her next album . . .'

Perhaps that was not the most tactful way to break it to the musicians. Had he had any hair left, Ron Baird at CAA would have torn it out months before. From the moment 'Boots' started picking up play, his phone had been ringing and with each week the offers increased, club dates, support slots, one-off country fairs. By the summer he had great offers for Shania to open from both Neal McCoy and Wynona. He told Mary that Wynona was offering $15,000 a show. Mary turned it down flat, told him that in a year she would be earning $100,000. 'I've never said "no" more times in my life than with Shania Twain,' says Baird. 'She could have played anywhere, every-where. We didn't turn down tens of thousands, we turned down millions of dollars. Shania always had in her mind that she didn't want to tour until, when she went up on stage, every song she played was a hit song. She was betting on her career and this was an extraordinarily risky way to do it.'

Naturally her refusal to tour was sneered at by Music Row. This proved she was just a producer's puppet, she couldn't sing live and probably hadn't sung on the album in the first place. At Mercury they knew differently, for Shania, Mary and Mutt had told them directly, 'Do you want us to work up a tour? Or do you want us to make up another record? Which one?'

That was easy. Record companies do not make money out of touring. It also gave Shania and Mutt the chance to confront a more serious problem. What to do about Mary?

CHAPTER SEVENTEEN

Goodbye, Old Friend

T he very thing that had made Mary such a good manager for
Shania was also her greatest weakness. Mary had believed in
Shania when she was still Eilleen, when nobody else did.
When money was tight and they had to share hotel rooms it was Mary
who slept on the floor so that Shania could get a good night's sleep. It
was not a take-take relationship, because Mary gave willingly. Her
Achilles heel was that she loved Shania too much.

'She was like my daughter – I never had one,' says Mary. 'And I just
believed in her so much, and so I just wanted her to be best. Probably
that parent thing, you know: you want to go to the ends of the earth?
Count me in, I'm going with you. I just was so proud of her, I loved
being with her, taking her somewhere and having her walk into the
room, knowing that she's just carried herself and presented herself so
well, I was never embarrassed by her.'

Most daughters grow up and leave home. She and Shania had
argued, but that was normal, natural. She forgot, or chose to forget,
that Shania had left her twice before, only to come back when she
needed help. But that is what daughters do so naturally it can be
forgiven if not quite forgotten. Now things were going so well, Mary
reasoned, there was no need for Shania to leave again. It was Shania,
Mary, Mutt and now Luke Lewis, the Four Musketeers versus Music
Row.

Mary adored Mutt Lange, indeed she still does. Mutt never preaches,
he leads by example. Mary was almost as captivated by his inner
strength as Shania. Willingly she became a vegan and began to study
the same spiritual path. As sales for *The Woman in Me* built, it quickly
became apparent that here was a monster record by an artist with a

green record-company boss and an inexperienced manager. The opportunities to blow it grew every day. The person in the weakest position financially and logistically was Mary.

To begin with, she did not have time to notice. The management office on 20th and Grand was soon under telephone siege. When a record explodes out of nowhere, attention focuses squarely on the manager. Yesterday nobody returned her calls. Today every media outlet, TV and radio station, every promoter, every back-street T-shirt manufacturer and two-bit hustle merchant hit the phone. Of course Mercury and CAA were fielding most of the traffic, but in the end every decision that might fill Shania's diary had to be OK'd by Mary. Musicians had to be booked and confirmed, their travel arrangements sorted. Mary hired Gillie Crowder, an expat Brit who had worked for concert promoter Harvey Goldsmith on tours for Queen, Elton John and Bob Dylan, and Julie Kerr to run the Nashville office, and her eldest son Bobby helped out. Up in Toronto she employed Patty Lou Andrews, the daughter of an old friend, to deal with press and promotion inquiries. The office was so cramped that Mary's bedroom and bathroom were soon invaded by boxes. Gillie could never start her day's work until the phones stopped ringing at 6 p.m.

Although Shania was living in St Regis Falls, she was not content to let it all happen for her. Every Tuesday morning at nine (Nashville time), no matter where they all were, there was a conference call between Mary, Gillie, Patty Lou and Shania. The call lasted until every item of importance had been discussed. While Shania had strong opinions on what she should or shouldn't do, she was also perfectly amenable to discussion and could be persuaded to change her mind. Once committed, she never gave less than 100 per cent. 'Shania is perhaps the most professional and the hardest-working of all the artists I've worked with,' says Gillie. 'When she was working on the road, she was never demanding, as long as she had her vegan food.'

Mary had cash-flow problems. Suddenly she was running an office, paying three salaries, flying between Nashville, Canada and upstate New York. Money was pouring out with none coming in. Royalties on record sales, songwriter's royalties and performance fees are accounted twice a year (usually 31 December and 30 June) and monies owed may not be paid up to a further ninety days. Furthermore, much of Shania's first royalty cheque from Mercury would have been eaten up paying back the advances she had received on the first album. Mary knew that, by the end of September, she would have more than enough to cover her overheads, but that did not solve the short-term crisis. Traditionally an artist with sales momentum goes on tour to generate cash flow. Shania was not going on the road.

Partly due to the poverty of her upbringing, Shania could never feel secure until she was financially secure in her own right, no longer reliant on a husband or a manager. (She has admitted that she didn't feel fully comfortable in her relationship with Lange until she had achieved her own financial success. 'There was no way I was going to enjoy life beyond my own personal means,' she says. 'He thought it was ridiculous. But I worked my butt off, and now I'm independent financially.') In fact, because she was married to Mutt, Shania had no money worries and could afford to wait for the royalty cheque. Mary could not. Bob Kasner had bankrolled the operation for a long time, but now it was placing considerable strain on the family finances.

Mary was inexperienced. She did not know the movers and shakers, the people who can settle problems with a click of their fingers. As far as touring went, she was a tyro. Soon after the CMA Awards in October 1995, Shania told Mary she should consider getting a partner who would concentrate on that side of the business. Mary agreed to try, though Gillie, who did know about it, told her she could learn that side of the business quick enough. Good tour managers are not cheap but they are always available. Mary looked around but found nobody who she felt could be trusted with Shania's career.

'I know I needed to take it to the next level,' says Mary. 'I only had so much experience and so many contacts. I did try and find co-managers, they were just not there, and I had a lot of disappointments. No matter where I went to find support it just didn't happen. It was frustrating. I never told Eilleen those things, maybe I should have, but I kept everything inside, because I felt she had enough on her plate trying to make records, she didn't need to hear my problems.'

Mary had lost the ability to communicate directly with her artist. 'She was half-way around the world, or I was up in Kirkland Lake, and we're trying to make things happen. I was so concentrated that our communication started to fade. So instead of us talking with each other, we ended up talking through others. Once you do that, it's over.' In business, as in love, when that spark goes, it is hard to rekindle.

Over at Mercury Luke Lewis had established a personal relationship with Mutt and Shania independent of Mary (Luke is the only other person to call her 'Woody'). 'I had a good relationship with Mary Bailey,' says Lewis. 'I didn't have a beef with her at all, we worked really well together, we had our squabbles, the normal record-company management shit. I felt like Shania did, that as supportive and as big a vision as Mary had, she didn't have the experience. We knew she had to go on the road and that she had to start working international.' He pauses and then cuts right to the heart of the matter. 'Neither Mary nor I knew how to do either one of those things, that was a flat fact. Somebody had to jump in – I guess one of us had to go.' However, it is generally the case in the music business that the head of the record company is both more important and more powerful than the artist's manager.

The tension increased. After Mary heard that Shania had publicly discussed asking a third party to act as her manager, on a salary plus bonus basis, she exploded. She sent a legal letter warning her off such a course of action, alleging 'tortious interference' (suggesting that she was trying to make a new contract while already under contract to Mary Bailey Management). As he had acted for both parties, Dick Frank refused to get involved, thereby cutting himself out of some substantial legal fees. By this stage the only solution was to sit down face to face and see whether the situation could be resolved.

In December 1995, Shania fired Mary. Mary will not discuss the circumstances. From that moment Mary was out of the loop. After she was fired, Big Bob Kasner went incandescent and vowed to use every penny he owned if it was needed to get what he thought was owed to her. Mary did not have the heart for a long-drawn-out battle. As she says, their relationship 'was never about money'. To her it would have been airing the family secrets to the world.

Mary did eventually receive money from the record sales of both *The Woman in Me* and *Come On Over*. She has now reached a full and final financial settlement running into millions of dollars.

At the 1996 Canadian Country Music Awards Mary was presented with the Manager of the Year award. Mainly out of bravado she took on a couple of new clients, including Joni Wilson from *A Touch of Broadway*, but her heart was no longer in it. It is difficult, when you have ridden a comet to step back to earth. A year later, she quit management altogether. 'My life deteriorated,' she acknowledges, 'because even when I was here [at home], I wasn't here. I lost many things that are really valuable to me.' The fallout almost destroyed her marriage. She and Bob split up for a while but have since been reconciled. Unlike his wife, Bob cannot forgive Shania, at the slightest mention of 'Eilleen' his face goes absolutely still, his body rigid and he retreats inside a bushman's silence that speaks bibles. Mary has found solace in her faith and refuses to dwell on the negatives, rationalizing that while Mutt took something valuable from her, he gave her back something worth much more.

She insists that she now bears Shania no ill will, that it was all for the best. At the time, she admits, she felt hurt, but as she now says, 'Perhaps she had more common sense than I had. They had to do it. Sometimes when the party's over, the party's over.' Yet when she says those things a shadow of darker memories flicker behind her eyes. It still hurts, because it was so personal. She loved . . . and however much she rationalizes it, she cannot help but feel that she was betrayed.

To Mary Shania is still the daughter she never had, though she now sees that so many of Shania's strengths – the focus, the determination, the sometimes humourless pursuit of a goal and a ruthlessness in obtaining it – are more usually perceived as male characteristics. 'We all have weaknesses,' she says, 'yet I have no idea what hers are, because I never saw any. She's so very strong in many, many, ways. It's the wolf in her. In the end,' says Mary, 'you live with the choices you make.'

Was Shania right to fire Mary? The people now around her obviously thought so. Luke Lewis admits he 'wasn't particularly upset' while Ron Baird adds: 'It was an appropriate point in her life and career to go to a world-class manager. She needed to have someone who had a perspective that was as big or bigger than hers. There was no way that Mary could have that, because she never had that experience.' By December 1995, doubtless in part caused by the steady drip-drip of doubts being poured into Shania's ears, the rot had set in. Other managers have been incorporated into a larger set-up, but that would not have worked. Mary cared too much. She was always professional, but to her it was personal. To Shania it was business first.

Such things are seldom handled well. Shania Twain was thirty years old, she had been trying to make it for ever and now that she had it within her grasp, she was not going to let emotion stand in her way.

As she has always done, Shania moved on. She had too much to do to worry. 'Change is normal,' she said when asked about Bailey. 'I like to go forward. I'm not a stand-still kind of person. I don't get caught in the comfort zone.' In the short term, Shania determined to manage herself with the aid of her New York assistant, Sheri Thorn, with Patty Lou Andrews doing press, all overseen by advice from Mutt and Zomba. It worked fine as far as Mercury were concerned. 'I was concerned about her not having a manager for a while,' says Lewis, 'but as it turned out, it brought the three of us closer together. We started talking even more together, so we never felt out of touch. I was able to translate her concerns to the staff.'

Because she was not touring, Shania's videos had taken on an increased importance and so did their budgets. It was the only way for anybody to get a glimpse of what she was like, and how she was as a performer. She took it seriously. 'Most artists,' says Retta Harvey, 'the less time they can spend doing a video the better. They look at it more as an annoyance, and not a means to an end. They're greedier, they'll only go two or three hours into it, where Shania's like, "I will sit here and I will watch, I want to make sure that everything is done the way we need it to get done."' It took five hours to fit Shania into her skin-tight bell-bottom pants for '(If You're Not in It for Love) I'm Outta Here'. During the shoot for 'You Win My Love' the crew were all flagging by hour twenty-two. That was the point at which Shania announced, 'Let's do this one more little thing, I think it will look really cool' and started to do a series of somersaults, cartwheels and backflips in front of a gigantic black and white chequered flag.

For the third single, 'The Woman in Me', Luke Lewis, who had been impressed by Billy Ray's clip shot at the Grand Canyon, and needing something to placate Polygram's international companies, shocked Retta Harvey by asking her, 'Where can we go that is completely distinctive, some place that's larger than life, that you have never seen before in a country video?' It was a rhetorical question as he then announced. 'You go to the Pyramids.' The shoot was indeed exotic, with Shania filmed in the oldest mosque in Cairo, in an ancient tomb and riding a horse across the desert 'dodging Pyramids', wearing a flowing white veil. Despite its lavish appearance, the budget was relatively low – only $150,000 – because director Markus Blunder had shot in Egypt before.

The three-day shoot was gruelling. In July, the daytime temperatures can reach 49 degrees (C). Shania had to be up at 3 a.m., so she was made-up and ready when dawn broke at 5.30 a.m. Shooting continued all day until the sun set at 9 p.m. Mary Bailey was knocked over by a wild horse and ended up with a badly infected elbow. On set Shania could not eat any of the food. Every day, the crew had chicken kebabs and she had to make do with plain rice and bottled water. Fortunately, the Indian restaurant in the hotel knew how to do vegetable curries. There were more than a few cultural differences, as Shania wrote in a diary for *Country Weekly*, 'All these women were around me. They were in black, I was in white. In Western culture white is always the sign of innocence. In Egypt white is considered a flamboyant colour, whereas black is a humble colour. We did some magnificent scenes with the women. They were wonderful. If my shawl was to come off, or if I took it off for a second, the women would run up to me like mothers and cover my shoulders for me . ... The mystery of the place just got to me. I got choked up for a bit while we were doing a take.'

She continued to do showcase gigs, award shows and TV shows (*The David Letterman Show* twice in six months) using the core of musicians assembled by Dave Malachowski. Her insistence on playing live might not have impressed the folk in Nashville, but at the *Billboard* Music Awards on 6 December 1995 they had Tina Turner swaying and grooving in the aisles. At the American Music Awards in LA (30 January 1996) the host Sinbad complimented Dave: 'You guys are bad, you're the only ones playing live and you're bad!'

By the time Fan Fair 1996 rolled around, Shania was the biggest country star in America. Mindful of how important it was to silence the doubters the eleven-piece band rehearsed their five-song set at Sound-check in Nashville. On Tuesday 11 June, Sammy Kershaw introduced Shania and her band. As she was about to lead off into 'Any Man of Mine', her earphone monitors packed up and she was unable to hear what any of her musicians were playing. Roadies scurried around trying to sort the problem but as Fan Fair operates on a tight schedule, with no more than five-minute gaps between acts, Shania realized that she would have to put up or walk off. Quitting was not an option, so she went ahead performing the short set without monitors. It went OK, especially in the circumstances, but it was not the triumph everyone had hoped for.

Videos and TV shows might have put her face and her songs out to a huge audience, but they do not connect with fans in the way personal appearances do. At Fan Fair 1995 (where she gave a short three-song set), the queues for Shania's booth stretched way back. While most artists give up two hours at the most, Shania spent a minimum of four and never cut her line off. Like Garth Brooks, she stayed there until everyone got their moment with her. For disabled fans she gave extra time; she stood up walked in front of her table and addressed them straight, eye to eye, treating them as individuals not objects of pity. On those days it was not the fans who caught the edge of her tongue but industry people who believed there was more important flesh to press. On 21 September 1995 Shania performed 'The Woman in Me', backed by the Vancouver Symphony Orchestra, at the opening of General Motors Place, a giant shopping mall. 25,000 fans went berserk. Seeing that success, Mercury (Luke Lewis gives the credit to John Grady) suggested that she make a personal appearance at the Mall of America in Minneapolis.

It was a calculated gamble; PAs, especially in the middle of winter, can fall flat. Minneapolis was her biggest market. On 10 February 1996, the main atrium was packed out; over 20,000 came to see Shania. She had not intended to sing but did a couple of acapella numbers. The experiment was later repeated at an outdoor mall in Dallas to over 30,000 fans. Both times she signed autographs for hours, talked to the fans and posed for photos with them without ever complaining. Every person who came to the front of the line had her photo taken with Shania by a member of the Mercury staff. That was PR at its purest, reaching directly to the heartland. Such gracious behaviour has a knock-on effect that creates loyalty that can last for ever.

It was a marketing coup that spread Shania way beyond the country market, positioning her ready for a crossover into pop. In 1987, Debbie Gibson had been introduced to the teen market by touring and playing in shopping malls. Her records had then exploded up the pop charts. To launch *Come On Over*, the mall signings were hyped up into Fan Appreciation Days, and Shania went back to Minnesota, Dallas, Toronto and Calgary. A year later, Jive Records, part of Zomba, followed a similar blueprint when breaking Britney Spears. Were they copying Shania's success? Or had they had input into the idea in the first place?

Shania works like she walks. Fast. When she is working she becomes absolutely focused on what she is doing, to the exclusion of all else. People working with her are expected to do the same and if she does not complain, she sees no reason why they should either. Nor does she stop to air-kiss, and pass the time of day, for that is wasted time. In an industry where back-slapping and brown-nosing are essential social graces, such behaviour can be perceived as cold and snobbish.

Luke Lewis believes she is misunderstood. 'I've never met an artist who worked harder than her. Ever. She never misses a beat, to the extent that some people think she is cold and stand-offish, because they get around her when she is hyper-focused. She is not going to stop and pat somebody on the back, especially cohorts. Label people had to get used to the idea that she wasn't going to stop. As a result, some people have the impression she is icy or cold, which is not fair.'

By Christmas 1996, *The Woman in Me* had sold over 10 million copies, overtaking *Patsy Cline's Greatest Hits* to become the biggest-selling record by a female country singer ever. Shania had also surprised the business by appointing her new manager. Looking after her own affairs was only ever a temporary option. She had been looking for the right professional heavyweight management company for a year. Shania had been courted assiduously by most of the industry's major players, including Bryan Adams' manager Bruce Allan. (Adams says that, at times he wishes he had never helped Mutt meet Shania, as the producer is always too tied up with her records to make time to write with him!) Her choice was a man who had never had any dealings with Nashville. However, Jon Landau did manage Bruce Springsteen, one of the most respected artists in America, and had done so for over twenty years.

Starting out as a journalist, Landau entered music business legend when, in 1974, he penned the line: 'I saw rock and roll future – and its name is Bruce Springsteen.' He started co-producing Bruce's albums the following year and became his manager, officially in 1977. Landau and his business partner, Barbara Carr (a former Columbia record executive who is married to Landau's journalist buddy Dave Marsh), have built up a formidable reputation as serious movers and shakers in the industry. They are artist builders and supporters, not manipulators out for a quick kill. Their experience with Springsteen's heroic touring schedule and the worldwide success of *Born to Run* gave them the international nous and infrastructure Shania needed to get to the next level.

It was Shania who approached Jon Landau Management, probably on the recommendation of Clive Calder. (Zomba had administered Springsteen's song catalogue outside the States for some years.) 'I approached them because they had international experience, which not a lot of management does, because not a lot of artists are interested in being international. They had maintained success and integrity with a class act,' said Shania. 'The reason I chose Jon is that he was very receptive to the direction I was already headed. I wasn't interested in somebody who was going to reinvent my career. He was willing to join, as opposed to take over. There was a mutual respect that I appreciated.'

For Landau it presented an interesting challenge, taking on an artist who had already sold 10 million albums. He likened it to jumping on to 'the middle of a fast-moving train'. He never dreamt how fast and far the train would go. To start with, Shania needed career guidance in a medium that Mutt Lange could not provide. During 1996, her past had come back to haunt her. Following close in its wake, scenting blood, came the tabloid hounds.

CHAPTER EIGHTEEN

Bad Blood (and Tabloid Hacks)

L ike everything in life, stardom has a downside. The longer you're up there, the easier it becomes, but at the beginning it is emotionally exhausting, equal parts exhilaration and fear. The early days of celebrity are also the times of fraud. While the star has all the trappings of celebrity, the money isn't there, they inhabit a film set – it looks wonderful but there is no substance behind the front. The fear lurks behind the designer shoulder-pads, whispering in the ear: 'This could all end tomorrow.'

Once you become a star, your greatest ally flips overnight and becomes your enemy. Once you had time on your side, now you have none. No time at all, because everyone wants a piece of you. Every TV chat show, every radio DJ, every magazine with a circulation higher than ground zero demands a piece of your life as if it were their constitutional right. In America the celebrity culture no longer allows for privacy. Public face in public place equals public property. Success begets jealousy. Overnight success begets a spawn of green-eyed monsters with honey on their lips, poison on their breath and talons dipped in venom. A new star needs help from people who've walked down the street before and can see where the puddles end and the sewer begins. Shania had none of that. Sure, she had heavyweight supporters, like her super-rich, super-successful husband and the boss of her record company, but in Nashville they were both outsiders too. To Music Row minds they weren't real country people . . . and nor was Shania. To their minds she hadn't paid her dues, hadn't waited her turn. She had not toured. Knocking about bars and country fairs when she was scarce big enough to hold her guitar did not count. She broke all the rules that had been set up to keep country pure (and a few people very rich). She didn't live in town, she didn't hang with and kiss up to the right people, attend the right functions, she didn't spread the wealth by covering lots of different songs, she flaunted her body, she was too sexy. (One must never forget that Nashville is a deeply conservative town; its biggest industry is not country music but printing bibles.) What really rankled was that Shania had been proved right.

'Mutt and Shania don't pay songwriters here,' says Sandy Neese, then Senior VP of Publicity at Mercury. 'No matter what anybody else tells you, that's not popular, because nobody else in town has a piece of them. They were totally self-sufficient. If you're part of the Nashville community, you know the songwriters and the publishers, the producers and all those people are going to vote for you. And then she didn't tour right away. You've got to be out there touring to be Entertainer of the Year, that's part of the total package.'

Nashville chose to teach Shania a lesson by ignoring her. Despite the success of *The Woman in Me*, she did not win anything at the 1995 CMA Awards. In 1996, after having sold 9 million copies, it was the same story. Three nominations and . . . nothing. No album of the year, not female singer, not even video of the year as a consolation. (Shania might have revolutionized country video, but the award went to Junior Brown's 'My Wife Thinks You're Dead'.) She finally received her first – and to date only – CMA Award, Entertainer of the Year, in 1999.

'In a sense, she was never embraced here,' says Luke Lewis. 'There is a carpetbagger thing in the South. I came here from California and some people thought I was going to Californicate the place. I am a bit abrasive and brash and not very good at politicking and we didn't get recognized here, truthfully, until she had won some BMI writer awards, which you earn and they are not political. Finally she wins Entertainer of the Year – 30 million records later. I don't think she was bitter about it, though she and I have laughed about how naive we were and also how jumpy that we were going to step on a landmine somewhere. We knew we were in a minefield but we didn't know where any of the mines were – it's that sort of town. I guess we were running so fast we missed most of them.'

There is an old industry cliché which runs 'Where there's a hit there's a writ.' In today's celebrity-obsessed world it has a further twist. 'Where there's a hit there'll be a hack digging in the dirt.' In America the real muck-digging is left to tabloid magazines, and in 1996, Shania was only just starting to blip on the radar of the *National Enquirer*, the *Globe* and the *Star*. The country press preferred to operate by innuendo. As the Milli Vanilli saga was still fresh in people's minds, that was the best place to start. In 1989, Rob Pilatus and Fabrice Morvan, two pretty-boy disco singers, had enjoyed a worldwide smash with 'Girl You Know It's True' and collared the Grammy for Best New Artist. Then their German producer, Frank Farian, revealed that they had never been in his recording studio. The boys were stripped of their awards and cast into outer darkness (Pilatus eventually committed suicide in 1998). Mutt Lange, who was a similar Svengali target, stayed resolutely silent which fuelled the rumours.

'The press,' recalls Sandy Neese, 'was trying to hint, ". . . well, he's a tremendous producer, she can't sing, she didn't really write these songs, he did," and bait her into performing. Her whole reason for not performing at that point was she didn't have enough songs to do a full set. She was the number one artist in the format, so it wasn't like she was going to go out and open for somebody so people would stop writing about her. Then it became an issue: "She's not touring because she can't cut it." I'm sure there were lots of times when she was really hurt.'

One of the most-quoted, and to be fair wittiest, putdowns, came from Steve Earle (an extremely talented singer who all but squandered his career on drugs and booze) when he ad-libbed in an interview: 'It doesn't take a rocket scientist to figure it out. She's America's best-paid lap-dancer.' Shania had waited and struggled for too long to let such sticks and stones goad her. But the whispering campaign did arouse interest in her past.

On 5 April 1996, her image took a major knock. The unlikely source was the Timmins *Daily Press*, which opened a sensational front-page article with these hard-hitting words: 'The *Daily Press* has learnt that Twain has woven a tapestry of half-truths and outright lies in her climb to the top of the country charts.' The nub of the story was that Regina Nutbrown, her paternal grandmother, claimed that, since she had got famous, she had ignored her relatives. 'All she talks about is this Indian man,' Regina told the paper. 'But what about her real father? What about us? I wrote about a year ago, but once she started going good, she never wrote. I wish she would. I don't know what's happened to her.'

For a small-town newspaper to attack its most famous daughter so openly guaranteed international coverage. The country music press who, star divorces and booze and drug addictions notwithstanding, make a big deal about roots, tradition and family values, promptly came over all sniffy. It was not that big a deal. Complaints that stars ignore their relatives are as regular as a new moon and about as interesting. There will always be another one along soon. The revelations about her bloodline were more interesting. So Clarence was her biological father, not Jerry, and there was the damaging suggestion that she had lied about having Native blood to advance her career.

The irony, which might have amused Jerry, who had endured enough prejudice in his lifetime, was that while a Native Canadian country singer was exotic news, an Irish Canadian country singer was not. Not telling the world that Jerry was her adoptive father was hardly criminal fraud. The media like things simple. Trying to explain the complexities of her family background to interviewers with the attention span of a sound byte was too difficult. (Most still do now know Clarence is not Jill's father, nor that Darryl is actually Jerry's nephew.) It was no big secret; some of her friends knew, some did not. Children do not run around telling all and sundry they are adopted. They want to belong, not to be different.

Did Shania deliberately pretend to be Native to arouse interest? Nashville had made a meal of her heritage. Yet when she was recording with Harry Hinde, she had infuriated him by refusing to exploit it. With John Kim Bell she was billing herself as a Native singer. Bell knew that Jerry was not her father, but says he was very surprised to learn that she might have no Native blood at all. Ever since the story broke, Shania has maintained a consistent line. Sharon told her the Edwards had Native blood. Why should she not believe her?

In the final analysis emotional truth must win over literal truth. As a child Shania desperately wanted to believe that she was part Native. Sharon did too. Shania once told May Thompson, 'I don't know why, but my mother always wanted to be around the Indians.' She was five when Jerry came into her life; she had no memory of Clarence, except in the quarrels that stalked her nightmares. Her grandmother Eileen died when she was seven and the only living relative she knew was her Uncle Don. Along came the Twains, who loved her unconditionally, and she loved them back. Small wonder she wanted to belong, to really belong. She loved and admired Jerry. She wanted to be his daughter, if not by blood then by word and by deed. When she had refused to change the Twain name it was *his* memory she was honouring.

Dick Frank, her former lawyer, put his finger on the crux when he said, 'It was very upsetting to her. She looked upon [Jerry] as her father, and she was very proud of her Ojibway heritage. Her biological father had [left] her mother very early. Eilleen has just drawn a curtain over that part of her life. I think it was terribly painful to have that curtain ripped open. I think she felt that it dishonoured her father who raised her and sought to diminish his role as a father.'

The controversy also affected the Twains, who had endured a miserable time since Jerry's death. They were just recovering from a double tragedy. Tim Twain had died of leukaemia in July 1994. He was only thirty-six. Gerry passed away a year later, diagnosed with cancer but finally succumbing to pneumonia. Attacked in her hometown, the one place she felt secure, Shania went on the offensive, issuing this statement:

'I've never had a relationship with my biological father, Clarence Edwards. From about the age of two years old, my mother and Clarence were separated. Soon after, Jerry assumed the role of being our father from that day forward, even though it wasn't until a few years later that my mother and Clarence actually divorced and she and Jerry married. My father Jerry then legally adopted us and to this day remains the only father I have ever known; emotionally or in any other way. He was the only one who was there for me on a daily basis, through thick and through thin, until he died in 1987 in the car accident that also killed my mother.

'Although I was briefly introduced to Clarence a couple of times in my teen years, I never knew him growing up. My mother did not deprive us of the knowledge of his existence. She let us know where he lived, what he did for a living, a little about his family background, and that there was some Indian heritage in his family. That's what I was raised to believe and know from her to be true.

'I never deliberately avoided contact with the Edwards family, but my father Jerry's parents loved us as though we were their very own grandchildren and we were equally accepted by his other relatives. That's the family we belonged to. It was my Gramma Selina who made my stage clothes when I was a kid. It was my Grandpa Gerry who spent hours with me in the woods teaching me to track rabbits and telling me all his bush stories. It was on the Mattagami reserve that I spent many summer weekends playing with my cousins. Therefore, I never felt the need to seek the love or support of another family, because I had it from the Twains.

'I don't know how much Indian blood I actually have in me, but as the adopted daughter of my father Jerry, I became legally registered as fifty per cent North American Indian. Being raised by a full-blooded Indian and being part of his family and their culture from a young age is all I've ever known.

'That heritage is my heart and my soul, and I'm very proud of it.'

Faced with that, the newspaper caved in and issued a front-page retraction, waffling about 'a misunderstanding' and finishing off: 'the Daily Press sincerely regrets any suggestion that Ms Twain lied.'

While the fuss went on and commentators, both white and Native, pontificated, nobody bothered to ask the Ojibwe at Mattagami what they thought. 'When the fuss broke, we never questioned her for a minute,' says Willis McKay. 'I was on the phone to her in the States and I said that there was never any question about her roots. In the days that she was around here she mingled with everybody and everybody accepted her as a Native person, regardless of whether she was white or not.'

Legally, too, Shania was laughing. 'I remember we had one problem with immigration when she was coming back in from Canada,' says Dick Frank. 'We had to go into action through Washington, but happily she is a registered Ojibway. The Ojibway nation originally populated both sides of what later became the Canadian/US border. Under our Native American laws, Ojibwe are citizens of both countries. It made it very simple.'

That should have been that. But it had opened up the whole can of Chapleau worms. Now the tabloids knew where to go if they needed some dirt on Shania. In 1996, all the juice they needed was being supplied by Mark and Darryl.

The boys had a bad reputation in Huntsville. 'They were trouble-makers, delinquents, into petty theft,' recalls one girl who knew them. 'They were basically partyers and while I don't think they would have hurt anybody they were teenage boys causing a ruckus for something to do.' One day, Celia Finley was driving along Main Street heading out of town. 'Mark Twain ran over this little puppy. And they both stood there staring at it. I stopped on the other side of the road, got a blanket from my car and got the puppy on to it and I gave it to them and said "You go straight to the vet's with this dog."'

In such a small community such behaviour will not be tolerated for long, no matter who your sister is. On New Year's Eve 1995, the pair were pulled on suspicion of driving a stolen car and Mark refused to give a breath test. On 5 January, they both pleaded guilty of impaired driving and taking a vehicle without consent, were fined and had their licences suspended. On 6 May 1996, Mark was in trouble again. He was drinking with his girlfriend at Deerhurst and kicked up a fuss when the bartender refused to serve him any more. The row spilled over into the parking lot, he smashed the window in his girlfriend's car and when the cops were called he swung his backpack at a policeman and hit him in the face with it. He was charged with assaulting an officer.

Two weeks later, Mark was arrested again, along with his brother and two friends, Darrell Stock and Paul Bartz. At 4.30 on the morning of Monday 20 May, police were called to the Festing Toyota dealership on Centre Street in Huntsville after a neighbour was woken by the noise of the men trying to steal cars. Three vehicles were damaged before the four were caught leaving the area. All four were charged with theft over $5000 and possession of burglary tools. Darryl, Stock and Bartz were released on bail on the Tuesday and after a court hearing given suspended sentences. For Mark the consequences were far more serious. On 5 June he was sentenced to six months in jail. After his release, the brothers took the hint and left Huntsville.

The media jumped all over the story, which was embarrassing for Shania. While she was livid in private her public comments have remained consistently sanguine. 'I have two naughty younger brothers,' she said in 1999. 'They are doing OK right now; they have stayed out of trouble. It's not an excuse, but when my parents were killed it completely wrecked them and getting into trouble was part of that.'

To Shania keeping the family together is still as important as it was in November 1987, or further back in the days when the heating was turned off and there was only bread goulash to eat. In private she worries about the boys, where they are and what they're doing. She tells friends, 'Darryl will be Darryl and Mark will be Mark,' meaning 'It doesn't matter what I do, nothing has changed. They have to learn for themselves, they have to be responsible for their own lives.' Darryl has tried her patience many times, but she remains faithful to him, because she hopes that one day he will grow up and become a man.

Another savage attack on Shania came in June 1997 with the publication of Laurence Leamer's book *Three Chords and the Truth*. In it he suggested that Shania's story was 'a brilliant reconstruction . . . a virtual past,' that she had made up or exaggerated the poverty of her childhood to give herself a real good country image. Leamer's target was not specifically Shania, for he took on the whole country music industry, raking over bodies and spraying good old-fashioned vitriol over icons like Wynona, Vince Gill and Reba McEntire. In the reviews and publicity surrounding the book Shania was scarcely mentioned. Leamer had fastened on minor inaccuracies and inconsistencies in her interviews and from that determined her whole story was a pack of lies. He was wrong, which went a long way to undermining his whole thesis. Jenny Bohler, Reba McEntire's spokesman, dismissed the book, which never sold well, with 'I think a better title would be *Three Chords and Half-Truths*.'

After *Come On Over* went nuclear and Shania crossed over into pop, the tabloid hacks returned to the forest of northern Ontario in force. Chapleau was invaded by journalists from the *Enquirer*, the *Globe* and *Star* looking for some dirt and offering hard cash for it. Clarence refused to say anything at all, especially after a photographer staked out his camp and snapped him urinating off the front porch. Other members of the family were more forthcoming, especially if they had been bought a few drinks. After years of frustration and hurt festering away, the stories that poured out were not kind about Sharon, but nor did they reflect well upon the Edwards clan – except Clarence.

Goaded into replying by the revelations, Shania stated in interviews that she had only met her father very few times, that he never contributed financially to her upbringing and that when he tried to call her after Sharon and Jerry were killed he was 'inebriated'. All true, but to the Edwards she sounded so unforgiving. The family had their own perspective.

In 1972, Clarence settled down with Shirley Caby, two years his senior. Under Shirley's influence he tried to re-establish contact with his daughters. The problem was, every time Shania saw him or his family, something went wrong. Basically Sharon and the Edwards clan hated each other. When Eilleen was about seventeen, she and Sharon were passing through Chapleau and stayed the night at Desi Edwards' house. Clarence chose to stay away, his elder brother did not. Gordon turned up drunk as a skunk and proceeded to tell Sharon what he thought of the way she had treated his brother. 'I said what I had to say to her,' he says. 'I said, "I know you like a book, don't bullshit me," told her that she hated my brother so much because he left her, she'd put poison in the girls' heads. I don't think Eilleen was too impressed with me, probably thought, "There's another uncle, there's another drunk," but that's the way it was for me in those days.'

'Clarence loved his daughters,' insists Lori Edwards. 'He wanted to be involved with both of them, but she was so obsessed with him that he wasn't going to. She poisoned them against him. He told me when he was leaving my dad's place, "Do you know what it feels like to be crazy? You feel like you are wearing a baseball cap and you have that tightness around your brain." He had that for a long time.'

After Sharon and Jerry were killed, Clarence's mother, Regina Nutbrown, did make some effort to forge a reconciliation. (She was no sweetheart. In 1971, Harold was told by a doctor in Sault Sainte Marie that he would die within six months if he didn't quit drinking. On hearing the news Regina walked out and moved in with another man, whom she later married. Harold drank himself to death within a few months.) 'Her grandmother would come to town once in a while for shopping,' says Helene Bolduc, 'and she would call Eilleen and say, "Do you want to meet me for lunch? I'll be in Timmins." They would have lunch together. I think the grandmother really wanted the father and the daughter to become close and it just wasn't realistic. That happened a couple of times a year maybe four or five in all.'

Encouraged by his mother, Clarence phoned Eilleen every few months. He was reaching out to her with no ulterior motive. The problem was that the only way he could pluck up the courage to call her was to reach for the bottle first. That did not make for much meaningful dialogue. 'A few times her father tried to make contact with her,' says Helene, 'but every time he would call, he was drunk. She had a lot of mixed feelings about him. I think at one time she would have liked to get to know him, and she did have a lot of respect for her grandmother. But after all this stuff in the paper, she thought, "What is happening?" '

Shania's reaction to the stories in the *Daily Press* was natural enough. She considered that Regina and by implication her father had betrayed her again. Life was too short and she was too busy to spend time mending fences that appeared irretrievably broken. When Regina died in 1998, she did not acknowledge it in any way, did not attend the funeral or send a card or flowers. Naturally this incensed the family again.

One catalyst came after Shania was interviewed on *The Oprah Winfrey Show*. Clarence sat drinking in the bar of the Sportsman Hotel, watching. 'He was here when she told Oprah her dad was an Ojibway Indian,' says Lori Edwards, who was working behind the bar. 'Clarence never said a word but he was weeping. A while later he dropped six pictures of Shania and him on the bar saying, "Let her deny this." '

One of the photographs was of Clarence standing next to Eilleen and Carrie Ann. She is wearing a yellow gown and about to attend her prom night at Pinecrest in 1979. 'You see that dress?' said Shirley. 'Well, we bought that dress.' This tallies with Shania's comment: 'The very first time I remember meeting him very briefly was when I was thirteen.' Another time Shirley says she and Clarence took the girls clothes shopping and they all went out for a very civilized supper. Sharon offered to put them up for the night, made up a bed in the living room with pillows and blankets. In the middle of the night they were woken up by Sharon attacking them, kicking, punching and screaming abuse. Shirley, who is not a physically aggressive person, stood up and told her, 'You cannot do this to him any more,' and they left the house at four in the morning. Another time, according to Shirley, they took the girls to supper and Eilleen ended up having a major row with her mother screaming 'Shut your mouth, mind your own business.'

The tabloid stories presented Clarence as an innocent party and Sharon as a loony nutcase. Kenny Derasp, who lived with the Twains in Hanmer, recalls matters slightly differently. 'Sharon talked about him a couple of times and had nothing good to say about him. I was there one time when he turned up in town and he called Sharon, wanting to see the girls, and she was really upset. She spoke to the kids who totally refused to see him, they wanted nothing to do with him. I read the stuff the tabloids printed about Sharon: one said she was a crazy woman, one said she was an alcoholic.

'There is no way that woman could have been an alcoholic. I've tossed a few beers back with Jerry, but Sharon seldom drank at all. There was no alcohol abuse in the family.' Smoking was a different matter. 'The store was a mile away, and if Jerry was out in the car, I could see her start to get fidgety when she was down to half a pack. She knew it would take fifteen minutes to walk there and twenty to walk back, so she started to get very raggy, scared she was going to be running out. Sharon was really passionate. She was quite excitable, we had a lot of laughs together.'

Two years ago at a family Thanksgiving dinner, Clarence got a little tanked. After a couple of drinks he turned to Lori's mother and said, 'At least you have your kids.' Lori said to him, 'Clarence, it is not necessarily all your fault that you don't have them.'

Except that in the end it is. Clarence made his choice when he abandoned his family and disappeared for six months. Probably he did contribute more than his daughters ever knew but at that moment he opted out of their lives. If Eilleen had not grown up to be Shania Twain, it would not be so bad and they might have reached an understanding. But because she is a star, every time she does anything, it is another wound, another reminder of how he failed as her father.

He lives 50 kilometres out of town in his bush camp, living off his railroad pension. He has no phone but he has a generator, a four-wheel-drive, a skidoo for winter; he hunts and fishes and does not drink so much any more. He has thrown in the towel and accepted that his daughter wants nothing to do with him. He says of her, 'She's written me off. What can I do?' He could have cashed in on her fame, sold his story, but he will not do that, for he doesn't want to torment her any further. In his way he is an honourable man.

When Timmins held its Shania Twain Day in 1996, he and Shirley attended, staying right at the back so she did not have to see him. When other members of the family tried to make him go and say hello he refused to move. All he said was, 'She knows who I am.'

CHAPTER NINETEEN

Come on Over . . . and Over Again

S hania had been working on the songs for her third album for years. In early 1996, she was playing early versions of 'Rock This Country!' and 'Black Eyes, Blue Tears' to Sandy Neese. She wrote the words to 'You've Got a Way' upstairs in Michael Bolton's house in New Jersey, when Mutt was working with the crooner back in 1994.

Once she started working with Mutt, Shania had to learn a new means of writing. He was as interested in her half-formed snatches of melody and phrase as he was in complete songs like 'When', a clever reworking of old clichés into a new hit which was composed when driving in the car with Mutt. By the time they reached their destination two hours later, the job was done.

Shania has refined her techniques over the years. Everywhere she goes, she carries a notebook and usually a small tape machine or mini disc recorder to sing down snatches of melody ideas. 'We write everywhere,' she says. 'When we're driving to the grocery store we write. Sometimes I come up with a melody when we're in the car and if I didn't bring the tape deck, I have to sing it all the way home so I don't forget it. When I get home I run up to the tape deck to record it.' Her note book is full of jottings, a word or a phrase that stuck in her memory the moment it was uttered. 'It's the way she does it,' says Helene Bolduc. 'When people are talking, she's always observing and listening and trying to pick up on something to write a song. She's always scribbling away. And when she's ready to write songs, she'll get ideas from the book or maybe she can pick up a title from it.'

The lyrics on *Come On Over* were clever and sassy, managing to sound more intimate than they really are. They had moved on from the previous album and a long way from the standard country formula. 'It's basically my personality coming out in my lyrics,' says Shania. 'My husband is partly responsible for that, he encourages it in me. I haven't always been brave enough to say some of the things I've said through my songs. I'll show him a song and he'll say "You've got to say it like it is. Be Yourself. So come up with all these lyrics that are fun, and independent." '

'Writing's like colouring. Kids like to colour. They don't have a reason to colour – they just like it. They have no inhibitions. They are totally open to being creative. That's how I feel about songwriting. It's a chance to just create without inhibitions.' Shania's writing is much like her personality, she writes as she speaks. When she first wrote songs, the process was an escape in itself, part of her did not care if nobody ever heard them. 'I never wanted anyone to hear things unfinished,' she recalled. 'My mother used to try so hard to catch me songwriting and I would just get so mad at her. I'd take my guitar and I'd go write out in the bush somewhere. That's the way I was.'

'I'm not really sure why I was so guarded about that sort of thing. Even today when I warm up vocally I have to make sure there's nobody around or I just cannot relax, I can't do it. I've always had a real shyness and lack of confidence in myself musically and it's very strange, that. I mean, when it comes to stage, I've learnt to jump into another skin, but when it comes to something intimate like to just sit down and sing something to someone, it's very awkward.'

Lyrically and thematically both Shania and Mutt are united in that they are determined to accentuate the positive. Just drawing on Shania's personal history would provide enough material to drown a listener in their own tears, but even her most heartfelt songs like 'God Bless the Child' and 'Send It with Love' do not strip her soul naked, lay her past out on the train tracks, the way Alanis Morrisette does. Such songs do exist in Shania's vaults, but that is where she intends them to stay, unheard even by her husband, which may be a pity. 'There are some things I won't want to share,' she says. 'I'm not that dramatic, I don't feel the need to communicate my innermost feelings – and people wouldn't get it, so what's the point? I only want to release music that people relate to. I write a lot of music I don't share, for the same reason people have diaries. It's not a creative thing. It's therapeutic.'

Just because she was married to Mutt did not make it any easier to pitch song ideas. He was always so busy that timing is everything. 'He has his own projects and he's not always with me. Actually he's not with me that often,' she says. 'We have to be together for more than one week to really get writing. It's impossible not to see each other for a whole month then get together for five or six days and expect to write anything. We're together and we don't have to plan when we are going to write. We write best when we are sitting around relaxed and almost bored. Then we'll start. It's quite fun. It's relaxed, there's nothing contrived and it's really natural. If anything, when you know each other so well, there are fewer inhibitions, because I would be afraid to reveal so much to someone else.

'Our writing styles complement each other. We both come from different places. Lyrically we think differently enough to make it interesting. He's the type of guy who almost never puts the guitar down. He's always got it on him, he walks around with it. He's great on the guitar and while I write on the guitar as well, I'm not a great player. The up-tempo ones come from him most of the time, but we bank our ideas. When he's writing music, I'll ask him, "Who's that for?" If its not for somebody specific I might say, "I like that, maybe we should do it on our next album." If its for somebody specific I'll let it be.'

As with its predecessor, the song titles on *Come On Over* were snappy captions, taglines and manifestoes in their own right. Exclamation marks were scattered like confetti over 'Whatever You Do! Don't!' and 'Man! I Feel Like a Woman', while the bracketed titles returned in 'I'm Holdin' on to Love (to Save My Life)' and 'Don't Be Stupid (You Know I Love You)'. The '(You Know I Love You)' part of the title was added later by Mutt, a neat twist turning reprimand into reassurance. Such puns and gentle *double entendres* have long been part of the Lange repertoire – Bryan

Adams' 'The Only Thing I Like on You Is Me' is an earlier example. 'He was always the master of the *double entendre*, if ever there is some kind of sexual ambiguity in the lyric, it's down to Mutt,' says Ralph Simon, who believes his lyrical influence is much underrated.

The original title of 'Love Gets Me Every Time' was 'Gol'Darn Gone and Done It' which cracked Mutt up when he first heard it. It was changed because the record company were worried that radio DJs would trip up pronouncing the tongue-twisting words. At times, the songs come perilously close to carbon dating themselves. 'I'm Holding on to Love' is packed full of knowing references to psychics, the Internet, Dr Ruth and psychiatrists while 'That Don't Impress Me Much', with its famous nod to Brad Pitt, loses its impact if you don't find the Hollywood star *du jour* sexy in the first place. The words to 'You're Still the One' are autobiographical, an oblique look at her relationship with Mutt and 'the nice feeling that we've made it against all odds'. 'If You Wanna Touch Her, Ask!' and 'Black Eyes, Blue Tears' are as close as Shania ever gets to overt feminist statements. The former is about respecting women's personal space and is a definitive slap in the face at gropers – something she had personal experience of back at school. 'Black Eyes' issues a manifesto on domestic abuse less dramatic than Garth Brooks' 'The Thunder Rolls' although cynics might argue about the merits or hidden meanings behind the words 'I'd rather die standing than live on my knees, begging please . . .'

When the time came to record, Shania and Mutt resolved to take their pop-country to its fullest extent. Most country albums are around the twelve-song, forty-minute mark. They determined to record six-teen songs with nearly an hour of music. 'When we decided to put the band together,' says Paul Leim, who was appointed session leader, 'Mutt phoned and played every song for me over the phone, just him singing and playing guitar. It took most of the evening. He called back about an hour later and started talking about players, asked me about this one and that one. Then he called me back and told me who he wanted.'

Joe Chemay, who had played with the Beach Boys, Pink Floyd and Leon Russell, took over bass duties, while the guitar parts were divided up between Biff Watson, Dann Huff and Brent Mason. Pedal steel duties were split between John Hughey, Paul Franklin and Bruce Bouton while fiddlers Rob Hajacos and Joe Spivey were augmented by Larry Franklin and Stuart Duncan.

For the sessions at Masterfonics Tracking Room in Nashville Mutt had even more specific ideas on how he wished the songs to sound. This time there were no budgetary restraints and he determined the record would take as long as he thought necessary. 'On the first record he wasn't that specific, because he felt under a time constraint,' says Leim. 'In my opinion it's a little bit more Nashville, you can hear the players contributing a little more. He said it was frustrating to him to have to finish it so fast, but I love that album, it really sounds like what we cut. The next one obviously sounds like what we cut, but he took it to another level of perfection . . . But once again the proof was in the pudding, there's a fine line between perfection and soulfulness, which is what he tries to find. Mutt brought a whole new level of professionalism and expertise to this town.'

Once again, Shania was in the studio adding her vocals to every pass, every take on the backing tracks. One day, Mercury had scheduled some interviews, and Shania was really pissed off that she had to do them while the band were cutting. She came back in the session and apologized, 'I hate it when they schedule something like that when I'm trying to work.' She hated it because it interfered with the creative process and she wanted to be part of that.

'Mutt thinks more along the line of production than I do,' she says. 'When we're writing a song, we might throw ideas out. I might say, "This would be great with a fiddle," or he will say, "This is the type of guitar sound we should go for on this song." We'll talk through stuff like that during the songwriting process, but it isn't until you get in the studio that you start experimenting with it. You don't always know what your best points are and what your weak points are. Its hard for a singer to be objective about herself. A good producer knows what those elements are. I know what sound I want, but he's the producer. I don't go into the studio to tweak the guitar sound for ten hours. I can't even be interested in that, but I can tell him creatively what I want.'

There is a trick with empty plastic bottles where you hold it behind your neck, tilt your head to one side and then pull hard on the bottle, which cracks sounding like you have broken your neck. One session Dann Huff was out in the hall drinking from a plastic bottle of Evian water and decided to treat the film crew chronicling the recording process to his performance. Dann sat just behind Mutt in camera shot. As he started massaging his neck, Leim called, 'Dann, what's wrong with your neck?' Mutt looked around as Dann replied, 'I don't know.' Crack! While the sound was more of a dull crunch it got a big laugh from everybody. A few moments later, Mutt, who had been bursting to speak, announced, 'You know if that had had a little more highs on it, it would have sounded more like you were really popping your neck.' Paul laughed, 'Listen, he's producing the joke'. Mutt went bright red to increased laughter.

For the musicians the routine was the same: sixteen tracks, sixteen days, starting at 10 a.m. and finishing whenever. 'I was aware of Mutt, but I had never worked with him,' laughs Joe Chemay. 'I didn't know that everything I had heard was actually true. He's such a perfectionist and likes to go over it so many times. But after working with him, I realize why he does that. He's working out the arrangement the whole day, he is concerned with perfection, but that's his method of getting every note exactly the way he wants it.

'It wasn't hard at all. Sometimes it can be when you have somebody making you play a certain way, but Mutt is such a gentleman that I was happy to do whatever he asked. He knows exactly what he wants. Not by the brand of guitar, but by sound. When he put the call out, he just said bring everything you have. I have seven or eight basses that travel with me in a trunk, and we went through and listened to all of them. At the beginning of each song, if the one I picked didn't sound exactly the way he wanted, he'd ask to try a different one.'

Mutt did let the musicians add their own touches. He knew that he wanted Joe to play fretless bass on 'You've Got a Way' but other than that he let him have his head. 'We cut that all day with just a trio,' says Chemay, 'just drums, bass and acoustic guitar. The fretless bass allowed me to slide and make gradual note and pitch changes. I had quite a lot of input on that song.

'Mutt's arrangements separate all the instruments nicely; the song will play along and there will be a steel part, and at that point everything drops away from it. It's not clashing with anything else. It sounds like you can mix it with a yard stick, push everything up and instruments would pop in at the right times without actually having to mix them.'

In fact, it is the mixing process where Mutt's record budgets soar, when he insists that that separation Chemay talks about is absolute. The biggest sonic change in the recording process on *Come On Over* was in Mutt's use of Pro Tools, a computer program that enabled him to bring his perpetual search for perfection one step closer. If the advent of digital recording technology and computerized mixing desks changed the way records were made, Pro Tools changed the way songs were edited.

In the analogue days, when everything was recorded on magnetic tape, moving a guitar riff to another part of the song was laborious; it had to be re-recorded from the master tape on to half-inch tape and then 'spun in', literally cut into position by hand. It was so hard to get absolutely right that generally it was quicker to get the musician back in, except that a 'perfect moment' cannot always be recreated to order. Using Pro Tools, the only limitations were the size of the hard drive and the extent of the producer's patience. With Mutt patience has never been an issue.

Pro Tools is a software program that edits songs the way a word-processing program does for words. Chunks of music ranging in size from a full string section to a half note on the hi-hat can be cut or copied and then pasted wherever the producer wants. If the bass guitar and the bass drum were absolutely together for nine notes, but out by a millisecond on the tenth, the mistake can be fixed. Once the producer has the performance he wants he can move it half note by half note until it is precisely the way it should be. And in the exact part of the song it should be. Vocals, too, can be differentiated, fixed differently, backing vocals enhanced again and again until they sound like choirs of angels; a note that's a touch flat can be tweaked, but the better the original recording, the less obvious the tweak. Mutt's production on *Come On Over* was cutting-edge and the credit 'All Programming, Pro-Tools, Sequencing & Editing and that extra Swedish Swing: The Excellent Olle Romo' says it all.

However, Hal aside, computers have no soul. While Pro Tools can varnish the sound, it still cannot turn wood into platinum. In the end it comes back to moments of magic, the original song and the playing still have to be there. At the base of all Mutt's best work, for all his nit-picking, lies soul.

The album's full-scale romantic ballad was 'From This Moment On'. The genesis of the song was anything but romantic. Shania was curled up on the sofa while Mutt was busy watching Inter Milan play on the satellite channel. Shania started scribbling away and then disappeared into the kitchen to grab her guitar and finish the job. She never did find out who won, but she came back with a powerhouse ballad she thought perfect for Celine Dion. As the pair developed the song they realized it worked best as a duet. Shania's first choice for a partner was Elton John. Instead of bringing in an established country superstar, they chose Bryan White, a 22-year-old from West Virginia, who had been making waves without cracking the top echelon.

White leapt at the opportunity. He travelled up to the Langes' home in New York. 'I'd never actually collaborated, as far as a duet, with anybody before,' he said, 'so it became a lot of fun. They let me do exactly what I wanted to do, and I think we blended real well together. I got to work out all kinds of different arrangement things with them. I say "them" a lot because I think of it as not only working with Shania but also with Mutt, who's so much a part of her sound. They were always both there. Basically, a lot of her (vocal) part was already down when I arrived. That meant I, mostly, did my part to her track because she had already finished. Vocally, it was extremely challenging. That's what made it so interesting and fun.'

Shania later described Bryan as having 'the best male voice in country music. Beyond country music! He's an excellent singer. So he needed to be on this record, because the song soars. It demands that. It demands dynamics.' Bryan's is the only vocal on the album not sung by Shania and Mutt.

When it came time to promote the album, the success of her Fan Appreciation days encouraged Shania to repeat the experience. On 4 November 1997 she returned to the Mall of America. The lines started forming at 6.30 a.m. and 20,000 fans turned up to welcome her back. On 9 November she took over Santa Claus' North Pole area at the Southcentre Mall in Calgary, Alberta, the heartland of Canadian country music. 27,000 people showed up to see the singer, who, dressed in black pants, matching crop-shirt baring her belly button and a baby blue jacket, did not hide behind security. When she was asked to wave to some fans not in the autograph line she marched to the front of the stage and climbed on top of a speaker. Several times she walked into the crowd to greet a fan in a wheelchair, she picked up babies like an aspiring presidential candidate, hugged children and posed for photos. When the scheduled end of the autograph session approached with thousands of fans still in line, Shania – who did not take a single break – insisted on staying until everyone got their autograph.

The marketing was carried out very differently in the USA and the rest of the world. While Europe went straight for the pop market, America chose to break *Come On Over* out of country and then crossover. 'Love Gets Me Every Time' roared to the top of the country charts quickly followed by 'Don't Be Stupid', which made it into the top ten. Mercury then stacked a series of album tracks one after the other. By Christmas, some country stations were playing fifteen songs off the album.

The crossover single was always intended to be the third release, 'You're Still the One'. It took off like a scalded cat. At one point her record was being played on five different radio formats: Country, Regular Adult Contemporary, Hot Adult Contemporary, Pop, and CHR

(Contemporary Hit Radio). Some of the country stations got very pissy; Shania was hot and they wanted to be the only wavelength in town playing her records.

'All of a sudden they wanted to own her, wanted to be the only one that's bringing you Shania Twain,' says John Grady. 'The record came out of Nashville, on a Nashville label so the country stations got very proprietary. Suddenly we were fighting a war at radio, and they made threats about her music, they made threats about all of our music.'

Taking Shania off the playlist would have been cutting off their noses, but boycotting less popular Mercury products could have had serious consequences for the label. Lewis and Grady held their nerve and stuck to their position as the record raced to the top of every chart available. Once the record was crossed over there was little country radio could do except keep on playing. Eventually there were to be nine singles released off *Come On Over* and the album sold over 17 million copies in the USA. In May 1998, Polygram sold out to Universal. It made no difference to the album, which kept on selling. Mutt and Shania did have a long chat with the new big boss, Doug Morris, and explained that they were happy with Mercury, Nashville, who continued to work the record.

From the outset, Mercury knew video was going to be an essential part of that crossover. The country feel was dumped from the off as Shania determined to go glamorous, whether it was classical sophistication ('From This Moment On'), flirting with half-naked hunks in moody black and white ('You're Still the One') or playing the cabaret decadent in top hat and gloves ('Man! I Feel Like a Woman').

'In the early days she always had a say in how she looked, in terms of clothing and hairstyle and make-up,' says Retta Harvey. 'And it just got progressively more so, because she knew who she was, and how she wanted to be presented as a performer. Now when we do videos, she's pretty much running the show, she's figuring out who she wants. She's calling the directors, she's dealing with the ideas with them directly, and I'm basically here to make sure it's all taken care of, financially and contractually. I handle all the nightmare phone calls.'

The average video budget was US$350–400,000. 'You're Still the One' was the most expensive. It was shot in Malibu, and bad weather required an extra day's shooting which kicked the budget over the half million mark. Half the cost of each video is recoupable against her royalties, the other fifty per cent is considered a company marketing expense.

'Shania knows that half of it is her money, she wants to get it right, and she's a perfectionist, so she's going to do it till it's done. She's a trouper. We've had times where we've shot twenty-two, twenty-three hours, because she wants to make sure it's done properly.' The killer video was 'That Don't Impress Me Much', where Shania, wearing a somewhat improbable fake leopardskin ensemble, hitches across the Mojave desert, turning down a series of lifts from increasingly more gorgeous guys riding Harleys, Jeeps and stallions. It was a camp classic which programmers, VJs and viewers adored. The work of a woman who knew how to exploit the medium to the full.

That only left Shania two worlds to conquer. The stage . . . and the rest of the planet.

CHAPTER TWENTY

On the Road (At Last)

S hania Twain's Come On Over Tour began at the Sudbury Community Arena on Friday 29 May 1998. The day before, when everyone else was worrying themselves into a frenzy, Shania drove out to Hanmer. She stopped by Proulx Court, took a stroll along the trail she once walked to go skating on Onwatin Lake and on a whim dropped in on her old school, Redwood Acres. It was lunchtime and she happily chatted to the stunned kids and had her photograph taken.

The night of the show, Shania was the calmest person backstage. She went through a meet and greet ritual, shaking hands with contest winners and well-wishers and found time to talk with her old friends in her dressing room. On the second night, Lynn Bond, who had come to see her backstage, managed to lose her tickets on her way back to her seat. During the show Shania announced, 'Lynn did you find your seat?' Despite all the palaver, she had taken in the information that her childhood friend was in a state.

In the minds of the media and the Nashville music industry Shania's refusal to go on the road had taken on a ridiculous significance. She had always known that she could deliver live but being Shania she had left nothing to chance. Failure was not an option. To Shania record sales were just numbers, not personal like the Fan Appreciation days. 'I haven't had the opportunity to feel the audience's response,' she said. 'There's a void for me and I want to see people respond to my music, live. Just to get out there and just, I don't know, vent. Just get out there and physically put myself into my music . . . I can't wait for it.'

Once she had made the decision not to go out until she could headline, Shania started formulating the plans for her stage show. She drew on everything she had learnt. The big Pink Floyd and Rush shows she had loved as a teenager, the pure showbiz Vegas glitz that Deerhurst had hinted at, the touches of intimacy that were so important to a country audience. Aware that if she used too many hydraulic sets and special effects the critics would once again accuse her of hiding behind technology, she resolved to focus on 'lights, sound and performance'.

In 1996, on a promotional trip to New York, she described her show to Sandy Neese, telling her, 'I don't want it to be about special effects. I want it to be a big party, I want the audience to be as involved in it, have as much fun as we are on stage, I want a band that's energetic and works as hard as I do. I want to do something for the hungry in every city. I want to bring on the local choir, I want to bring somebody up from the audience who can sing . . . if somebody had given me a chance like that to get up on stage and sing when I was a kid . . . well I'm going to do that.'

Just as she does with her videos, Shania came up with the basic concepts for the show and then found the best men to sculpt them in reality. Jon Landau, who loves to get involved in conceptual planning, was an essential sounding board. Along with Jon came another Springsteen veteran, Tour Director George Travis. Travis' last three projects had been world tours for Bruce, Madonna and Mariah Carey, representing a wide cross-section of diva demands, complex staging and sheer stamina. 'George is a remarkable fellow,' says Ron Baird. 'His whole job was to translate into reality her visions, desires and direction and sometimes to tell her, "There's no way to do that." I think he did a spectacular job.' Shania spared no expense and gave him *carte blanche* to hire the best, most experienced people. The show used the very latest technology, revolving treadmills; the video screen was a proto-type built in China, all state-of-the-art equipment. She and the band might have been big-stage virgins, but the guys behind the scene knew how to make the Pope rock.

In today's marketplace the most successful concert tours are no longer just about the music. They have to be an event, a spectacle, part

Broadway show, part theme-park ride, a combination of high energy and effects that assault the eyes as well as the ears. However, while constant touring is an integral part of country music, the live shows have remained traditional, visually as dull as ditchwater – grizzled old bloke in hat, jeans and cowboy boots stands still and plays jolly well. Shania was determined that her live band break the mould.

The trick was to keep the country sound but present it as if it was something new. The players had to be accomplished, versatile musicians capable of playing the complex song arrangements but to look young, cool and funky. 'I can't have anyone in the band who doesn't have my energy,' said Shania, explaining her choices. 'I don't want people who have been on the road for years and are just doing it in order to do it. And I like a clean band. I don't like drugs. I don't like alcohol. I like to have clean-living people around me.'

After he had finished remixing *Come On Over* for Europe, and Shania took off to promote it, Mutt took on the role of musical director. He only kept two musicians from *The Woman in Me* days: pedal steel guitarist Marc Muller and fiddle player Allison Cornell. From Nashville's young scene he recruited guitarist Brent (B. B.) Barcus and drummer J. D. Blair. Blair was a six-foot (1.83 metres) black guy in wrap-around shades and dreadlocks who looked like he had stepped off a street corner in Compton. His resumé was equally impressive, mixing up funk with Bootsy Collins, gospel with Take 6, Lyle Lovett's Large Band and Shelby Lynne's R&B-flavoured country. There were two Australian expats who had fetched up in Tennessee: guitarist Randall Waller, the joker in the pack, and bassist Andy Cichon, once a member of Oz hard rockers Rose Tattoo.

By late January 1998, Mutt's attempts to find a keyboard player who could double on percussion and accordion and sing high had floundered. B. B. recommended Hardy Hemphill, with whom he had played behind Steven Curtis Chapman. Hardy was cooking dinner at home when he had a call suggesting he learn 'You're Still the One' fast and get out to Los Angeles even quicker. After borrowing a friend's CD and an intensive day rehearsing, he was invited to play with Shania on Jay

Leno's Super Bowl show two days later. Fiddler Cory Churko, a native of Moose Jaw, Saskatchewan, who also doubled on guitar, mandolin, keyboards, percussion and vocals, quit his job as a computer animator to enlist.

The final recruit on fiddle was Roddy Chiong. In February 1998 Chiong, who also acts and had appeared as a Chinese hitman in Mel Gibson's violent thriller *Payback*, was at a loose end when he got a message to call Brent Barcus. Roddy was not too enthused when B. B. talked about a possible country gig he had, saying, 'Do they know that I'm an Asian guy with long hair? I don't like to play fiddle music too much. More rock kind of stuff.' When the name of Shania Twain came up, he blanked it. Something nagged at him all night, so the next morning he looked her name up on the Internet. Minutes later he was back on the phone to Brent. Then he rushed out, bought both Shania's albums and spent the next two weeks practising the songs.

In March, Roddy flew to Albany, where George Travis picked him up for the three-hour drive to the studio in St Regis Falls. 'When we arrived at the very large house,' writes Chiong on his website, 'I said hello to everyone and we started playing right away. I almost didn't have time to be nervous. There was a very pleasant man at the front of the room telling us what to do and he was obviously the leader. I didn't know who he was – which ended up working to my advantage because it was Mutt Lange, Shania's husband. The first song we played was "Don't Be Stupid". This was fine by me because I had practised that one the most. But I was in for a surprise – the version that we were going to play was a new version called the "international" version, which would require me to relearn the song in a slightly different way. Slightly enough to mess up my whole audition (so I thought)! Incredibly, the power went out and nothing was working, so everybody took a thirty-minute break – just enough time for me to figure out the new parts! It went smoothly, and we continued to play most of the songs from the album.

'My playing seemed to be up to what they were looking for, and next Shania wanted to know if I could sing. We were just about to get started on that, but something in me felt like I wasn't quite ready and I needed some time to warm up, so I asked if I could have five minutes. Incredibly again, a one-hour lunch break ended up being called! There was no way that I was going to pig out on lunch and then try to sing. So, I went into the exercise room, jumped on the stationary bike and did some easy pedalling while warming up my voice and learning the harmony parts to the song "No One Needs to Know". Well, that one hour did the trick because when Shania and I got together, my voice was there where it needed to be.'

Chiong was hired. His first gig was the *Divas Live* show on VH-1, after which the band settled down to five weeks of intensive show rehearsals in Lake Placid. Apart from J. D. all of the musicians wore microphone headsets allowing them the freedom to roam the stage while recreating the complex vocal harmonies on the albums. For Mutt the sound was everything. Early in rehearsals it became apparent that the complexities of his arrangements made mixing the front of house sound too much for one man.

'Due to the sheer number of inputs and the fact that we are trying to duplicate the record mixes as close as we can, it was decided that we needed another sound engineer,' explained John Kerns, another Springsteen alumnus, who started the tour. 'The show is pretty hectic because there are so many cues – about fifteen to twenty per song for each of us.' His co-engineer was Nigel Green, who has mixed a large amount of Mutt's studio work. Green concentrated on Shania's vocals, while the second engineer provided a series of sub-mixes which were then placed in and out of the overall balance. Despite press stories that he was attending the World Cup finals in France, Mutt was omnipresent in the first days of the tour, adding little tweaks, minuscule touches on faders in a series of last-minute adjustment. Once it was up and running to his satisfaction, Mutt left the tour. There are too many variables in live shows for his comfort.

After a month, Shania invited Ron Baird, Luke Lewis and other key Nashville personnel up to Lake Placid. Ron, who had had the hottest act in country on his books for six years and not earned a penny, was nervous. 'I was curious,' he says. 'I didn't know how good it was going to be. She did a dress rehearsal for twenty people in this arena, and it was fantastic, so much better than I could have ever hoped for. In thirty years I've seen thousands of shows, but clearly from the very beginning this was one of the very best shows I've ever seen.'

The first casualty of playing to an audience of 30,000 is intimacy. The first fifty rows have a great time, but to those at the back up close to heaven the figures leaping around the stage might as well be Lowry matchstick men cavorting in hell, while the sound in the worst aircraft hangars can be better in the car park. Giant video screens and Mutt's painstaking rehearsals solved some of those problems, but not the physical one. Fans come to see live shows because they want to – or imagine they might be able to – touch the star.

During *A Touch of Broadway*, when Shania had entered the hall from the back of the audience, the effect was always electric. On tour as the band struck up the opening chords of 'Man! I Feel Like A Woman', silhouetted against a waterfall of tumbling fireworks, she was borne to the stage on a platform, a queen sitting on her throne, but a queen who reached out to touch her subjects as she passed. Some nights she walked through the crowd, or leant down off the runway signing autographs as she sang, collecting flowers and gifts, acknowledging the giver without missing a beat. Before the third number, 'You Win My Love', she stood behind a giant yellow spotlight and swung it into the audience, eventually focusing on the very worst row of seats in the auditorium. The folk caught in the beam were then invited down to take new seats in the front row. It was a trick Garth Brooks had used but its effect was the same – she won their love. At other predetermined points throughout the concert Shania invited little kids or fans up to sing with her – something that did not always work musically. The intimacy of watching her face in close-up on the big screen was magnified, as one could see how her gaze rose and fell, focusing once in a while on a particular person, accompanying a shy smile with a tiny wave of the fingers.

The show blurred the country boundaries from the off. Shania wore tight outfits, revealing her world famous midriff for at least half the set, tirelessly working the stage from side to side, from back to front. For the quick changes before 'Black Eyes, Blue Tears' and 'From This Moment On', Helene was waiting in a booth just off the side of the stage. 'We had it all down pat,' she says, 'because we had a minute and twenty-eight seconds to do it.' The musicians all wore skin-tight T-shirts or vests – except the 'Groove Regulator', J. D. Blair in his outsize headphones and ski goggles – displaying buff muscles, tight buns and firm abs, not a paunch or a denim in sight. Musically the show bore as much relationship to country music as the Police did to reggae: the instruments were familiar, but the groove was pure pop. The final number, 'Rock This Country', did Def Leppard proud, complete with guitar posturing and pyros going off in all directions.

At the climax of Marc Muller's juddering lap steel solo on '(If You're Not in It for Love) I'm Outta Here', Shania stood on top of a giant bass drum and with a flash of smoke disappeared down it. Moments later, she appeared in the middle of the auditorium, being carried back through the crowds to finish the song. Michael Jackson employed a similar magic stunt on his Bad Tour and the reaction from the crowd was always the same – how did she do that?

Away from performances, Shania's relationship with her musicians was friendly but distant. 'Before every show we would do a vocal warm-up,' recalls Marc Muller, 'usually the gospel vocal breakdown on "God Bless the Child". Then Hardy, the appointed band preacher, would say a prayer asking for a great performance and continued band unity. Then we'd all say a huge "AMEN!" and go to our spots off-stage and wait for the lights to go down.' There were practical jokes played on stage. Allison Cornell got her own back on Shania one night by 'making a rude picture pop out of the Polaroid camera when she thought I'd just photographed her with a fan'.

Once the business was over, Shania headed for her bus, while the band, who were only allowed alcohol after the show was over, headed for their own. Shania's bus was custom-made. It cost a million dollars, complete with a cinema, a media room with a state-of-the-art communications system so she could do interviews when travelling, fully stocked kitchen, plus a bedroom, bathroom and kitchenette at the back for her assistant. Shania's bedroom, complete with a large fixed bed, en suite toilet and hot shower, was at the front of the bus, away from the noise of the motor and the pumps. The only personal security Shania would allow on the bus was her German Shepherd Tim, a trained guard dog fiercely loyal to the mistress who issued all his commands in German.

Just before midnight one Sunday night, Helene Bolduc had returned home after an exhausting twelve-hour shift in the Emergency Room at Timmins and District Hospital. The phone rang. It was Shania saying, 'Are you ready to come on the road with me? It's my first tour and I'd really love to have somebody personal with me on the bus, you and Larry would be great.' Larry, who was driving for Sears, came in at three and saw Helene sitting on the floor. Once he realized that nobody was sick, he blurted out, 'We're going on the road, all this getting the tour ready, I just had this gut feeling she was going to ask us.'

So Helene, who admits she 'didn't know a thing about anything', went on the road with her as her personal assistant. 'I was in for a lot of surprises. I took care of the bus. Larry was driving it, but he was driving at night when we were both sleeping, and then in the morning he'd park that bus at the next venue and go to sleep in a hotel room.

'She wanted a bus on the road, so she would have her own home, her own set-up the way she wanted it. If she was on the bus, she was not disturbed, because everybody had to come through me. If she was sleeping, I wouldn't disturb her for anything. The minute she had one foot out of that bus, everybody wanted her, it's like "Shania, Shania, Shania," a thousand times in a few hours. She was not having an easy life. And I think when she got tired, she was even worse. A few times I'd have snapped. She never did, she won't.'

Once a day, Helene and Shania sat down to go through the stacks of requests that had built up. 'She'd do interviews, a whole ton of things, unbelievable, nobody knows what a star has to do. Some days I would just look at her and I'd say, "Why do you bother going through all this?"

On the day of the show she would do a sound check at five o'clock. Then she would have to get made-up to do television interviews, sometimes as many as five. There were nights when it all got too much and she said, "Helene, I don't want to do this," and vented her frustration.' The meditation techniques that Mutt uses have never been so effective for Shania. She is too impatient when things do not happen easily or the way she wants them too.

After Mutt went back to the studio, they would talk on the phone every day for hours. She had hoped to write some songs on the road, but there was hardly enough time for that. 'After the show we left immediately, and she would just shower get into her PJs and then we'd just talk, not about the show, I'd talk about the family, the cottage, talk about anything else and that would unwind her.'

Helene's role was mother as well as confidant. One of her most difficult jobs was making sure that Shania ate enough – her high-octane performance burned thousands of calories which her vegetarian diet did not easily replace. 'Sometimes she would feel weak or tired, and I'd tell her, "You've got to eat more," I'd make her shakes in the morning, rich with cream, because she could use the calories. I'd leave food every-where, so if she was hungry, it was there to snack on. Every night I'd make her meals. Before a performance she didn't want anything heavy, just a lot of vegetables, soups and stir-fries with Tofu in them.'

Shania's diet contains no meat, no fish, no eggs. Wherever she travels a blender goes with her, so she can make fruit and vegetable drinks. Her concert rider is spartan in its simplicity. In her dressing room she required, 'Six large ripe California oranges suitable for juicing, six lemons, three papayas, three mangoes, eighteen apples, six bananas, one pineapple, one cantaloupe, one honeydew melon, one small water-melon, ten pounds carrots, three medium beets, two bunches celery, three heads broccoli, quarter pound ginger root . . . and a kettle for boiling water.' Other requirements included salt and vinegar potato chips, two packages of Mori-Nu Silken Style Soft Tofu, orange cheese popcorn, assorted herbal teas, twenty-four small bottles spring water (at room temperature), twelve cans Diet Coke, six cans of Ginger Ale

(Canada Dry if available), six cans Orange soda. If Helene was not preparing her vegetarian dinner it had to be cleared with the road manager in advance. Pasta dishes had to be cooked with angel hair pasta made without eggs. Desserts, cobblers cakes had to be eggless, as did the dozen home-made cookies and muffins demanded. Shania has a sweet tooth and likes her candy as much as dill-flavoured potato chips.

Shania's greatest extravagance was bringing her horse Dancer on tour. Dancer, an Andalusian pure bred, had his own special trailer, and Shania took off on him at every opportunity. That put her personal injury insurance premiums sky-high. 'He's my knight, beautiful, regal with a very powerful high action,' she enthused. 'Dancer has had special training, on his passage and gait and all that special stuff. He's a ballet dancer, very muscular and strong with a swan neck. He gets frothy at the mouth and very excited. He's great fun to ride but quite intimidating.'

Helene instructed Shania from the off to tell if she wasn't up to the job. Her worst blunder came towards the end, when Shania was flying to Europe for the Party in the Park and the concerts in the UK and Dublin. It was right after Shania's show in Timmins, and everybody was all over the place in the post-gig euphoria. Her wardrobe was shipped with all the equipment. The problem was that she was meeting Prince Charles and didn't have a thing to wear. Instead of chilling out, Shania had to buy a suitable outfit – everything she liked was either too long or didn't fit right. Jan Stabile and Barbara Carr, from the Management Office, were frantically sewing, hemming and making the outfit as they drove in the car to meet the Prince. 'I was supposed to think of those things for her, and I goofed there,' says Helene. 'She never said a word about it, nothing.'

Shania is a perfectionist who demands the same standards from those who work for her. When she makes decisions, she expects action right away, but throughout the tour Helene never saw her lose her cool. When she got angry she bit her lip and then quietly told the management what had to be changed. Her brother Darryl was originally employed as a pyrotechnics assistant on the show, but once his behaviour became unacceptable – turning up late or not at all and then reminding his colleagues of who he was – he was warned and finally fired.

In the 23-strong set the highpoint for musical drama was 'God Bless the Child'. Shania was joined on stage by a local choir. Beefed up by dramatic tympani and extra verses, the song was moody and powerful, so very different from the gentle, heart-tugging a cappella version on record. This was swiftly followed by a clip of Shania performing as a child, which in turn introduced a performance by a local child. To some it was a twee interlude which sat uncomfortably next to the navel-baring rock that went before and after. To others it was the one point at which she revealed her intimate feelings.

Shania does not often wear her emotions on her sleeve but the way she talks about child hunger should silence the cynics. It comes from her guts, from a physical memory of the time when her stomach was empty. To help assuage that emptiness she has given hundreds of thousands of dollars away. The royalties from 'God Bless the Child' are split between two organizations – Second Harvest Kid's Café in the US and the Canadian Living Foundation, who are also given a portion of all proceeds from T-shirt, calendar and poster sales. In the States the money she has raised has helped launch twenty-two separate Kid's Café programmes. In addition she donates tickets to every concert so local food banks can run raffles, while a donation is also given to a specific local charity. In Timmins the money went to Mattagami First Nation, the local food banks and the hospital. In Europe she donated to the War Child fund for Kosovan children.

'A lot of stars support different charities,' she explains, 'but only a few deal with poorer families and underprivileged people. One reason that I contribute so publicly is to raise awareness. Only a relatively small part of society can really understand what it means to be truly poor, when you can't afford the most basic things . . . Other charities are fine, but they often don't deal with people who are in a really needy situation. And I know from personal experience what it means to be poor. I was one of those people who couldn't afford basic essentials. People who are well-off don't know what it's like. They can be ignorant of the fact that there are people out there who are really hungry. Food is one thing you can't get by without and there are a lot of people who can't afford it.'

'I was that hungry kid,' she explains. 'My goal is to save kids the humiliation, the anguish of feeling inferior.' Backstage before and after every performance Shania worked her way through a line of dozens of well-wishers, including sick children and terminally ill fans. 'A lot of artists [wouldn't meet with a dying fan], and I can understand why,' she says. 'But I've been through enough in my life that I can relate to people very well. I'm not tough. I'm strong. And I think there's a very big difference.'

On 11 May 1999, the day of her show at Fiddlers Green Amphitheatre in Englewood, Colorado, Shania paid an unannounced visit, with no media publicity, to the hospital where five high-school pupils were still recovering from the appalling massacre at Columbine High School three weeks earlier. She had decided to make the visit when she learnt that one of the wounded, a student who had hung from a second-floor window during the shooting, was a huge fan of hers. The kids screamed with delight when they saw her, and Shania gave each of them a signed photo and a portable CD player. When questioned about her visit later, all she would say as she fought back tears was, 'Well you do what you can.'

The tour was a triumph, elevating her from country star to pop superstar without missing a beat. Between 29 May 1998 and 16 January 2000, Shania Twain played 165 shows in five countries (primarily the USA and Canada; she also gave seven concerts in Australia, three in the UK and one in Ireland) to over 2.5 million people. The tour grossed $86 million, the highest-grossing country tour in history (Garth Brooks actually played to more people but pegged his ticket prices to $19.50). Only the Rolling Stones were a bigger draw.

Not bad for a little girl who, when she started to perform around Sudbury, had to be forced on to the stage . . . and who had often left it in tears.

CHAPTER TWENTY-ONE

Shania Twain Superstar

I n January 1998, Shania Twain was a huge star in the States, 15 million albums big and rising. But she was a country star, and if record companies know one thing it is that country doesn't sell in Europe. Capitol had spent a ton of money to make Garth Brooks' *In Pieces* a hit album, but none of his succeeding records had broken the top ten. Country has to be sold as something, as anything, else.

Being part of a niche market was not on Shania's agenda. She was determined that with *Come On Over* she would become an international star and that she would do whatever was necessary to achieve that. On 3 January, she arrived in London to stay in the Milestone, a small, discreet hotel on Kensington High Street, a low-key beginning to one of the most effective marketing campaigns in recent times.

'Not a lot of American artists are interested in being international. I am,' she said without any trace of bravado or arrogance. It was a simple statement of intent. At that point, *Come On Over* had sold about 10,000 copies, all imports, to die-hard country fans in the UK. 'I am Canadian. A lot of Canadian acts have had success in Europe first, so I am acutely aware of the rest of the world.' Twenty-four months later, the album had sold a further three million copies in Britain, 30 million around the world, and Shania was a bona fide pop superstar, the C word forgotten, mixed out of her CV as adroitly as the fiddles out of the European mixes.

Shania was always different from the usual American country stars. There was a formality, a cool reserve about her; she spoke softly in an accent that did not spit grits and chitlins. Her handshake was just that: a nod of her head preceded a slight pressure on fingers and palm, then quick release. No fake bonhomie, no air hugs or multiple space kisses. Shania preferred to keep her distance. What struck was how poised, how pretty and – when she stood up – how petite Shania was. Instead of the usual cowboy chic and big hair, she wore a beige sleeveless high-necked ribbed sweater that accentuated her figure but focused attention on her face, with its perfect cheekbones and flawed nose. She was gorgeous, but real, a woman of thirty-two with a real *Angela's Ashes* life behind her, not some teenager mouthing Spice Girls soundbites. The hunger that blazed in her belonged to an aspirant, not a woman who had no need to work again. She had control, power and money . . . and one thing was quite clear. It was not enough.

In a different era, *The Woman in Me* might have gone international. As one might expect, it did brilliantly in Canada, selling 1.8 million copies (it is now double diamond selling over two million) and it went platinum in Australia. 'The pattern was to get a crossover hit in America before we took it international,' says Luke Lewis. 'Billy Ray Cyrus did that with 'Achy Breaky Heart', which went pop over here before it went overseas.' Lewis believed he could break out with the title track, 'a ballad which everybody over there was hollering for', which is why he sent Shania to shoot the video in Egypt. It didn't happen. 'I don't think they felt it was right,' he admits, 'which left Mutt and me frustrated out of our brains.'

Luke's enthusiasm did get to David Munns in London. Munns, who was Polygram's Head of International, got Shania and saw the potential. On 5 July 1995, she made a short promotional tour of Britain playing lunchtime gigs at three small clubs – the Renfrew Ferry in Glasgow, La Gitaine in Manchester and Venom in London. The reaction was positive but building a buzz involved interesting the media. They were not that interested. As the record continued to sell in the States, Munns refused to give up. What the record company had to do was not so much think outside the box as chuck it away and build a new one.

In September 1996, Munns contacted Richard Beck at LD Publicity. LD are one of the most well-respected PR companies in Europe, whose client list has included the Rolling Stones, Tina Turner, Peter Gabriel and Janet Jackson. Once again, interest was hard to arouse, though they managed to book her a slot on the major prime-time TV show, *The Des*

O'Connor Show. Just prior to coming in, Shania had to return to Canada for major surgery on her wisdom teeth and the show was pulled. Soon after, she appointed Jon Landau Management and Munns decided to wait until there was a new album.

Once a record goes multi-platinum in the States, there is a great deal of pressure on the overseas companies to duplicate that success. However, many American artists are not prepared to devote the energy and the time necessary and cannot be bothered to tailor their sound and image to the demands of an international market. Mutt and Shania were.

Once *Come On Over* was completed and delivered to Mercury Nashville, Mutt spent the next four months remixing seventy per cent of the album. This involved diluting or removing the twang elements. On 'You're Still the One' the obvious fiddle and pedal steel parts were cut right back and the pop elements of the song brought to the forefront, and it is one second shorter. The running order was also resequenced: the US version began with 'Man! I Feel Like a Woman', the international with 'You're Still the One'.

Great Britain is still considered as the taste-maker for Europe. Germany may be a bigger market, but Britain has a national media – newspapers, music and style magazines, radio and TV stations – that reach the whole country in one hit and pride themselves on spotting and selling trends. While over the last decade the singles charts have changed to reflect saturation marketing campaigns – records regularly enter the charts at number one and sink almost as quick – there is still a prestige to getting a UK hit.

David Munns hired LD Publicity, and they set out to formulate a radical campaign. 'All the press photos were of her with a horse and it was so country,' says Richard Beck. 'From the start I refused to do country media, because I knew they would buy her record anyway. Luckily I was backed by the label and by Shania herself.' The American artwork, all bleached out and flying hair, was rejected, and George Holz did a new photo session. The new cover was very simple – Shania, head turned towards the camera, with dishevelled hair, a half smile and a bare shoulder – and very effective. Hinting that coming on over might be very rewarding, it was sexy, but not overt.

'David Munns gave us *carte blanche* to do what we wanted on the act,' says Beck, 'so we went all out. She had been marketed as a country act in the past, so the first thing I suggested to set her aside from the country thing was doing interviews with *FHM* and, for credibility, *The Times.*' Beck had already confirmed the photo session with *FHM* before he had met Shania. At the time the magazine, while an important player, was not the lads' mags market leader selling some 300,000 copies an issue. Its content, a mixture of sexy photo shoots, irreverent, nudge-wink articles on sports, beer and sex ('The World's Sexiest Women' leading into 'How to Tell if You Have Genital Herpes') was nowhere near Shania's American profile. Fortunately, she agreed to do it.

For Beck, the *FHM* session with Barry Hollywood was nerve-racking. The results exceeded all expectations. Shania came out looking beautiful in a bustier and a white suit, showing cleavage but not leg. Everybody loved the shots. *FHM* ran an eight-page feature and a poster campaign on London buses. Shania had Polygram buy the rest and they were used as press shots for the European campaign. 'The pictures made her mainstream. People would look at her. From being a country girl she became this sexy diva,' says Beck, who credits the *FHM* session, *The National Lottery Show* and *The Box* with being the three factors that helped her crack Britain.

Shania had made her own personal impact on the promotion campaign. On 8 January the record company had hosted a party for her at Alberta's, a chic bar over the Alberta Ferretti showroom at 205–206 Sloane Street, London. A true professional, Shania worked the room, speaking to every media person, TV, radio and press no matter how small. She was particularly charming to Richard Park at Capital Radio (the most important independent radio station in London). Within a few days 'You're Still the One' was on high rotation at Capital.

The BBC's *National Lottery Show*, which regularly pulls in 12 million viewers, desperate to discover whether they have become millionaires, is a great place to showcase a new single. Shania's performance on Valentine's day had its problems. She was singing live to a backing track, and after three run-throughs announced, 'I'm not happy with the sound I'm getting in my ears.' The management called Mutt, who had stayed in the hotel, and sent a car to pick him up. The sound engineer, who was getting very twitchy, almost had heart failure when Mutt walked in. Any union regulations were forgotten as Mutt spoke to Shania over the foldback. Within thirty seconds, she was happy with the sound and did a perfect take. Whether this was his magic touch or the placebo effect, Mutt never said.

The Box is a cable TV show in which the viewers dial up and request the video they want to see. It is the most-watched satellite music programme in the UK, with six times the viewers of MTV. More importantly it has a very young demographic; it is the channel the kids watch and they are the people who still buy singles. 'You're Still the One' was an instant favourite, quickly getting 2,000 requests a day. The song entered the charts at number ten on 28 February 1998.

Two days after *The National Lottery Show*, Shania flew to Austria on a two-week promotional tour of Europe designed to follow the template that had been set in Britain – glamour, credibility and selective dyslexia when it came to the C word. After a week in Germany, Switzerland and Scandinavia, she flew into Edinburgh, where she got into a Mercedes mini-van and spent the next two days crossing the UK. The first day they visited Glasgow, Newcastle and Manchester; the next took in Birmingham, Bristol and London; before she took the Eurostar to Paris and further promotional work in France, Italy and Spain. The routine was the same: start at 8 a.m., visit local radio and TV stations for interviews, accompanied by a local journalist who would interview her in the bus between venues. Aside from one impromptu walkabout at Watford Gap service station to buy some new videos to watch on the bus, Shania was on the go all day, doing phone interviews until she reached the hotel late at night.

'There was never a moan, she would do whatever was necessary to break this record,' says Beck. 'This was an artist who had incredible success in America. *Come On Over* was at two on the *Billboard* chart and she was in the back of a bus schlepping it out like any other band in a transit van. She is the most professional artist I have ever worked with. Her regime, her lifestyle, her work ethic are stronger.'

It was a low-key affair, high on work-rate and low on drama. Her entourage was never more than four people. Barbara Carr and Jan Stabile from Jon Landau Management, Cyril Lanoir to do hair and make-up and Beck. To begin with, the national record companies were surprised, and a little put out, by some of her requests. Breaking long established traditions, she did not like to be met at the airport with all the attendant fuss and would sometimes decline meetings with company personnel, reasoning they would be more productive in their offices than at her hotel. She was a strict vegetarian and so the ubiquitous record company dinners became an ordeal. When she is on show and working, Shania does not like eating and talking at the same time, so she started to eat in her room first and then would just pick at the dinners. At the end of every trip Shania sent a personal signed thank you letter to the major executives of each record company. In a business where thank yous are generally perfunctory, such small courtesies are major motivators.

During the two years that she was promoting *Come On Over*, as well as making her first-ever concert tour, Shania made nine promotional trips to Europe, unprecedented for an artist of her stature. In April 1998, she flew down to Australia to do the TV show *Hey Hey Saturday*. As her appearance was also tied in with the Australian Grand Prix, 60,000 people turned up. That kicked the record into the stratosphere down under. In Europe, Germany was the first territory to rack up the hits, followed eventually by the rest of the continent.

Even as she got bigger and bigger, Shania stuck to one rule. No bodyguards. Valuing her privacy, she realized that having personal security men draws attention. When she was staying in London, Shania often went out shopping in Kensington High Street, horse-riding around Rotten Row, or walking in Hyde Park all by herself, dressing down, perhaps by pulling a hood over her head. She bought an Aga and kitchen equipment for the new house in Switzerland at Smallbone & Co. on the Fulham Road and nobody recognized her – partly perhaps because she is so petite that people, expecting a larger-than-life star, simply look over her head, but as much because she walks very fast. Because she does not expect to be recognized, she is not.

Most evenings, Shania retired to her room to eat and be alone. When the party went out to dinner – the Bombay Brasserie is a particular favourite in London – she would first reflect on the day's business and discuss the forthcoming schedule. She loved to talk about her family and get into passionate discussions, for she has firmly held opinions about most things and can get loud when expressing them.

When she laughs it can still a busy hotel lobby, as Richard Beck recalls: 'We had an ongoing joke. I'd always told her, "I don't do bags and beans," and, of course, one day in Cologne I had done both. She buzzed my hotel room and asked me to come downstairs, where she said to me, "I'm really unhappy with the air-conditioning level in my room." As I walked away to sort it out, she started laughing with that laugh that stopped everybody in the foyer and said, "Get back here I'm only joking." Silly things, slapstick things, make her laugh. And when she laughs it is funny because she is so loud.'

For all the smiles, Shania does not like doing promotion – she would much rather be writing songs or performing. She regards it as a necessary evil, provided it has a specific point. (In 2000 a headline spot at the Brit Awards was turned down because she felt that the album had already peaked and she would only be doing it as a vanity exercise.) By the end of 1999 there were times when, behind her eyes, one could see the bone-dead tiredness that stars get when the promotion treadmill has run one single, one video, one interview too far. She felt as if her past was another country that has been invaded too many times. On those occasions she might have to be psyched up but she never threw prima donna tantrums, regarding that as unprofessional. When she does an interview, she gives it her full attention. In return those working for her are expected to measure up to her work ethic. She dislikes press conferences, as there is no one-on-one contact, but her major bugbear is television.

'I really don't like television, it makes me nervous,' she says. 'TV is restricting. Someone else is in charge. I have no control.' Not being in control always worries Shania, and when things go wrong, the warning signs are easily recognized: a thin-lipped non-smile interspersed with swear words. Once Shania starts effing and blinding, it is a sure giveaway, for she seldom swears.

'Anything to do with production, sound or visuals, is monitored and controlled,' says Beck. 'All I know is that there are no ifs and buts. Shania and Mutt know how they want to present something and that is how it has to be done. There is no room for the label to change or deviate from that at all.'

The only blip that marred the effortless rise and rise of Shania Twain was the release in 1999 of the tracks that she had recorded with Paul Sabu and Harry Hinde in Deerhurst ten years earlier. The album was originally released over the Internet and then marketed in the USA by Jomato Records on CD as *Beginnings 1989–90* by Eilleen 'Shania' Twain. (In Europe it was repackaged with a sexy cover as *Wild and Wicked*.) Shania was not impressed. 'I don't mind listening to my old stuff, but it annoys me that people make money out of that,' she said. 'If I met that person, I would slap their face, it is so rude. I feel like I've been betrayed by a fellow music person.'

The recordings were very poor quality, taken from an old tape and cleaned up. The mix was shoddy and most of the songs are simply not very good. The cover of Cher's 'HalfBreed' is excruciating. On the US sleeve the credits for the musicians are inaccurate. The record also stated that: 'A significant portion of the proceeds from the sale of this recording is being donated to Make A Wish Foundation and Second Harvest/Kid's Café.' Those may be Shania's favourite charities, but they have yet to receive any money, probably because Jomato has filed for protection from bankruptcy under Chapter 11 in the US.

To cap it all, from the first release of the record, Harry Hinde has been in dispute with Jomato and Paul Sabu. Harry's lawyer claims that 'Harry Hinde owns all the rights, title and interest in the masters and has never assigned these rights to any other party. If something has been done with these tapes, it is not with his permission.' Sabu, however, has alleged that he owns the copyright and half the publishing. For its part, Jomato claims it thoroughly vetted its legal status with the recordings, and the record company boss, John Edwards, says, 'We licensed this from Harry Hinde and Paul Sabu in April 1999.'

Harry, after trying to sell his masters to Universal and Shania without success, intends to release the recordings in the near future. In February 2001, he was back in Nashville remixing the tracks, replacing some of the outdated drum and bass sounds with his take on her current sound. The *Limelight Sessions* will be released by the end of 2001. It sounds a whole lot better than the *Beginnings* album, but it is still old material. There will always be fans willing to pay to hear an artist's early work (sales of the *Shania Twain* album are now up to 1.5 million). Shania, however, will remain unimpressed.

When the third single 'From This Moment On', was released in November 1998, *Come On Over* was already a platinum album (300,000) in the UK, a bigger hit than many had thought possible. In 1999, Shania's profile reached new heights. When she flew in for the première of *Notting Hill* in April ('You've Got a Way' was played over the closing credits but was never released as a single, as Mutt did not want it), Julia Roberts, a big country fan who was briefly married to Lyle Lovett, specifically asked to meet her. After a series of negotiations – Julia's agents wanted to meet in a private room – they met up at the cinema and chatted for a long time. At the same time, there was talk of Boyzone star Ronan Keating doing a duet with Shania, but nothing ever came of it.

'From This Moment On' pushed sales to a new level, but the killer was 'That Don't Impress Me Much', complete with tongue-in-cheek video. The song, released in June 1999, peaked at number three, and spread all over Europe like a summer rash. When Shania performed at Capital Radio's Party in the Park on 4 July 1999, that was the song that had them rocking, the number that had all the headline writers punning away. On 1 September 1999, eighteen months after it was released,

Come On Over finally made it to the top of the British album charts. It remained there for the next sixteen weeks.

The album sold over two million copies in Canada; helped by astute marketing and the use of special mixes it even cracked the Quebec market. It went multi-platinum in Germany. In Australia, after the longest stay in the top ten since ARIA began compiling charts in 1983, it has become one of only a dozen albums to have sold over 1 million copies. By the turn of the millennium, Shania had achieved an almost unique cross-section of the audience. She had the adult market that buys albums and the kids, young girls from eleven to fourteen who adored her image, indeed wanted to be like her, that buy the singles. Her music, in very much the same way that Michael Jackson's once did, engages children on a fundamental level. They don't care about the sub-text of the words, they just love the songs and the way she looks. To the late teens and early twenties she was certainly not credible, as far from hip as can be, but that has never been her – or indeed Mutt's – market. Their happiness shrapnel is now embedded the world over.

CHAPTER TWENTY-TWO

The Château

E arly in 1999, Shania and Luke Lewis were getting into their stretch limo following an awards show in Canada. She was wearing a sheath dress so tight that she could barely move her legs, let alone walk in it. Luke let her in first, and as she went to sit down, the leather seats and the slick dress material combined to create perpetual motion. She scooted the length of the car and landed flat on her backside. Luke's immediate reaction was to crack up laughing. Mid-howl he checked himself for he realized this had become a defining moment. How would Shania react? There comes a point at which a star turns into a prima donna, diva into demon. To them such things are not funny. Not funny at all.

Shania lay in the back of the limo, legs akimbo, in a most undignified heap . . . and roared with laughter. 'What I am living right now is probably the lightest time in my whole life,' she has said. 'I don't take myself too seriously but I take my music too seriously. I never have lived a normal life. I never will, I guess.'

She can still laugh at herself, still finds the idea of what she has become faintly ludicrous. That ability helped when the *National Enquirer* printed a story that, after her concert in Timmins on 1 July 1999, she had rekindled her affair with Paul Bolduc, offered him a job driving her bus and caused him to split up with the mother of his two children. When Helene read the story, she refused to tell Paul what was in it, because she was laughing so hard. So did Shania whenever the subject was raised.

She didn't laugh so much when Darryl sold a story and photos about the Lange Christmas celebrations to the *Enquirer*. The story can be best summarized as follows: no-meat, no-booze, no-sex, Indian cult with dead dodgy leader brainwashes superstar. It was all smoke and shadows. The link with the branch of Sant Mat led by the highly questionable Thakar Singh was intriguing but irrelevant, as Mutt is not one of his followers. Certainly Shania has become a stimulant-free vegetarian, but Mutt's previous history has always been letting his lovers make up their own minds. Perhaps Darryl wasn't so much worried about his sister as he was angry . . . and possibly broke.

What hurt Shania was the betrayal. She had invested so much in setting it up, inviting over all her family. Mutt's brother Bill flew in from South Africa with his wife and daughter. 'I'm going to have a great Christmas,' she had said the preceding October. 'I'm staying home, I could make a lot doing a show, but how much money does one person need? I'm bringing my whole family out to Switzerland. They have never been there. I'm so excited. For New Year I'm going to build a campfire in our yard, stare at the Alps and set off some fireworks.' They did all that. Everyone had a great time . . . and the good feeling lasted until March, when the story broke. Mutt, who cherishes his anonymity, was particularly upset and has found it hard to forgive Darryl.

Such is the price of fame. It was one of the reasons Mutt and Shania had moved to Switzerland in the first place. By the end of 1997, neither were enjoying living in upstate New York. Mutt missed England. He missed sport. Ice hockey, baseball and basketball were cold comfort for a man weaned on rugby, cricket and above all football. Mutt loves watching football matches – during the late 1980s, when enjoying a weekend break from recording in New York, he thought nothing of taking a Concorde flight home, watching either Spurs or Watford play and catching the plane back the next day. 'He loves all sport,' says Shania. 'He loves to talk about football and, like any good wife would, I listen to his football stories. He's very funny, he watched Manchester United all the time because a great friend of his would die for the team. He doesn't follow specific teams any more, he loves players. He watches the game very closely. Being from South Africa, he watches all their rugby games.' Mutt is also 'an avid gardener, it is one of his passions', and found the lack of variety in plants and flowers frustrating.

Even in their small community Shania felt under constant scrutiny. 'If I wanted to go to the mall and do my Christmas shopping I couldn't do that any more. It is not being recognized that bothers me – I don't find that obtrusive – but in the States people can get so assertive, like it is their right to talk to me, and they make a loud thing about it which causes a whole fuss. I hate that. I don't want to be treated like a star, I want to be like everybody else.'

The final nail came after Mutt fell foul of the local environmental policies. Although he owned 3,000 acres, he was not allowed to make any changes that might affect the welfare of the local wildlife without permission. 'He didn't damage anything,' says Helene Bolduc, 'he just made it more beautiful. It didn't stop the animals from going to drink anywhere, do anything.' The building was little more than a lodge and he wanted to build a bigger studio. Permission was refused to do the building work and despite employing lawyers to sort the regulations out Mutt was not prepared to fight it out in the courts. Instead, he decided to leave.

Mutt asked Shania, 'Do you want to be living like this?' and they got to talking about where they'd like to spend the rest of their lives, a place where they could have more privacy, a garden, access to lots of football games and generally live among people who were not as enamoured with fame. They considered moving up to Montreal, but the top-rate tax bracket in Canada was too high for such a high-earning couple to consider. Mutt wanted to be in Europe. Switzerland became the ideal compromise, for the Swiss make a virtue of ignoring celebrity.

During the summer of 1998, when Shania was on tour, the Langes quietly left St Regis Falls (which remains unsold), and moved to a château in the Vaud canton just between Vevey and Montreux, less than 100 kilometres from Geneva. Le château de Sully has been described variously as having a hundred rooms and costing millions. It doesn't (more like fifty) and it didn't – locals estimate the cost at around £5 million. It is difficult for foreigners to get permission to buy a house in Switzerland (Tina Turner rents her house in Zürich and Phil Collins, although married to a local girl, had to wait three years before he was officially allowed to buy). Because he was planning to build a recording studio and bring artists into the country, Mutt was considered to be a special case.

'We weren't looking for a place that big, but you are very restricted as to what you can buy,' says Shania. The original house was designed and built in 1882 by the Geneva architect Emile Reverdon for Baron Bertrand de Boucheporn, whose family had fled France during the Revolution. Intended as the permanent residence of the Baron and his family, it was designed as much for comfort as for show, far closer to a mansion than a draughty old castle (a real old-fashioned castle, La Tour de Peilz, is a few minutes' drive away).

The house was officially designated a 'château' in 1929 when its new owner, Zürich industrialist Wilhelm Escher, had it redesigned by local architect Ferdinand Kurz. The spectacular Byzantine swimming pool in the basement was transformed into an auditorium, an annex was added to the east, a porch to the north and a semi-sunken swimming pool to the west. The house then went through a succession of owners: a company who sold off much of the estate, the writer Joseph Kessel, Liliane Borle and then a public utility company.

What Mutt and Shania own is a big, but not massive, house with an imposing entrance hall and plenty of spare bedrooms. It is private but not secluded. It has its own recording studio and an attached farm – where they keep their horses – surrounded by a few acres of land. The view from the front looks over wine terraces that run down towards Lake Geneva. At the bottom of the terraces is the football pitch belonging to the high school with a gym complex right next door, a series of modern concrete buildings fortunately masked by trees.

Until July 1999, Shania had never spent more than a few weeks at the château. The previous Christmas, she had only a ten-day break between tour dates and New Year's Eve was spent on stage in Phoenix. Although she and Mutt had been married almost six years, they had never spent huge blocks of time together and never in a place that was truly their home. The union of two such formidable work ethics had been hard to schedule; they talked every day for hours but that is not the same thing as being in the same space.

There were times in the early days of their marriage when the gossips insisted she had only married him as a career move. If that were ever true, the doubts are long gone, for Mutt has a unique ability to make people love him. One of Shania's most treasured possessions is the rough draft of their wedding vows complete with all their scribbles. 'I've kept the draft and I've kept the actual vows,' she laughs. Mutt's other relationships ended because he was never there, and eventually love was not enough. For much of their marriage Shania was never there either, but what they shared was more than physical love. 'A lot of the time,' she said, 'it's true, he's not there and I'm not there. But the largest chunks of time we've been apart are over. I will never leave home for such a great length of time again, it's my reward. I don't want to do that any more. The key for him and me is that we share something so intimate and so unique in our music. It is something we're always going to have, it's not ever going to go away. It's not like a relationship where what we have most in common is our love of tennis and if one of us decided they don't like tennis, there goes the relationship.'

It took time to get used to each other. 'We're taking it slow. We're living together for the first time almost in seven years,' she told Radio 2 DJ Bob Harris at the 2000 CMA Awards. 'We eat lunch together, we eat dinner together, we take weekends off and we're having a life and making a record all at the same time. This one we are doing more together than we did the last two. Because I was gone so much, he would do bits on his own, I would do bits on my own, and we'd get together and sort of blend everything together and make it work that way. Now we are together all the time, so our ideas are melding right from the beginning, which is a new way for us to do things. I'm liking it a lot.'

Watching the two working together often makes Helene laugh, for in Mutt Shania has finally met her match. 'Mutt is more of a perfection-ist than her,' she says. 'Sometimes he'll make her start, and start, and start, and she'll say, "It's good enough, it's OK." He just goes: "No it's not." '

For Shania the hardest part has been learning 'how to chill. My husband is a great chiller. When he works, it is extremely intense, but he knows how to relax, to kick back, to be a couch potato all day. I can't do that. I can handle sitting and watching a movie but I'm not going to sit down for another hour and just flick through the TV channels. I have to be in the kitchen making something. I love to cook. When I'm at home during the day it is relaxing, therapeutic and I am doing something.'

Mutt never put any pressure on her to stop eating meat. After a while, she started reading and learning more about it and finally decided it was a waste to kill an animal when she physically didn't need to eat it to survive. She cooks with tofu, masses of fresh fruit and vegetables ('I'm a chopper, not a slicer') and the many new cheeses she has discovered in Switzerland. Vacherin and haloumi (from Cyprus) are particular favourites. 'I like to make soups, stews, comfort food, nothing too exotic.'

On a quiet day they eat breakfast out on the terrace looking at the Alps: 'They are gorgeous in the morning. Even in winter I can just wrap a duvet round myself and sit there for hours.' She rides one of her five horses (Tango, Dancer, Shadow, Thunder and Big Chief) for hours at a time. One New Year's Eve, they just sat out on the veranda and watched the fireworks going off up and down the Rhône Valley. Mutt has learnt to speak good French quickly, which drives her crazy, so she has regular lessons and insists Helene speak to her in French for at least two hours whenever they meet up.

In the early days, when Shania came back from a promotional trip, Mutt needed to know everything that had happened. She just wanted to go for a walk, smell the roses, anything but go over the details once more. 'He gets frustrated, because he is interested,' she said. 'Sometimes it can be difficult. He's so involved he wants things to be so great for me. Sometimes I can't escape the intensity of it, he wants me to be great all the time. I can feel that pressure. I am very hard on myself and I don't get to escape that when I'm with him. Sometimes I just don't want him to care about my career, but it's impossible, because he is such a part of it.' She made a rule never to talk business over dinner or in bed and teased him, 'I have great management. Call them.' He did, called Landau and Lewis, asking questions while she was lying next to him.

Otherwise they talk about everything under the sun. Mutt loves good conversation, he reads voraciously, knows his history and his sport and loves the movies. 'He loves fashion and likes to keep up with the latest of everything; he's very into the aesthetic of things, which is real fun for a girl when we're shopping.' The image that has been built up of Mutt as some shadowy recluse is a media invention. He has never done interviews, because he does not see the need (nor does Clive Calder). The Langes regularly make weekend trips to London for a mix of sanity and culture. Friday night watching *Swan Lake* at the Royal Opera House, take in a Spurs match with David Rose on Saturday afternoon, dinner at the Bombay Brasserie, back home on Sunday. Nobody, not the management, not the record company, knows. No fuss, no bother.

That is the way Shania likes it. On Saturday 5 July 2000, she stunned Timmins by turning up unannounced at her high school reunion. Helene spoke to her on the phone on the Friday night and should have realized something was up, because the conversation was over in two minutes . . . and Shania never gives up the phone that quick. The next morning, Helene was sitting on the deck out at her cottage on Star Lake when Shania came out of the trees laughing fit to burst. She had flown into Toronto, Carrie Ann had picked her up, they had rented a van, driven up to Timmins and stayed with friends.

Shania and Helene spent the day out at the cottage, yakking away before she went back into town and got ready for the homecoming. Shania knew that, if people were expecting her, it would change the whole tenor of the event. So she turned up without security, simply dressed in a sleeveless top, black pants, her hair tied back and only light make-up. She happily chatted away, signed autographs and posed for photographs with any of the 2,000 odd guests who wanted them. Then one of the organizers announced, 'She's done her thing. Now she's Eilleen, she's one of you guys, she's here for the same reason as everybody else, please let her have a good time.' The other alumni did exactly that; she mingled with her friends, chatted to former teachers and had a wonderful evening.

The next morning, she had breakfast with Karen Twain, Don and Jan Fraser, went to see Grandma Selina and left for Huntsville with her sisters. It was a most gracious performance. Small wonder Timmins loves her and was prepared to build a museum in her name.

At heart Shania will always be a tomboy, a jeans and sweats girl happy riding her horses, but she has learnt to accept the compliments of beauty. On 27 July 1999, Revlon announced that she had been appointed a company spokesperson – joining the ranks of such notable faces as Cindy Crawford, Melanie Griffith, Salma Hayek and Halle Berry. She starred in a series of TV and print ads to help launch the cosmetic manufacturer's new product range, ColorStay Liquid Lip and Crystal Glam. 'It's incredibly flattering to be recognized with some of the most beautiful women in the world,' she said disingenuously. 'My image and music fits their campaign perfectly and I don't have to compromise at all. The just let me be myself and that's what makes it the perfect relationship. Also, it's an extension of what I already do in my own job – dressing up and play acting. Except this time they are paying me to do it.' Shania earned some $3 million for the campaign, which was cunningly designed to tie in with the release of her single – 'Man! I Feel Like a Woman'. Part of the appeal was that both the photo session for the ads and the television commercial were shot by photographer to the stars, Herb Ritts. The sight of twenty flunkies running around after the flamboyant Herb amused her greatly.

Such over-the-top pampering has always made Shania uncomfortable. She knows how easy it is to get lost in stardom. Several times she has told Helene Bolduc, 'If ever you see that I'm going the other way, please make sure that I come back this way, bring me back to earth.'

She is worth at least $100 million. Depending on the value of his stake in Zomba, Mutt Lange is worth maybe three times that. For a long time, Shania was uneasy, not with having money, but with spending it.

'Finally she can go out and shop for expensive clothes and won't feel guilty about it,' laughs Helene Bolduc. 'She used to. Eilleen was so dirt poor, and without so much. She doesn't want to forget that. She would die before she goes back there. She makes me laugh every time but she still likes to find a bargain, it's a kick with her. She's all excited about that, she loves saying, "Hey, boy, did I ever get a good deal." '

Shania is certainly not stinting on her new 'cottage' on the Lake of Bays. She bought four lots of prime waterfront near Port Cunnington, forty-five minutes from Huntsville, tore down some of the buildings and had one refurbished in time for her to spend last Thanksgiving there with her family. The plan is for Carrie Ann and Jill to have adjoining cottages. The best-appointed cottages in Muskoka are close to mansions made from wood, beautifully appointed by craftsmen used to dealing with serious money. She has never asked for an estimate, just told them to get on with it.

She is generous to her close family and to those who work for her. If she gives a present, it is one she has personally picked out and paid for. She has a remarkable memory for details, and if anyone mentions they like a particular wine, there it will be in their Christmas hamper. The cards she sends have hand-written notes inside.

Switzerland may not hold her for ever. Its manufactured perfection of nature set against a stunning natural background may wear thin. It's easier there for her to fire up her chainsaw and light a fire, but it is not the same. She has a place in Florida and now the cottage in Muskoka where she can snowshoe through the woods and portage her canoe from lake to lake to her heart's content.

She is as close to happiness as she has ever been in her life, which scares her. 'Ever since I met Mutt, ever since I got married, I don't feel the need to struggle any more,' she says. 'A lot of the fight is gone. I find it hard to keep myself going. Sometimes I get so fluffy and emotional I don't like this person, it isn't me. I guess it is better to be sensitive than not to be. I am so much more aware of people around me, of things going on.'

Because they want nothing more of her than her attention, Shania can be more herself with children. She does not care if they are sick, dying even, but engages with them on their level, asks all kinds of questions. 'She is wonderful with kids,' says Helene, 'I see her with her nephews and nieces and she'll be with them hours, playing any game they want her to play, she's really good with that. Kids were attracted to her even before she became a star. She used to babysit here, and the kids just loved her. I don't know if it's that beautiful face she's got or her smile, kids would just automatically go to her . . . they need to touch her, they need to talk to her, it's always been that way.'

Her own childhood, she acknowledges, was largely lost and the memories of cold, hungry days haunt her still. But she has no regrets, for the past cannot be reclaimed, only remembered. 'When I look back at my childhood, I don't carry that grief with me,' she says. 'I feel like it was another person. I've gone through some very dramatic stages in my life, and I feel three different people lived through those stages. It's funny, I often feel like I'm on my third lifetime. My greatest fear is losing someone in my life, because I know what it's like and it is a very scary thing and I know how vulnerable life is that it could happen at any time.'

Kids were never an option until she was through the first part of her career, the tour was done and she was established. For the past three years she has agonized about having children, wanting them one moment, not the next. It is not an easy choice for Mutt is fifty-two and as wedded to his Muse as he ever was. The thought frightens her, for she grew up in a dysfunctional family – loving but dysfunctional – and she knows how easy it is to repeat the patterns of our past. She takes comfort from the way her sisters, albeit with a few hiccups along the way, have 'broken that cycle, raising their families in a higher standard of living than we were'. Mark, too, has put his past misdemeanours behind him; he lives in BC, works in computers and has his life on track. Darryl, now twenty-seven, lives in Edmonton with his girlfriend and a foster baby.

'I'd like to have a child,' she said in 1999, 'Mutt is open to the idea. He is not rushing to have one, but at the same time he doesn't want me to get to a point in my life where I then regret not having one. I'd like to have children . . . but when I don't know, we'll play that by ear.'

That time came sooner than most of her friends expected. The process of recording her fourth album proved very fertile. She told her close family the good news over Christmas, and it was officially announced in March 2001. Shania gave birth to a health baby boy named Eja on Sunday 12 August.

It became quickly apparent that her next album would not be released until the spring of 2002 at the earliest, assuming, that is, Mutt does not feel the need to do a series of 'baby mixes'. The old Shania might never have considered delaying her career for such a thing, but eventually even a wolf must answer to the cries of nature.

And Shania Twain has nothing left to prove . . . except to her child.

* NOTES AND SOURCES *

To avoid confusion, I generally refer to Shania Twain as Eilleen (her given name) until 1992, when she signed her record deal with Mercury in Nashville. Thereafter she is Shania unless I have quoted directly or used non-original material in which she is commenting on past events.

Occasionally quotes may refer to her as both Eilleen and Shania in the same paragraph. Such quotes are taken from previously published sources and not my own interviews.

Books

Deerhurst Resort, Laura Kennedy with Celia Finley (Boston Mills Press, Canada, 1996).

Jimmie Rodgers: The Life and Times of America's Blue Yodeler, Nolan Porterfield (University of Illinois Press, 1992).

Lost Highway, Peter Guralnick (Penguin, 1979).

On Her Way: The Life and Music of Shania Twain by Barbara Hager (Berkley Boulevard, New York, 1998).

Shania: Feel Like a Woman by Andrew Vaughan (André Deutsch, London, 2000).

Shania Twain by Peter Kane (Aurum Press, London, 2000).

Shania Twain: An Intimate Portrait of a Country Music Diva by Michael McCall (St Martin's Griffin, New York, 1999).

Shania Twain: On Her Way by Scott Gray (Ballantine Books, New York, 1998).

Timmins: The Porcupine Country, Michael Barnes (Boston Mills Press, Canada, 1991).

The Virgin Encyclopedia of Country Music, (ed.) Colin Larkin (Virgin Books, 1998).

Websites

Shania Twain is a true child of the World Wide Web; most of the minutiae of her career can be found on the Internet. Particularly informative are www.shania-twain.co.uk and the Shania Twain Online Fan Club (www.shania.org).

The official David Malachowski Zone! (www.davidmalachowski.com) provided useful background information and quotes on Shania's first backing band.

Roddy Chiong's personal Website (www.roddyonline.com).

The Mutt Lange Zone (www.internettrash.com/users.bigbrobasement/page1.htm).

For my take on Ojibwe history I am indebted to Lee Sultzman's First Nations Histories (see www.tolatsga.org/ojib.html).

Castles of Switzerland (www.swisscastles.ch) provided much of the background information on the Château de Sully.

The Media

Other than those from my own interviews, I have taken quotes from other interviews first published in: *Rolling Stone*, *Q*, the *Daily Mirror*, *The Times*, *Redbook*, *Macleans*, *Cosmopolitan*, *FHM*, *The Toronto Star*, *Country America*, *Music City News*, *Total Style*, *Country Music News*, *People*, *The Calgary Sun*, *Country Wave*, *The National Enquirer*, *Entertainment Weekly*, *Billboard*, *The Timmins Daily Press*, *The Sudbury Star*, *The Huntsville Forester*, *OK*, *TV Guide*, *USA Today*, *Total Productions* and *E-Online*.

TV and radio sources include VH-1 *Behind the Music*, the CBS TV interview *From Rags to Riches* and BBC Radio 2 interviews by Mindy McCready and Bob Harris.

* INDEX *